AT THE FEET

OF THE MASTER

A journal of life and studies with Jesus
from the perspective of
John the Beloved disciple

AT THE FEET
OF THE MASTER

A journal of life and studies with Jesus
from the perspective of
John the Beloved disciple

CAROL D. WARNER

DREAMSPIRIT BOOKS
TRAFFORD

Contact the author c/o DreamSpirit Books, Atthefeetof@aol.com
Co-published by DreamSpirit Books and Trafford Publishing
Printed in Canada

National Library of Canada Cataloguing in Publication Data
Warner, Carol D. (Carol Dianne)
  At the feet of the master
  ISBN 1-55212-718-4

  1. John, the Apostle, Saint--Fiction. I. Title.
PS3623.A76A83 2001   813'.6   C2001-910611-4

TRAFFORD

This book was published *on-demand* in cooperation with Trafford Publishing.
On-demand publishing is a unique process and service of making a book available for retail sale to the public taking advantage of on-demand manufacturing and Internet marketing.
On-demand publishing includes promotions, retail sales, manufacturing, order fulfilment, accounting and collecting royalties on behalf of the author.

Suite 6E, 2333 Government St., Victoria, B.C. V8T 4P4, CANADA
Phone   250-383-6864   Toll-free   1-888-232-4444 (Canada & US)
Fax   250-383-6804   E-mail   sales@trafford.com
Web site   www.trafford.com   TRAFFORD PUBLISHING IS A DIVISION OF TRAFFORD HOLDINGS LTD.
Trafford Catalogue #01-0117   www.trafford.com/robots/01-0117.html

10   9   8   7   6   5   4

DEDICATION

This book is dedicated to all of those who have helped inspire me to always strive for the highest manifestations of my ideals and purpose.

Most of all, it is dedicated to Jesus, the Master Teacher, who through his life, love and teachings, shows us the path to Love and Freedom.

— Carol D. Warner

June 18, 2001

ACKNOWLEDGEMENTS

THE PROCESS OF MANIFESTING THIS BOOK into its current form has been done with the assistance and inspiration of many people along the way, more than I can possibly give credit to here, but to all of whom is due my sincere gratitude and appreciation.

First, I would like to thank the people and village of Tepotzlan, who befriended me and loved me as I experienced my spiritual awakening so many years ago. I give my gratitude to the teachers who have helped to illumine my path, including Robert Van de Castle, Harvey Aronson, Jerome Bernstein, Corinne McLaughlin and Gordon Davidson, Susan Ulfelder, Alexandra Buckner (who helped me to face my inner promptings), and many in the Association for the Study of Dreams who have steadfastly believed in the power and guidance of the dream.

Many thanks also to the friends and family who have devoted many hours to reading and proofing the manuscript, and who have encouraged me to move beyond my doubts, including my mother, May Belle Warner, Bob Van de Castle, Rita Dwyer, Michael Balsamo, William Moore (and for his inspired cover art), Carolyn Amundson, Martha Molpus, Vi Jefferson and Helen Carter.

Appreciation and gratitude also go out:

To those visionary writers and organizations who have taught me and inspired me along the way, including Alice Bailey, Helen Schucman, William Blake, Edgar Cayce and the ARE, the Association for the Study of Dreams, Brent Baum, the Center for Visionary Leadership, and Unity Church.

To Christine Granville, for her gift of courage.

To John, for his Love.

To my friends and family who have supported and nurtured me over the years.

To Stephanie Glennan, for her beautiful cover design and for her patience with me in helping me to hatch this.

To Trafford Publishing, particularly to Bruce, Marsha and Margaret, for offering me this opportunity to publish this work in the full integrity of its original form.

And, of course, to Jesus and Mary, for their brilliance. And last. but most of all, to God, who has given me so much, and helped me through so many rough times...

PREFACE

IN THE MORE THAN EIGHT YEARS since I first wrote this book, I have struggled with how to introduce the material. After a variety of thwarted attempts at publishing, I began to realize that I could not continue to present the work as if I had penned it in an ordinary way. After all, what could a woman 2000 years later know of the extremely personal and subjective relationship John the disciple had with Jesus, and what manner of profound hubris would compel her to write about it in such an intimate way, even with the label of fiction?

As a psychotherapist in private practice, I combine my graduate and post-graduate training in religious studies with my clinical training to work holistically with clients on different levels of their being, emotional, mental and spiritual. Yet, despite an active imagination, and a love of writing, it would have never occurred to me to research John's story and to attempt to reconstruct the incredible relationship that he (and the others around Jesus) must have had with Jesus. This book was written in 1993, before the recent interest in the historical Jesus, that began with the Jesus Seminar and has continued until the present time. The paucity of personal information about either Jesus or John, and particularly about their relationship, was and still is, remarkable. Nothing in my experience or my training seemingly could have prepared me, led me, or, perhaps most importantly, qualified me to write such a story.

The narrator of this story, John the disciple, is a character who deeply loved Jesus, and through whose loving eyes Jesus' humanity and divine nature is made real to the reader. We learn the many lessons he learns through his apprenticeship to his Master, and through the mutual (if unequal) friendship that develops. John emerges as a character absorbed in his devotion, who is profoundly transformed by his association with Jesus. We, as readers, become aware of his need to be special, and of his very human flaws. It is perhaps because of his flaws, rather than despite them, that we can identify with him more readily. The practical and metaphysical lessons that he learns, as well as the growth of his love and friendship with Jesus, are chronicled in this narrative. The lessons about love and healing stand out, both in the specificity of detail, and in their power.

When I had a dream in 1991 about John reflecting, sometime soon after the crucifixion, on his life with Jesus, I did not know what to make of it. I have journaled and worked with my dreams since 1975, and place a great deal of importance on my dreaming life. The dream was poignant and profound. I found myself moved by the dream in ways I could not understand. I knew better than to dismiss it completely. Gradually, I allowed it to percolate through my thinking and to enter the space of my meditations. Though I was in Jungian analysis at the time, I found myself strangely resistant to bringing the material into my weekly sessions, as compelling as it felt to me. Eventually I felt that I could no longer avoid it. The movement that resulted from my opening to it in therapy, in my dreamwork and in my meditations, resulted in a clear mandate.

It is difficult so many years later to reconstruct exactly what happened when, but I do remember around this time sitting in a meadow on a bright sunny day, meditating, as I did on most days. During my meditation, I heard a clear inner voice telling me that I was to serve as a scribe and take down John's story, and that it would be given to me from start to finish. There was a profound clarity and inner peace about this voice. While it was expressing, all of my normal mind chatter was held at bay. I was told that it would become clear to me when it was time to start writing, and that I was to worry about nothing, except to sit down, pray and meditate to open to the words that would come to me. I was filled with a calm and a certainty that were beyond words.

Later I would question and worry and then question some more, but yet somehow the power of that experience in the meadow was so compelling and transporting, that I could only turn my doubts and my questions over to God, and trust that I would be given more information as it was needed. I knew something about channeling, from different points of view.

In my mid-to-late teens, I had a lot of exposure to the works of Edgar Cayce, a trance channeler whose medical and spiritual reading gave help and hope to many people. In my college years I had been fascinated with the artists and writers who claimed that their work was "given" to them through a process of inspiration, and that their work was not their own. These artists included musicians such as Beethoven and Mozart, and writers such as William Blake, on whom I wrote my senior thesis. It was his view that true Imagination was that which was given by inspiration of Spirit, and that all poetry that was not inspired was "pretense" only. In recent times, I had benefited greatly by studying the Ageless Wisdom teachings of Alice Bailey, who had channeled a Tibetan master. She made no claims for the veracity of the material which she channeled, and adjured the reader to decide for him or herself what was helpful and what was not. Despite these very positive examples with which I was familiar, the excesses of the New Age movement, and the ridiculousness of some of the channelers and their claims contributed to suspicion of this form of communication. Never had I aspired to "channel". This meditation message was on some levels quite unnerving, yet it also inexplicably left within me a profound peacefulness.

It was to be many months before I was instructed that it was time to begin. I had tried to put it out of my conscious mind, and simply to accept that when and if this were to happen, I would once again be instructed. I continued with my meditation and dreamwork, which sometimes dealt with John, but mostly focused on other areas of my life. Then, on a beautiful snowy March day, I went to a nearby park for a walk. The trees and stream were almost mystically beautiful with the snow covering them. The silence was profound. I was drawn to a circle of benches, where I had previously been quite moved while witnessing a group of nuns praying and meditating. I went over to a bench and cleared it of snow. There, I sat down, and began meditating, beginning as always with a prayer. It was during that snowy March meditation that I received word that it was now time to begin writing.

From that day forward, and for the next nine months, I took down the story as it was presented to me. I would sit at my computer for about an hour a day, five days a week. I would "hear" the words in my head, and take them down as if they were dictation. The material was presented at the speed that I could type, somewhere between 80 to 100 words per minute. The stories were often moving and absorbing, sometimes quite surprising. Often I could not remember details of what I wrote outside of the writing session. Between sessions I did not re-read the material, not even to check where I had left off. The material always re-commenced as if there had been no break, picking up exactly where it had left off.

I struggled deeply with many doubts and many fears about the material. On a daily basis, I wondered and feared the "dictation" would stop. The material seemed very beautiful and rich to me. I reasoned that if it was from some source in my "imagination", then I feared I could not sustain the momentum, especially when I put no conscious thought into it. On the other hand, if it were coming from some other "higher source" (which in its unlikely way by now seemed more likely!), and I was merely the instrument for the dictation, then perhaps due to some failure or unworthiness on my own part, I might not be able to continue with it. Further, I wrestled anxiously with whether the material was authentic. In order to keep my sanity, however, I decided I had to let go of the authenticity question. Instead, I decided to allow the process to unfold, without judgment, *as long as it felt safe and productive*, because otherwise the process was too tortuous. Yet, somehow, despite these and other doubts and internal struggles, every day when I sat down to my computer, the words were always there, like water from a deep well.

In presenting this manuscript to other readers, I make no claims about the authenticity of the material. These questions I cannot answer for myself, much less for others. I have come to the understanding that whether or not the scenes in the story actually happened is not what is most important. I believe the value of this material is that it presents a view of Jesus' teaching that may give depth and insight to the reader's understanding of this most holy of men, as well what his private teachings and relationships might have been. The story definitely enriched me in this way, helping me to imagine what it must have been like to live, love and learn in the presence of the Master. I have also taken many of the lessons I have learned from this book, and applied them in my psychotherapy practice, where appropriate, with very positive results.

I am a practicing psychotherapist with a thriving private practice, who is respected in the international dream community (I've been on the Board of Directors for the international Association for the Study of Dreams for many years in one guise or another, including serving three years as Chair of the Board). I have felt until now that I needed to keep the story behind this book under wraps. At one point, I told a friend about my struggles in the process of writing the book, and how l was extremely reluctant not only to scribe it but also to publicly speak about the process. He was very familiar with the Course in Miracles, and said my struggle reminded him of some of the things Helen Schucman had gone through. I knew nothing about her at the time, and though I had heard about the Course in Miracles, I knew nothing about it. Now that I am a student of the Course in Miracles, and have read about Helen Schucman and her resistance with being a scribe for the Course and going public with that fact, I identify with many of those struggles. I, too, have been concerned with my professional reputation, and how my integrity or even my sanity might be questioned. I have no defense to offer either for the book or for how it was written—I only know that it came of its own accord, and must stand on its own merits. Yet, I also know that it would be fundamentally dishonest to put forth this work and to say that I wrote it, for it is not mine, except insofar as I scribed it, and have lovingly brought it forth for publication.

This book has been through a number of edits, in order to make the writing more clear. Because of the nature of how the book was written, there was little attention paid during the scribing process to grammar or punctuation. Many of the original sentences were quite lengthy, and needed to be broken up, both for clarity and for readability. A number of different people graciously helped with the edits of this book. In each case, the editing was done with an eye to maintaining the material as close to its original intent as possible, while attempting to make the book smoothly readable. There were times when I wished to take out some material, but was guided to leave everything as is, for the sake of the integrity of the manuscript.

I was aware as I scribed the material that it was being translated from Aramaic into English, and that the translation was sometimes difficult or inexact. The rhythm and syntax of the writing is at times awkward in its English version, but I have tried to keep it as close as how I "received" it as possible.

The story is written as if it were John's journal, written in his later years, and reflecting on his experience with Jesus many years before. Beginning with the introduction, John is the narrator, telling the story from his perspective. (Out of all the disciples, John was the only one who lived a long life.)

I humbly offer you this book, and hope that you enjoy it and in some way may benefit from its many lessons.

— Carol D. Warner
January 24, 2000

INTRODUCTION

THIS BOOK WAS WRITTEN A VERY LONG TIME AGO, and had been hidden away. When I sat down to write it, I zealously wrote every night by candlelight to put down on paper the many thoughts and feelings I had about the multitude of experiences I was fortunate enough to share with this man that they call Jesus Christ. I want the world to know of my experiences, for I think that what I was taught and what I have been blessed to learn, can be of immeasurable value. My life and my vision have been so completely transformed by what I have experienced, that I cannot even imagine seeing out of the narrowness that used to be the complete scope of my consciousness. What I thought I knew, I did not know at all. What I do know now, as limited as it is by my all-too-human capacity, I owe to him whom I loved as I have loved no other.

I believe that it is now time to bring these words to the light of day. It seems that the time has come when all of us are more receptive to these truths than in those ancient times when so many were ruled far less by the Spirit inside than by the prevailing opinion of what one should think and believe. *The core of what I learned from this man of whom I write lies in learning to self-reference into my interior, into my very soul, to reach God and to reach the Truth.* I loved him so very much, and I grew to depend on him greatly. Often I wanted nothing more than to rely completely on him for my experience of God and of Truth and of Light. Much to my frustration, after the initial period of apprenticeship and then discipleship, he would not allow me to depend on him in this way. "The Kingdom of God is within you" was the first lesson, the middle lesson and the final lesson.

I am only a man, and make no pretense to be less vulnerable, or less error-prone or any less subject to the foibles of human nature than any other man or woman. I hope in the document that follows to share some of my extreme good fortune in being able to be so intimate with this God/man on a daily basis over a period of several years. He was a Master above all other Masters. His heartbeat is the heartbeat of humanity at its best. I can only hope to convey in bits and pieces the mosaic of love and divinity and hope that I have experienced through my incredible good fortune, and through my intense heartbreak as well.

CHAPTER I

I WILL NEVER FORGET THE DAY I FIRST MET HIM. It seemed I had been hearing so much about him. I wondered if I would ever set eyes on him so I could make up my mind for myself. People everywhere were in awe of him. They wondered if he could be who he seemed to be saying that he was, or if he were a deluded impostor who had incredible powers of persuasion. Tales of the miracles he performed spread rapidly from town to town: none of us had ever heard of anything like this before.

As for myself, I barely dared to hope that anything so wondrous could be happening here, in my homeland, and in my lifetime. I always listened as the townspeople talked of him; I listened very carefully and let myself take in all the various points of view. I would stand just outside the circle of people who were gathered, and wish I had more of an opinion on what they were discussing. The truth is that I just did not know. At times I felt this to be a deficiency within myself, for I felt if I were more learned, or wiser, that I would know the truth and be able to speak my mind with all the conviction with which I heard so many men speaking. I observed the women too. They seemed to be more open. Often, I noticed that they too refrained from offering opinions on this matter. With them, I assumed it was a higher wisdom that kept them from talking at this early stage of his ministry. I simply assumed that they would wait to see what transpired, and then make up their minds.

I was a young man, barely 19 years old at the time. I was of above average height, and had a very muscular build. My hair and beard were quite dark, and I had a fair amount of hair over my body. I took great pleasure in the day-to-day life of the body; in eating, sleeping and in working with my father Zebedee and my brother James as we fished and tended to our boats. I found much joy in this simple life, and assumed my entire lifetime would be much as it was on this day. I was a gentle young man. I was told I was handsome, and young women appeared drawn to me. Yet, I was very shy and unsure of myself with regard to women, and was happy to spend the day fishing with my father and brother. When I could find time, I loved to read and to study, and even to dream about writing. My family found me a bit unusual in this regard. I did not really seem to want the same things that other young men my age wanted. As much as I loved the simple life of the body, I also had a very active imagination that took me to faraway places and distant times. Sometimes my brother would gently chide me when we fished, for I would be there in the body but certainly not in the mind.

On this day, we were finishing up fishing for the day. We had a fair catch, and I was satisfied with my work. We had pulled in our nets, and were heading into shore. I was pleasantly tired, and looking forward to a hearty meal and the amicable chatter that always accompanied it. I looked up on the shore, and there I saw him for the first time. I knew immediately who it was. A powerful surge of energy went through my entire body.

With the wisdom of the intervening years, I can look back and say that all of the energy centers, or chakras, in my subtle body lit up at that instant. For that brief moment, my light body was activated. I had never experienced anything approaching this before. Intuitively, I knew he orchestrated it all. I felt enveloped in a profound sense of peace, love and understanding. My heart felt open in a way I had never before experienced. To a complete neophyte such as myself at the time, who was so immersed in the daily life of the body, these feelings and this experience took me into a complete other dimension. I felt strong feelings of wonder and awe. My vocabulary is truly inadequate to describe my experience. It will have to suffice to say that it was immeasurably profound and deep. In that instant, a very deep part of me knew that in some as yet completely undefined and unknown way, my life now belonged to him. Imagine such a moment, in which you could know in just an instant, and with profound feeling and conviction, that from this moment on, your entire life would be completely transformed and changed....

For all of the grandeur and the mystery of that inner moment, I revealed on the outside of me nothing of what I was experiencing. I looked up at him, into his eyes, now suddenly regaining my reason and doubting everything I had just experienced. For, as I have previously stated, I was a young man who was well grounded in many ways in the life of the body. This life did not leave much room for this kind of inner, intangible experience. As powerful and wondrous as it felt, I was also terrified by the momentary loss of my sense of myself. I was hoping, I think, to see in his eyes an ordinary, uncomprehending look that would tell me that what I had experienced was but a product of my own imagination. Then I could return to my ordinary life and see this moment as a wonderful aberration.

Instead, what I saw was a warm and gentle, yet very penetrating knowing. Immediately I felt that not only did he know everything that I was experiencing, but that he could completely understand and accept even my desire to flee. I knew that he had deliberately given me that experience, and that through it he wanted me to experience the wonder of God. He smiled at me, a very warm and loving smile. In that moment I felt completely loved.

But, my mind raced, these feelings are crazy! This man does not even know you, and you are allowing yourself the most outrageous imaginings! These denials that I felt were the product of what I now understand to be fear. Fear of what I was feeling and felt to be true, fear of what I knew would shake up my life to the very core, fear of mentally and spiritually moving outside the very comfortable world that I had carved out for myself, fear of an intelligence so vastly greater than my own, and also fear of losing my identity and being swallowed up into something much greater over which I would have no control. Yet, the love that he radiated was much greater than my fear. In some measure, I allowed the feeling of being so loved to penetrate my cells and my consciousness. It was in that moment that *I surrendered*.

I did not have any way of knowing at the time how pivotal that moment would be. All that I knew was that this man was unlike any other. At a deep level, the trust I felt for him was as if I had known him forever. So much was racing through me at the time, and (since once things started happening, it all happened so fast) it has taken me years to sort out my internal experiences. As Jesus stood on the shore talking with my brother, it seemed that he and I maintained a constant communication with each other. My mind was racing with a million thoughts and feelings. The human part of me was anxious to deny the import of what I had been experiencing. With each denial that my mind produced, a knowing and gentle answer would come into my mind that would reassure me. In some ways it felt that a revolution was taking place within my own mind. I knew that this involved a dialogue between this man and the higher energies that he represented, and myself. I felt calmed and nurtured by him. My fear, which seemed to want to take on a life of its own, was becalmed. In some deep, inexplicable way, I now felt that I belonged to him, or perhaps more accurately, to the divinity that he manifested.

It feels an impossible task to convey the intensity of those moments, especially since almost the entirety of this interaction and experience was on a nonverbal level. Never before had I experienced communication at this level, much less such a life-transforming communication. I was not then, nor am I now, a man who was easily swayed or persuaded. Always within me I have carried a strong sense of what I felt was right and just. I considered myself moderately religious, and preferred to look for evidence of God in the simple rhythms of life, rather than in the temples. I never saw myself as the kind of man who would go out and preach and try to convert people to his beliefs. I innately felt that people would come to their own conclusions regardless, and that my own beliefs were personal and would best be manifested in the manner in which I conducted my life. This was very much in line with what I had been taught at home. My father especially was a model for me in this regard. We were honest people, who respected God and others, and we tried to live our lives in the highest manner possible.

So, my being overcome so strongly and so quickly with this sense of linkage and bondedness to this man, was quite out of character for me. To my reasoning mind, it felt somewhat mad. However, deep in my heart I was moved far beyond any way I had ever been moved before. James and Jesus were standing on the shore, and James was talking with him about leaving his current life, and following him. This was happening incredibly fast, and it would have been total madness if this man were not who he was. My brother was later surprised that I had seemed to make my decision without any discussion with him at all: in fact, he said, I had seemed quite removed from the entire afternoon's event. I did not have the words to adequately describe to him what had happened to me; I could only tell him that I was moved beyond words and beyond fear and beyond reason by this man, and that I knew that I had no choice but to follow.

Father was saddened by the prospect of losing both of us at once, but I think he had been moved by this man as well, and knew that what we were doing was a good thing. Mother had dreamt of this ahead of time, and had been emotionally preparing for a while. She gave us her blessing with her tears.

Mother, of all of us in the family, was somehow the closest to God in her everyday life. Her simple unquestioning acceptance amazed me. Sometime before this day, and after the stories had begun circulating through our village about Jesus, mother had awakened in the middle of the night, and had told my father of the dream that had awakened her. The dream was as follows:

"I am standing outside on a beautiful, clear sunny day. The weather is of the kind that will not allow you to stay inside and ignore its calling. I am in a field, enjoying the special moments.

Suddenly, from out of the sky, I hear a most majestic musical sound, and see an angel materializing, and coming toward me. I feel no fear: I listen as the angel begins talking to me. It is hard to say, as strange as it may seem, whether the angel is male or female. It is almost as if the sex kept changing, and I saw both masculine and feminine aspects. In any case, I knew that this was not important for me to understand.

What I was told brought great joy but also sorrow to me. I was told that this man Jesus would come and ask my two sons to come with him and study with him and help him to spread his message. I was told that it was a very great honor that my sons had been selected, and that they would have an opportunity that many over time would wish to have had. I was told that we all had been in preparation for this for some time, and that it was predestined. I was being prepared in advance by this visitation so that I would know that this was a great thing, and that I should rejoice, but also so that I would have ample time to let go of my more human wishes to have the boys continue to be so nearby and available on a daily basis. I was told that they would be gone for long periods, and that there would be many difficulties ahead for them in their new work, but that it was all for the glory of God, and that I need never doubt this."

As mother told us this story about her dream, she related that when she told father about it, his response to her was a simple "so be it." He would have major losses ahead, for the three of us worked together to make a living. But, both of them had a strong yet simple, unquestioning faith, and if this were to be how things would be, then it was a matter simply of honoring God's will and letting go of the rest.

Even with the relating of this dream, neither of us could have begun to imagine the magnitude of the enterprise on which we were to embark. We knew from our experiences in the afternoon that this man was quite extraordinary. Certainly we had all heard stories, but we had little idea what we might be getting ourselves into. What we did know, each in our own inner experience of the man and of the day, was that we both felt we had no choice but to follow him. James had followed John the Baptist, and had been preparing for this, but how does one really prepare for something so monumental? We had to know what this was about; we had to serve. For the two of us to agree so completely and with such conviction, in such a short period of time, was in and of itself quite remarkable.

CHAPTER 2

I SLEPT LITTLE THAT NIGHT, for my excitement and youthful enthusiasm swept over me and kept me awake. I had a million imaginings of how my future would be, and intensely wanted to know *now* what I would be experiencing and learning. I knew I was embarking on the adventure of my life, and I was ready to have it start immediately. My brother did not seem to be faring any better with his sleep. Eventually we succumbed to our wakefulness. We talked throughout the night about Jesus and the decision we had made, or perhaps more accurately, the decision that had seemed to have been made for us. We were related by blood, as cousins, though we lived in different towns and had not previously met.

We marveled that we knew so little as of yet about his beliefs. We saw and we felt that he manifested the divine: that much was common to our experience of him. His energy field was unlike that any of us had ever experienced: we felt vitalized and our consciousness was raised when we were around him. There was an almost magical quality to his presence: we could not define this nor could we describe it any more clearly, but we felt this very strongly. We wondered at our rapid decisions, for this was so unlike us. We remarked repeatedly how qualitatively different this man must be from any other for us to have had the experience we did and to have made the choices that we did.

We were still talking as dawn broke. We both had people we wanted to say goodbye to, and we knew there would be many questions we could not answer. I was surprised over the course of the morning by the varied responses I received. Many were curious about Jesus, and were glad to know people who would be close to him, so they would hear of him from someone they trusted. Because it was two brothers who were going, I heard some comments about people wondering if this man had put a spell over us, and would he put us up to evil ways. A few seemed genuinely glad for us, but most people seemed to have mixed feelings and some misgivings. Many were concerned for my father and my mother, wondering how they would fare without us there to help out with the work that needed to be done.

My friend and neighbor to our family, Rachel, a pretty and soulful young woman, was happy for me, yet sad to see me go. I know she cared for me a great deal, and I admit to having feelings for her at the time as well. She seemed to understand better than anyone my need to go, and it seemed she wished she could go with us too. Tears came to her eyes when I told her I was leaving. I was grateful for the connection between us. It was in saying goodbye to her that I realized I had deeper feelings for her than I had previously thought.

Hardest of all to leave was my younger sister Naomi. She was very special to me. Whenever we returned from our fishing, I looked forward to seeing her. She was a loving young girl of 10, whom I adored and who adored me as well. She would always run up to me to greet me and I would catch her in my arms and lift her up (even though now she was getting a bit large for me to do this as comfortably). She had long, curly black hair and large dark brown eyes, and was beautiful inside and out. She taught me much about joy. She had a natural irrepressible cheerfulness that never failed to lift my own spirits if they were flagging.

Naomi took the news that we were leaving quite hard, sobbing in my arms for a long time. I reassured her that I would see her as often as I could, but for a while she was inconsolable. When finally she finished crying (and I will never forget this), she looked up at me with her deep brown eyes and said: "I wish you well. I know you have to go to do this and that it is for the good that you do. I only wish I could go with you." To me, her genuine good wishes for me and for us was an enormous sacrifice from the heart for a ten year old. Her heart was so big, big enough for an elder who has experienced many years of living and loving and sacrifice. She looked up at me with a smile, and in that moment, the love that we shared for each other wrapped around us and between us like a warm blanket.

We were to meet Jesus that afternoon on the edge of town, and travel with him on our way to Jerusalem. We could only bring with us what we could comfortably carry as we walked over the land, so there was not much we could do in preparation. We did not know when we would be back in town. I put on my sturdiest robe and sandals, knowing that they would have to last me for many days and months. Naomi gave me one of her most prized possessions, a small but beautiful stone she had picked up when we had been out on a walk together, just the two of us. She told me it always reminded her of that happy day together, and gave her joy. She hoped it would do the same for me when I was away and if I ever got sad. I was very touched by the love this girl offered.

Mother made sure that we had a large afternoon meal. She packed us so much food for our journey that we joked we surely would never be able to make it out of town without a pack animal to carry it for us. Father was proud, I could tell, but I could also see he was deeply sad, and missing us already. It relieved me to know that some other young men in the village, upon hearing we were leaving, stepped right in and offered to work with father. This offer he gladly accepted. I would have worried about him more had this not happened, but it seemed that God was taking care of things and looking after father, who had just freely made such a great sacrifice.

I wanted to leave quietly and without much fuss. It seemed the whole town knew now. People were coming by to speak with us and give us whatever words of wisdom they thought to offer. I endured this poorly, and grew irritable and impatient with wanting to be gone without this attention. My brother was much more gracious and forbearing than I, and I was grateful for him and his personable nature. Naomi stayed close to me, and I focused as much of my attention as I could on her. How I would have loved to bring her with me, if it would have been the right thing to do. Yet, it clearly was not, and she would be much better off at home, than suffering the many discomforts we would be encountering. I was to miss her most of all.

I focused my attentions on the events ahead of me. My excitement and also my fear ran in strong currents through my nervous system, and it was all I could do to contain them. It was as if they pulsed in alternating currents through me. No doubt James was experiencing equally strong and consuming feelings. I was able to manage by taking step by step the details I had to attend to that day. The day went quickly, yet paradoxically seemed to last forever.

At some point, I remembered a glimpse of a dream I must have had during one of the brief periods of sleep I had managed to have during the previous night. In my dream, I was with Jesus, and felt very bonded to him, as if he and I shared part of the same soul. I experienced boundless contentment and love, and a sense of expansion in which I knew that all men somehow participated in the sharing of this soul. I experienced this knowledge as a great revelation, for I had always viewed humans more in terms of what separates them than what binds them together. At this point the dream ended. I do not know what triggered the recall for me, for I had not remembered this dream earlier. But now, having this recall served to reassure me that what I was doing was right, and encouraged me that the journey on which I was embarking would be one of great positive learning. It strengthened me, and fueled my curiosity even more as to the great mysteries that lay ahead for me and for my brother.

As the afternoon wore on, we said our last goodbyes and made our way to the edge of town. There were those who wished to walk with us, but we both felt we wanted to begin this part of our new journey with just us two. As filled as we were with ideas and feelings and wonderings, it was a surprise to me how silent we were as we made our way out of our immediate neighborhood and onto the road that led to the outskirts of town. I can speak only for myself in this: I know it was hard to let go of my past, for I knew that truly nothing would ever again be the same. What was happening felt cataclysmic. However, my reasoning self told me that this feeling must surely be larger than the reality of the situation warranted. It would be a long time before I developed a stronger trust in my feelings and intuitions. Nonetheless, I did know I was on a new adventure, that I was leaving my old life behind, and that what lay ahead of me would change me in ways I could not imagine.

CHAPTER 3

IT WAS LATE IN THE DAY WHEN WE ARRIVED at our destination just outside town. The warm, clear afternoon was turning into a balmy twilight. When I first saw Jesus, he was standing under a tree, talking with two other men who were gathered there with him. With my inner eye, I perceived a radiance around him, like a gentle golden glow surrounding him. He turned toward us, and welcomed us over. He introduced us to the men who were with him, and told us these men would also be accompanying us as we journeyed over the land. These men were Andrew and Simon Peter, whom we already knew from our lives as fishermen. Apparently these men had been traveling with Jesus for a short period of time. There would be others to come in the months ahead.

We began walking towards the direction of Capernaum. As the sun set and the stars began to become visible, I marveled at this new situation in which I found myself. Jesus talked at first of God, and of the unfolding plan in which we would all be taking a part. He did not get into too many specifics on this walk. In general, he emphasized that we would be given divine guidance at each step along the way, and that he would teach us how to access this information in the clearest manner possible. As we walked, he taught us to visualize a light coming down from the heavens that surrounded all of us. This visualization was invoked by prayer and by the power of our imaginations. He told us that the purpose of this light was to keep us focused in our individual and collective beings on our divine purpose. It would also serve to protect us from those who might wish us harm.

I was surprised to see how strongly I felt the supportive force of this light around us. I was not accustomed to tuning in to such subtleties, and yet, once I was tuned in, I was surprised how very real these forces felt. It was clear to me that Jesus was extremely powerful at potentiating and activating these forces. My curiosity was aroused as to how he did this. My concentration and my focus seemed unusually clear. I had the impression that this had something to do with the field of energy that surrounded us.

We sat on the ground and ate supper. My brother and I shared the food that mother had given us. I was glad we had something to offer, since we were in the position of students who would be taking so much of what Jesus and the others had to offer, especially in these initial days. As we ate, Andrew talked of some of his recent experiences. He was especially enthusiastic about what he was learning about healing energies. There was almost a boyish quality to him as he spoke, so eager was he to learn all he could. I was glad he was such a talker, for I was more than happy to sit back and listen tonight. I felt blessed to have been chosen to accompany Jesus, yet I also felt empty in the sense that I did not feel I had much to offer.

I was beginning to observe that Jesus did not always do a lot of talking either. For example, as we relaxed this evening, he sat back and listened to the conversation, and occasionally joined in. He did not seem to need to be the center of attention, or in any way to monopolize the conversation. Yet when he did talk, we listened, for his words were always of value. There seemed to be a rhythm to him; at times he would be inward, and at times he would come out and share his wisdom with us. This felt comfortable to me. It seemed that there was room for me to be myself. I must admit to feeling inadequate, but it was a great comfort to have my brother with me, for we were true friends. We all told our stories to some extent that night, but James gave the general picture of how we had met Jesus, and what we had to do over the past 24 hours in order to get here.

My curiosity about Jesus was intense, and my focus kept going over to him. Perhaps I stared too much, but I was anxious to know more about him. I sensed that he felt this, and I somehow felt his patience with me, and tolerance for my anxieties and curiosity. I could not say that at this point I was growing accustomed to feeling that he knew my mind, but it was beginning to dawn on me that this would be the case. This was a bit unsettling (as I imagine it would be to anyone), and frightened me somewhat. Yet, paradoxically, it did not feel intrusive in the way it might have if there were a feeling of criticism or disapproval involved. In fact, even at this very early stage, it seemed perhaps he was able to accept me and support me in a way I could not accept myself.

As the men talked, I observed myself letting go into a preliminary acceptance that the boundaries of my mind as I had always known them would be changing considerably, and that my very intense private inner life would now be viewed by someone else at times. As a check on myself, however, I vowed that if this ever struck me as dangerous or wrong, I would speak up in whatever manner I could. Telepathic communication was a new idea to me, and I was open to it with Jesus because it had felt positive so far. However, I was adamant in my feelings that I did not want to ever feel coerced or pushed.

The tone of the conversation was changing, and Jesus said that he wanted to share some words with us before we slept that evening. I found myself very eager to hear what he had to say, but observed a resistance in myself that I did not understand at the time. I know now that it was fear of the unknown, and fear of the changes I knew I would have to make in myself. Part of me welcomed these changes, yet another part did not want to move in any new directions.

I think it was very much a part of my character at the time to be circumspect and somewhat guarded, and fearful of the workings of the human heart. My family had been a loving one, and I had felt very much loved and cherished within that circle. Yet, for some reason I always carried a reticence and reserve with me that perhaps went beyond a normal degree of wariness. I have no doubt that part of this had to do with my high degree of introspective self-awareness, and how it simply seemed that for me, my consciousness registered shades of gray and ambivalence within my own psyche that it appeared most simply did not notice within themselves. (I am including these observations within this manuscript, for it has been my observation throughout my life that it is this resistance and fear in the human psyche which, through ignorance and lack of understanding, can lead the unsuspecting human into some of the most horrible deeds imaginable.)

As Jesus began talking, I came out of my reverie. He was saying the Light of God was within us always, and we must strive to always stay connected with this Light. He said that if we did so, we would always be close to truth and to goodness, and we would always know how to act and what to say in any given situation. He led us in a prayer, in which he asked God to allow his Light to manifest in us and through us, and that we be able to feel God's presence within. I was not accustomed to thinking of God as residing within, and was made dizzy by the sensations that were occurring within my body and mind. The sensation I had the previous day of being lit up from within recurred, and was intensified manyfold. I felt one with God and with my companions. My head almost buzzed with the sense of expansion beyond my ability to comprehend. There was a blissfulness and peace in the heightened awareness that made me feel alive in a way I had never before known. I truly felt in the presence of the Divine in a way that was tangible and real, and far from the abstract heavenly God of my imaginings.

As Jesus ended the prayer and thanked God for having shown Himself to us in such a clear and present manner, I marveled at this man and his ability to help us to connect with such formidable energies. He prayed that we be led in each of our actions to serve as best we could in our capacity as emissaries of God. He asked God to watch over us as we slept and to fill us with his goodness and grace. He thanked God for having gathered us all together in service. As he closed the prayer, I felt joy in my being for having been so blessed as to be able to take part in this venture, and that my brother James could be a part of this as well. I looked at James and we smiled a knowing smile at each other. I knew he was feeling similarly blessed.

It was late now, and I was completely exhausted. The lack of sleep the night before, and the intense emotions and changes I had been experiencing over the past day and a half had worn me out. I looked forward to the next day, but barely had time to wonder about what would be in store for us before I drifted off into the soundest of slumbers.

CHAPTER 4

I AWOKE EARLY THE NEXT MORNING. It was not yet light, and the stars were still visible against the sky. At first I did not know where I was, and then when I looked around me and gained full consciousness, I smiled inwardly. No one was yet awake, and I took a few moments to relax and enjoy the changing sky as dawn approached. The others started rousing and moving around. James, who had been sleeping next to me, greeted me and immediately rose. He always had such a strong energy about him, even so early in the morning. It took me a bit longer to get myself going.

I remembered my dream from the night before. This was two nights in a row that I had dream recall, which surprised me a bit, for most often I did not remember any dreams at all. This dream was also brief, but left a strong impression on me. In the dream, I was walking alone with Jesus up in the hills somewhere. There was a strong bond between us, as if we were more than companions but also close friends. The dream ended with me having the definite impression that we were on this walk because there were some things he wanted to share with me that he felt were important and also pertaining to me somehow. My waking thoughts about this were in wondering if we would be developing this kind of special and intimate bond. However, I had the inclination to dismiss this, and to think this would indeed be something I would love to have happen, but that it would be unlikely.

We had a long walk ahead of us this morning, and gathered up our belongings in preparation. Before we set out, we gathered together in prayer, and encircled ourselves with the holy Light of God. I could not seem to take my eyes off Jesus. The dream memory and feeling lingered with me. I wondered a great deal about what kind of personal connection we would develop. My initial thoughts about him had been more along the lines of what I would learn from him and how I would be able to help him in his work. However, after this dream, my musings began on a more personal dimension as well. I began speculating about the personal relationship that would develop between us. As I pondered, he looked over at me and smiled so gently, and with a knowing yet reassuring look that I would become very familiar with. I was a bit unnerved, yet also felt encouraged.

As we began walking, I chatted easily with the others. We had a specific destination, but no particular plan of what we would do when we got there. Our role was to learn as much as we could of what we would be taught, and then to teach it in turn to others as time went on. *Our behavior and our words had to be consistent.* It was assumed that in this early stage, we would be putting most of our energy into observing, learning and beginning to master our own instruments, ourselves. Conversation was light-hearted and yet often purposeful. Jesus had an easy sense of humor, and a ready laugh. Just as quickly, however, he could get very serious and intent on communicating what it was that he needed to share and teach at that moment.

Jesus was a very handsome man. His shoulder-length curly hair would have been dark brown, but it had lightened in the sun. His skin was olive. He was of medium build and size, yet his stunning presence made him seem bigger than his actual size. His eyes were deep pools of liquid brown, and seemed extraordinarily clear. When I looked into his eyes, it was startling always, because it seemed I could somehow see into infinity through them. They were definitely the warmest eyes I had ever seen, the kind of warmth that is born of the blending of compassion and wisdom into love.

Jesus had more presence than anyone I had ever known or seen. It was impossible to be around him and not to feel it. The only way I know how to describe it is to say that to be around him felt like being in a sacred space, a space where one's thoughts and aspirations and confusions were healed and uplifted, as if raised out of the mundane into an entirely different level. I was to learn only later about energy fields and the transforming effect that they can have. His energy field was enormous and extremely vitalized, and it was this energy field that accounted for the effects I have just described. Later I learned how to see this field, and it was truly startling. His conscious control over this field was also astonishing, but I am getting ahead of myself. My ability to perceive these levels of energy fields was virtually nonexistent on this morning walk. All I knew is that the energies I was experiencing were very different and very much more powerful than anything to which I was accustomed.

By mid-morning, we were hungry and thirsty. We had some food and water with us, and stopped to partake. The morning had been cool, but it was clear that it was going to be a quite hot day. I was glad to be able to rest, and to enjoy the company in which I found myself. Jesus told us that the next few days would be fairly easy ones for us. This would give us time to get better acquainted with each other, and to acclimate to the new level of energies in which we would be finding ourselves.

Jesus said that with the raised level of vibrations we would be experiencing, the body would be going through a physical adjustment period in which it would be cleansing and realigning. He explained that the body gets accustomed to operating on a certain frequency or rate of vibration, and the frequency on which we had been operating would be raised because of the influx of higher energies. During this period of readjustment, we would find ourselves more easily exhausted and weakened, something which he explained would be nothing to worry about. The others told James and myself how they had experienced this as well, and were still going through it, and how unsettling this process felt at times. These were men who were accustomed to depending on the natural physical strength of their bodies, who had found that this natural fount of strength felt much more exhaustible during these times of transformation.

I was surprised at the emerging complexities of what we were working with on a daily basis. I suppose that I thought it would all be simpler somehow, perhaps because the decision to follow had been made so quickly and so easily, and without complicated thought. I thought I had learned much in my early years, but now I was beginning to believe that my mind was more like an empty scroll. In this moment, I felt overwhelmed by what I had to learn and experience in order to understand even a portion of what this man had to offer. I could not even begin to comprehend how much he had to teach me. However, this momentary glimpse made me realize I was truly in the presence of someone who could transform the infinite into a form that would be understandable for someone like me who was so much more comfortable with the tangible and the known.

We gathered ourselves up again and resumed walking. James was avidly interested in finding out what the experiences of each of the others had been thus far. It seemed to me he felt that if he could learn what had happened up until now, he could have a better idea of what was to come. I listened as he questioned, yet my main interest was to find out more about Jesus' history, and was glad when we could move the conversation around to this.

He told us the story of his conception and birth, and his parent's flight into Egypt. He did not remember a time when he was not aware he would be playing a special role,. Those around him spent many hours in preparing him spiritually, mentally, physically and otherwise to become the most perfect instrument he could be to contain the energies that would later be radiated through him. His experience of his childhood was that he was given enormous amounts of love and nurturing. He spent many hours in meditation and prayer even as a young boy. He wanted to learn all he could possibly absorb, for he knew it would later all be needed. His direct experience of the divine began at a very early age, and he received guidance often through prayer, dreams and through direct transmission. He credited his mother Mary with the strongest faith he had ever known. She taught him the experience of faith and belief in its most fundamental ways.

He studied many scriptures and many lessons, and appreciated greatly this kind of thorough grounding in sacred texts and writings. But, from an early age, his avid interest was in direct experience of the sacred and divine. This was something he could not learn in texts and in classrooms. His mother's experiences with the divine fascinated him, as did the many preparations that she had gone through in their religious community in order to prepare herself to be the physical and spiritual channel through which he was to be born.

Daily prayer and exercises for connecting with God were a very important part of his early preparations. He felt most comfortable at these times, and looked forward to them. He learned a great deal about his role past, present and future from these times. Jesus also found that his dreams were extremely helpful in keeping him informed about various aspects of his life. He gained much valuable information about his past lives both from his dreams and from meditations. Both his parents and the rabbis helped him to sort out the information he received, and to assess its relevance or usefulness to his present situation.

Beginning in his mid-teens, Jesus became very aware he would need to travel a great deal in order to study and learn more of what he would need in order to embark upon his mission. He knew that the time of his leaving would be several years hence, and that he would know when the time had come. When that time came, he left and continued with his studies in each place he resided or visited. He traveled many miles, into many lands in the East, where he studied ancient traditions unknown in our region. He studied with Masters and learned all he could from each one. They unlocked many doors for him, and taught him about the one God we all share, about healing, the various energy bodies, meditation, prayer, creation, telepathy and other mental powers, reincarnation, and many other matters. As much as he learned mentally, he also learned through direct experience. While in the East, he had learned to master his body and its energies. He learned to consciously travel into the past and into the future, and how to use this information wisely to guide choices.

When it was time to journey back home, it was with the knowledge that his time of learning and preparation was over, and that it would now be time for him to begin to fulfill his purpose. The journey back from the Himalayas took many months, which gave him time to pray, meditate and pull together all he had been taught and had experienced. His gratitude to the Masters who had taught him along the way was enormous. He thanked God often for having given him such extraordinary teachers and mentors.

I was fascinated by this story, as were the others. How rich this man's experience had been! I felt very fortunate to be in this position, in which I could learn from someone who had experienced and seen so much of the world, and the spiritual riches it had to offer. I was anxious to begin to learn more of these practices and how they would be applied in our lives.

CHAPTER 5

THESE EARLY DAYS WITH JESUS PASSED VERY QUICKLY, and were full of excitement. We would camp outside towns or villages by night, and by day we would travel and go into the towns to meet with the people there. It seemed to me that I could never learn enough of what was being presented. I welcomed our private time together as a group when we were united in prayer and teaching. I was learning so much. My body, mind and spirit were alive with many new energies and ideas. I loved to watch Jesus in action, and learned a great deal from seeing and hearing his responses to people.

On one of these early days, we had ventured into a small town, and into the marketplace. I watched as he moved among the crowds. He was very tender to an older woman, his gentleness emanating from him. As I watched and continued to scan his energy, I felt awe. As I felt the awe, I scanned my own self for traces of my own identity, and realized that at this moment, I had allowed myself to be completely eclipsed by him. This was surprising; for this was a degree of trust I had never allowed myself to feel before.

As I watched him, I observed light all around him. I was beginning to be able to see energy fields, and I could see that his body was composed of bright light. What happened next was completely unexpected, and took me totally by surprise. As I felt and saw the truth of his body being composed of light, it was as if many layers of caked-on crusted mud, which had accumulated over many centuries, suddenly broke off from my heart. It was a sudden, extremely wrenching pain. I literally cried out in the agony of complete surrender. I knew somehow that he had directed this experience, and that it was a necessary clearing out in my energy field. The pain and inner reality of what had just happened was extremely startling. I know no way to better describe in words the intensity of this experience. The noise of my cry was lost in the crowd, for their focus was on him as he used his hands and his energy to heal.

This brief but brutal initiation marked a definite shift in my acceptance of him as a Master. Whereas before I had accepted him as a Master, on this day I accepted him fully as my Master. I have thought about this experience many times over the years in an attempt to understand what happened. I learned many times over in my years with Jesus that a Master has the ability to teach and direct experience in a number of arenas at the same time. What might seem impossible for the rest of us was not at all so for him. In this case, he was focused on the old woman, but could also be focused inwardly on a teaching experience that would be directed towards me as well. I have spoken earlier of the unusual degree of guardedness and reticence which I carried within me, and how it did not seem to be a product of experience in this life. I have learned that it was a product of many centuries of pain and suffering, and that I carried this thick layer of protection in my energy field, and especially around my heart.

When I perceived with my inner eye that his body was composed of light, I perceived with a new clarity the reality of his divine nature. Previous to this, it was impossible for me to perceive this through the very clouded lenses of my normal perception and the guardedness of my normal personality. In order for me to truly take this in, the clearing-out had to occur, and hence the sudden wrenching sensation of pain which I experienced. *It would be many years for me to understand both what had led up to the necessity of my having this experience, and the impact this would have on my life.* What I did feel in those moments was a new sense of openness to Jesus and to what he had to teach me on an inner level. I was not accustomed to allowing someone so fully into my heart or into my being. It was clear that from here on out, our relationship would be qualitatively different. It was as if I could now allow him to reach me, or I could allow myself to truly reach out to him.

I never spoke of this experience to anyone. There were times later when I was tempted to ask Jesus about it, but it almost seemed redundant and superfluous to do so. It had changed me deeply. From this time on, I began to feel closer to Jesus on an emotional level.

My focus shifted from my inner experience to what was happening in the outer world. Jesus had healed this woman, who was now testing out her legs. She appeared dumbfounded that she was actually able to walk freely on them. The crowd was amazed to see this old woman, who had been crippled for many years, now walking. She was crying for the miracle, and crying for the release of her pain. I was touched by her tears and by her feeling, and found myself crying as well. At that moment my compassion for her was so strong that I could almost feel her relief, and the release and letting go of the pain she had carried around with her for years. She asked Jesus what she could do or what she could give him to thank him for his help, and he said: "You can thank God for your faith, for it is through your faith that you have allowed yourself to be healed. If it were not for this working together of you and God, this would not have happened."

I was so impressed by this double example of spontaneous healing, and so touched by both experiences, that I did not take in much else of what was happening in the square. As we left the marketplace, there were several people who walked with us and wished to talk about what they had seen. One of these people, a woman, offered to fix us a meal. Jesus agreed to go to her home. We walked down the narrow streets to her house, which was a modest stucco structure. Jesus, Peter, James and myself went in and she led us into the main room where she bade us to sit down. We sat on a rug on the floor, and she brought us something to drink while she went to prepare a meal. Her husband and two daughters were out visiting a relative, she told us, but would soon be back and she would very much like us to meet them.

I enjoyed relaxing in this woman's home. We talked comfortably there, and reviewed what had happened that day. I could tell that she wanted to hear as much as she could about what we were discussing, for she seemed very interested in the healings she had seen take place that day. When she brought the meal in to us, Jesus blessed the meal and this woman for having provided it, and we began eating. The bounds of Sarah's seemingly endless curiosity appeared to be matched only by the depth of her faith. She wanted to know what it was that Jesus was teaching that was different from what the rabbis taught in the temples, and how it was that he could heal. Jesus was very patient with her. I listened very carefully, for I knew these were the kinds of questions that would come up repeatedly as we journeyed.

What was different, he said, was that he was teaching that God and His kingdom reside within each individual, and not only in the temples and in the rabbis. What gave him his special ability to heal and to help others, was that he had spent many long years learning how to access this God within and to make it manifest. Because of this, God had bestowed on him a special dispensation. He said that what he taught was not so different from what she had learned so far, but that there were different emphases.

In order to accept and to access the Kingdom of God within, there must be love. Without that love, the divine cannot manifest or be heard. Therefore, much of his message was also focused on people loving each other and forgiving each other, and accepting that the nature of the human condition is to fall short. The old woman in the marketplace who had been crippled was someone who for many years had been unable to forgive herself for some of the mistakes she had made in the past. The longer she carried this burden of self-hatred with her, the more it manifested as this extreme pain in her body. He stated that she, himself and God formed a powerful triangle of energy, and he poured into her forgiveness for her mistakes, and divine love and healing. In the moment of healing, she was open to believing that she deserved to be healed, and was able to accept the influx of divine love and forgiveness. She was forgiven, and she forgave herself. She was loved, and she was able to love herself.

As Jesus talked, I thought back to my experience of watching the woman in the marketplace cry as she was healed, and understood from a new and heightened perspective her tears of joy. I also understood on a new level why I was moved to tears myself, for in her tears there was a release of the physical pain, and also of the tremendous emotional and mental burden she had been carrying with her for many years.

We finished our meal, and had the opportunity to meet briefly with Sarah's husband and daughters. We then left, and went back to the outskirts of town where we would meet with the others, and rest for the evening. This had been quite an extraordinary day. I was spinning inside with what I had learned and experienced.

CHAPTER 6

As THE DAYS WORE ON, I WAS CONSTANTLY LEARNING, and constantly surprised by the genius of this man called Jesus. To say that I was in awe of him would barely convey the depth and complexity of my sentiments. Jesus consistently told us it was not his power, but the power of God working through him and within him, that enabled him to do the things he did. I suppose I was so accustomed to thinking of God as an externalized force that it took quite a bit of getting used to for me to even begin to grasp the concept of God within as well as without.

Perhaps one of the most difficult challenges for me to accept at first was to look at the subtle energies, and to begin to take responsibility for those that I created. As I began to develop auric sight, I began to see blockages that were around me and had been there for many years. The incident in the marketplace had been a radical introduction in this respect. Yet even more difficult to accept was the idea and the reality that the negative thoughts and emotions I experienced and generated had a life and an energy of their own, and that they could definitely have an impact on others without either one of us knowing. An early incident comes to mind that demonstrates my dawning awareness of this principle.

I was washing my robe in the stream early one morning. I suppose I must have been nursing some resentment towards my mother over some incidents long over. I was barely aware of this; it was more like a musing of the kind that people so often do with little awareness. Just then, Jesus came towards me and described a brown and red angry cloud that he saw emanating out of my aura. He said that as he watched, the cloud grew larger and larger, and was beginning to send streamers out in the direction of my hometown. I listened incredulously as he went on to say that, left unattended, these thoughts would continue to gather momentum until my mother would be affected. She would find herself in much the same manner thinking resentfully and angrily about me, without having any more awareness about the process than I did.

I felt many feelings at the same time. I felt shame and humiliation for having been seen so clearly and for not having better mastery of my thoughts. I felt angry that I could not have my own private thoughts without intrusion, but then I was glad that if I was indeed participating in something that could truly be harmful, that I had the opportunity to learn how to stop. I was confused, for I had barely even been aware of my thought process, and how could I possibly learn how to stop that which I hardly knew I did?

I asked him, "Master, what is it that I can do to correct this, and to make this cloud go away? I do not wish to harm anyone, least of all my mother."

What he said then took me by surprise. He said: "Based on what I observe and sense in you, I think it would be best if you would go home and see your mother and spend some time with her. I have felt over the past few days that you were not truly free to be here, and we have much hard work ahead of us. Go, and spend some days there until this matter no longer occupies you so. Then you will be ready to put your full concentration on the work that lies ahead of us."

I felt stung by his words, but knew he was right. We were close to my home, and this would be the perfect opportunity to visit, for we would be journeying farther away in the weeks to come. I wondered if I had failed somehow, or if this would be a reason to keep me away, but truly I felt from him that he wanted me to clear this so I could be back with him.

I took my leave, and went back home for several days. The time at home was well spent. I made sure to have private time with my mother so we could heal together. I had no idea how to approach the subject, other than to tell her exactly what had happened, and what Jesus had told me, and how he thought I should spend some time at home before moving on with him. We did not get into details beyond this, but assured each other of our good will and love toward each other, and prayed that our energies together work only towards good.

People were curious why I was home and why James was not with me. They wanted to know everything about Jesus and what he was doing and teaching, and what were my thoughts and opinions now that I had been exposed to him night and day for many weeks. I shared with them what I could, and took some pride in being the center of attention for this short while. Soon enough I would be giving all of my attention again to someone else, and it was nice for now to have people focusing positive attention on me. It was also nice to have the comforts of home for these few days, and to be around Naomi and have time to play with her.

One day, I went out fishing with Zebedee. He had missed us greatly, though he had been pleased with the young men who were now fishing with him and for him. It was a pleasure to return to work with my father, and to be able to experience our father–son bond from a very new perspective. He was a hearty soul, and always a pleasure to be with. Over the years, I had always looked up to him to teach me, and I had learned so much from him. Today, though, it was different. He was seeking to learn from me about my experiences. He had many questions about Jesus, and what I thought about him, and what it was that I saw happening. Rumors and stories were continually flowing through town, and he had no way of sorting through them by himself.

I did not have the language or the ability at that time to even begin to describe to him my experiences. What I was able to tell him was that I thought Jesus was an extremely learned holy man, and I believed he was in contact with God at all times. I described what he taught, and told my father of the healings I had seen thus far. I told him that in my short time with Jesus, I had learned and experienced more of God than in many years of studying and worshipping in the temples. I told him I felt blessed to be able to be an apprentice to this man, and that I hoped I would be able to prove myself worthy as a disciple as time went on.

Zebedee seemed relieved at what I was describing to him. Though he had inherently trusted the decision James and I had made, and had given us his support, it was important to him to have this kind of follow-up, and hear for himself how this venture was going. He had been concerned when he first heard I was back in town, but now was only glad to be able to hear the news.

We walked back home together. A number of people stopped us to ask me why I was back, and what I thought of Jesus now that I had been around him. The first question I managed to skirt around, saying only that I now had an opportunity to visit before we journeyed far, and I thought I would take advantage of the time to see my family. The second I answered in various ways, depending on who did the asking. My basic answer was that Jesus knew much of God and love, and that he taught of both through direct experience. Many questioned if I thought he was God. I told them that God spoke through him always; that there was a direct link between the two of them. I told them he lived his life in perfect harmony with God's will, and if this made him God, then this was who he was.

I had time at night, in the privacy of my thoughts, to take stock of the awesome responsibility I was taking on in my life. No longer content to be a simple fisherman, I had now entered a world of complexity that seemed beyond my grasp. The incident that had precipitated my homecoming was far from forgotten in my mind, though the feelings had been resolved. I was astonished that the impact of one's thoughts and feelings could be so strong, and had serious doubts if I would be able to take on the kinds of complex mental and spiritual responsibilities that would be asked of me in my new role. I had had no idea my private life would become so open in this sense, and that on this path of spiritual development my thoughts and feelings would count on the same level of importance as my actions. The message was that my thoughts and feelings were actions, if on another, more subtle plane. I had to be as cognizant of them as of my behavior.

The more I thought about it, the more I realized that, difficult as it might seem to be moving in these far more subtle worlds, I had already embarked upon this path. I was not sure that even if I wanted to, I could go back to being the fisherman that I had been. I remembered how gentle Jesus was with me when he was teaching me in this most recent incident, and how supported and cared for I felt, despite my shame. I realized that, since I was already on the path of these understandings, I would never find a better and more brilliant teacher than the one I now had. So, despite my own insecurities and feelings of inadequacy, I remembered that, for some reason, he had chosen me, and it only made sense for me to move on in the path I had already begun. I wondered if he had any idea about my ambivalence, then laughed to myself when it occurred to me that of course he did. He would have known that I would have needed this time to sort this out as well. No less than a complete commitment was needed for the work I would be doing.

When I headed back the next morning, it was with a sense of renewal that surprised me. There were many levels of choices to be made in this work. It seemed I had made many already, yet there were many more to make. I had thought it would be as simple as making the decision to follow, but in this, as in so many things, I had no idea of the complexity involved. I was very eager to return to be with Jesus and my new family of brothers. When I saw them from a distance, I quickened my step in order to be with them just a little bit sooner.

CHAPTER 7

I WAS WELCOMED BACK WARMLY, and quickly felt I was back in my true home. I looked over at Jesus, and we exchanged knowing glances at each other. It is true that, at that moment, I felt much lighter than previously. I had not even known I had been carrying a burden until now that it was gone.

It seemed there was an unusual amount of activity. James quickly informed me that we were in for a few days of hard traveling, to arrive at the region around the Dead Sea. There we would be in retreat for several days, for there were some lessons that the Master was planning on sharing with us. We would each have some work of our own to do. I was puzzled by this, but there was not much more information to share. During the few days I had been gone, Jesus had chosen several more men to follow him, and now we were up to six, excluding myself. These two, Phillip and Thomas, seemed as uncertain of themselves as I had so recently felt, but seemed likeable enough, and appeared ready and eager to learn what they could as quickly as they could.

Some women who had been among the crowds the day before had offered to bring food for a meal before our journey. It seemed as time went on, no matter where we went, there were always people, particularly women, who recognized the light and the truth that Jesus brought, and who were eager to nourish the bodies of Jesus and the men in his entourage. Though it was men in this world who made the journeys and spread the word of God, it was women who seemed closer in many ways to spiritual realities. Women often formed the majority of the crowds that gathered to hear Jesus speak, and watch as he performed miracles of healing. Women accepted more naturally what they felt and what they experienced, whereas my observation of men was that they far more readily scoffed at the manifestation of the divine, as if it were manly to adopt this pose. I suppose I felt a more natural affinity to women in these ways. As time went on I grew more respectful of their ability to accept the unseen and the unknown, and to act out of their faith. My particular affection extended to older women, especially women who had sustained many losses and sufferings in their lifetimes, for I found their faith to be the deepest of all. Their ability to see Jesus for who he was, and what he had to offer, was the greatest of all. That early experience with the crippled woman in the marketplace had made a very deep imprint on me. I never forgot the tears I shed for her, and the space in my heart that she opened.

Though much had happened in the relatively brief time since I had been a part of Jesus' retinue, it was still quite early in my apprenticeship to him. I really did not consider myself a disciple as yet, for to me that would have implied a level of understanding and mastery which I as yet felt I was nowhere near attaining. James felt quite the same way on this matter. Both of us shared the feeling that the longer we were around Jesus, the less we felt we understood of the world we had so long taken for granted.

James' sense of humor was quite keen. He had a way of poking fun at us and our little span of knowledge, that left me very amused and also feeling supported at the same time. It was very good to have him beside me in this journey; he countered my seriousness and my intensity with a spirit of fun that was irrepressible. He helped me to take myself less seriously, and to put our situation into perspective. I was grateful for his good spirits, for I could always count on him to bring me up when I was feeling at my lowest.

If it had not been for James, I suppose this adventure would have felt a great deal more frightening. As it was, I was ready now after my brief break to take on whatever was to be coming my way. James did not know why I had gone home, and I did not share the details with him. I did give him news of home, and greetings from everyone. We were close in many ways, but I kept private the experience I had with Jesus that led to my visit home.

The long walk towards the Dead Sea was hot and dusty. There were times, however, when Jesus was talking that I would lose track of time and of my fatigue. I had a sense of excitement about the days ahead, for it seemed this would be an important time of learning. I found myself positioning myself close to Jesus often, as if the nearer I got to him, the closer I might become in spirit. I felt more alive and more whole around him than I ever had around anyone else. This was despite my trepidation that if he got closer to me and saw more about my human shortcomings and failings, he would reject me or not want me to continue on as a disciple. As I think about it now, I think it was in part my humility that he saw as a positive in me, for the more realistic I was about my human shortcomings, the more open I might be to spirit working through me. As Jesus once told me, with a grin on his face: "a full vessel leaves no room to be filled."

I devoured the stories he told and the lessons he taught. I found, as time went on, that I adored this man. I loved how he was with people. He was gentle, patient and nonjudgmental. However, he did not suffer fools lightly when they tried to push people around or to take advantage of others. I think it was during this journey that I truly began to love him. Because of my recent experiences, I was more vulnerable around him. I felt he truly understood me in his sending me back home to heal unresolved feelings before we moved on to the next stage in our journey. Yet, I know there was more to the deepening of my feelings than this. I don't know what was touching me so deeply, but I found myself focusing most of my waking attention on him, and admiring him so much that my heart ached sometimes. How can you help but love someone who is the very personification of love and goodness? It took me time to see and believe this, through observing the way he conducted himself in those everyday encounters that speak so much about a person's character. It was on this trip that I began to feel in my heart for him a love I had never known or even dreamt of before.

CHAPTER 8

AFTER SEVERAL DAYS OF HARD TRAVELING, we finally arrived at our destination. It was hot and dusty, and it seemed there would never be a time again when we would feel clean and cool. I was full of anticipation, wondering what was in store for us. Jesus said we would be fasting for several days, and doing much praying and focusing on God. This would be a very special preparation and cleansing period. It would be very important to our ability to work in the future in the way that we would be needed. This sounded full of mystery to me. Any doubts I was having about my ability to do what I would need to do were swept along in the confidence I was feeling through my connection with Jesus. He gave me so much strength. I was beginning to feel that, when I was with him, I could do anything I put my mind to.

After a night of the kind of solid slumber one gets when one is weary to the bone, I woke up and immediately joined with the others in prayer that linked us to the preparatory prayers of the night before. The sun was just coming up, and the air felt alive with God's presence. The colors of the dawn combined with the charged atmosphere to create a special mood. In this ambience, I felt surrounded by a loving and benevolent universe that would readily lend to me the experience I would need at the time. It was with this confidence and sense of readiness that I opened myself to the experience God would be giving to me.

Jesus led the prayer. He opened by having us sit in a circle and close our eyes. He asked God to protect us and open our hearts to what we needed to experience, and invoked a circle of light to surround us. Within each of us, he asked that we connect with our inner light source. We were to visualize ourselves as linked to each other and to

God through this source. God, he said, was at the center of our circle and also at our own centers. We then linked ourselves to the center of the circle. The energy was intense as we proceeded with this work. It felt almost like the vibrational level lifted me out of my self and into another dimension of being. We sat with this experience for what seemed to be both a brief while and a very long time. Then, Jesus told us we were experiencing what it was to know that God was within us and without us. The power of the individual to know God was multiplied manyfold when a group gathered together to focus its energies. I was simply amazed at the level and intensity of energies that were manifesting through us, and which I could feel so acutely within my own being.

While we were still in this state, he said God had selected us for this very special work. We were gathered here today so that each of us might internally begin our preparations for the time ahead. We would meet together at night, but during the days we would go off in silence by ourselves to commune with our God nature, and to listen to the guidance we would each individually receive. He asked God and our angels to watch over us, and to furnish to each of us that which we needed. He then closed the prayer, and we rose up to go on our own.

I got up hesitantly, feeling suddenly diminished with the closing of the prayer and the pulling away of these powerful group energies. I wished desperately that I could accompany Jesus, for I believed my experience would be tremendously heightened around him. I observed my own thoughts and feelings, and was suddenly quite surprised at the intensity of the dependency I was developing for this man. This was quite unusual for me. I felt longings in my heart for closeness and intimacy that I had never before experienced. Of course, I knew I had to strike out on my own like the others, but at some level I wanted only to be with Jesus and to absorb whatever I could from him. It was as if I felt that I could benefit just by breathing in the air around him that was charged by his essence. There was a level of poignancy in what I was feeling that made me feel like my heart was crying just from aching to be with its beloved. With these very human thoughts and feelings about the human relationship that I so desired,

I turned my mind toward the mission at hand. Reluctantly, I released my fantasizing and opened my mind to guidance as to which direction I should walk.

I walked toward the water's edge, and gazed over the large span of salty water. I mused about what these few days might bring, and let myself experience the charge in the air. There was a crispness to it, not in temperature, but more in clarity. My senses felt keenly alive. As I turned from the water's edge, I saw a spot up in the hills where I felt pulled to walk. The varying shades of brown blended into one another, and I strolled with some eagerness toward that path above.

As I walked, I was aware that I was not alone. The presence with me felt reassuring, though I could not ascertain what it was. I was just beginning to learn to accept impressions and not question them as much as I was wont. I supposed it was likely this unknown presence that was leading me in the direction in which I was going. I made the assumption that it had a better knowledge than I of what lay ahead. Going on these thoughts, I eagerly moved into the terrain in front of me. I was moving quickly at this point, and let myself be pulled and steered by the forces I was feeling.

Just then, up ahead, I saw it. I was stunned and amazed, and could not believe my eyes. When I closed my eyes and opened them again, still I saw the same phenomenon up ahead of me. What I saw was intense, and intensely unbelievable, but undeniably there. As I watched, it grew larger. I sensed that despite the substance of the vision, the energy vibrated at a higher rate and therefore did not have the same density as matter to which we are accustomed. As my inner eye scanned this level of the reality in front of me, my outer eye was captivated by the size and majesty of the lion in front of me. I had never before seen such a beast. The animal stood proudly in front of me, almost showing off its glorious golden presence. Surprisingly, I did not feel fear, but only admiration for this creature. I searched the manifestation for any signs of threat or malicious intent, but found none. Instead, I had a few moments to revel in the sheer visual enjoyment of its sensual magnificence and splendor before the vision disappeared in front of my eyes.

I was struck by the power and the brilliance of what I had just seen. I was at a complete loss to explain or understand it, yet I felt I had been greatly honored by having been allowed to see it. In my body, I felt a surge of powerful energy that felt sensual, sexual and spiritual, all at the same time. I felt for these moments that I was sharing in the experience of the energies of that mighty lion. It was surprising to me that these energies blended together so harmoniously, each complementing and enhancing the other so very completely. I was accustomed to separating out the overtly sexual and sensual from the spiritual. Here, they were all combined and merged in a way that felt very powerful. I experienced my manhood in a newly enhanced manner. It was as if I had become more than myself by partaking of the instinctual energies of this beautiful animal.

I continued with my walk. The sensation of participating in a sharing of the energies of this animal stayed with me for quite a while. All of my senses were heightened and amplified. I felt more one with myself than in my usual mode of existence. I lost all sense of time, and my energy seemed boundless. It was as if this animal had generously lent to me its spirit, and now I was carrying it inside me as I roamed through the hills. My mind wanted to understand what this animal was, and why it presented itself to me in this manner. My body and the blood pulsing through it seemed more than satisfied with staying with the experience, and feeling the power and the beauty of it for as long as it lasted.

I must have wandered around in this state for hours before I felt my inner voice telling me it was time to turn around and return to the campsite. I had carried the trait with me from my earlier years that I could easily lose all track of time, and remain entranced in whatever world I was visiting that day or that hour. I realized at this point with some surprise just how far gone into my inner reality I had been, and how ravenously famished my body was. I picked up my step, for I had hours to walk before I would be back with my new family.

CHAPTER 9

WHEN I RETURNED, MOST OF THE OTHERS WERE ALREADY THERE. A strange quiet pervaded the atmosphere. I guessed that I had not been the only one who had been blessed with an experience of the other world. I wanted to hear what everyone had experienced, yet I also did not want to break the spell of the day by talking. Silence seemed to feel more comfortable to all, for though we made attempts at speech, we always fell back into a quiet that felt more serene and more right at this point than verbal communication.

By the time we had all returned and gathered together, it was already dusk. The stars were beginning to show against the sky. James was the last one to straggle in. I could tell by the look he gave me, and by the look in his eyes, that he had journeyed far. Jesus led us in a prayer, thanking God for what each of us had learned today, and thanking God that we had each other to depend on, to learn from and to give each other strength. There was something in the way he said the part about giving each other strength that made me think the times ahead of us might be much harder than I had previously imagined. I did not dwell on that thought, and returned my focus to the magic of the gathering at hand.

Our prayer ended with a period of collective silence, and again the combined impact of our energies was dazzlingly intense. I did not know if it was the divine energy that Jesus was able to summon through his perfect channel, if it were the combined energies of this many dedicated men in prayer, or if it was a combination of both of the above, that made these group experiences so powerful. Whatever it was, I felt very grateful and blessed to be a part of this group in this time and this place, and to be able to participate in this very special series of experiences.

I think it was this profound sense of gratitude that I experienced the most strongly of all this night under the star-lit sky. The temperature dropped rapidly after the sunset, and we wrapped up in what coverings we had. I watched the sky as I lay waiting for sleep, and felt insignificant in the context of being one man in one time in such a vast universe. And yet, I knew that Jesus, as one man also, was tremendously significant, and that his impact would be felt for many years to come, in many different places and by many different people. I could not imagine how, but as I let my imagination go, I knew this was true, and true far beyond my capacity to imagine.

As I pondered, I kept returning to my feelings of gratitude for having been allowed to participate in this unfolding drama, and I thanked God for having put me in this situation. I looked over at Jesus, almost instinctively. As his eyes met mine, I was gripped by the knowing that he was aware of my feelings. He smiled at me with the most tender smile imaginable. I felt his love like a blanket warming me, and touching me in my heart. A tear came to my eye. I smiled weakly, and turned back and closed my eyes. I was not accustomed to feeling so vulnerable and so transparent, nor was I accustomed to a love that reached so deeply inside of me. It warmed me from the inside out. I wondered as I drifted off to sleep how it was that I was so fortunate as to have been selected to be a part of this wondrous journey.

I must have fallen quickly into a sound slumber, my body and my mind exhausted from the day's events. I dreamt a most unusual dream, which haunted me for many days to come. In it, I was a soul, not yet a man in a physical body. I saw ahead of me a very intense and brilliant white light that drew me to itself with an irresistible pull. This light felt incredibly beautiful, warm, and full of love and goodness. I had no choice but to let myself go, for its force was completely overpowering, and I felt with all my being that I wanted to follow. I had the sense, as the dreamer, that it was the draw and the call of this light that led me into this incarnation as John. I felt I truly had no choice in the matter, or, if so, I had made it long ago.

When I awoke, I pondered that this dream was telling me it was not an accident I was in my current situation. It was my destiny, the reason for which I was born into this life. I assumed, after a period of thinking about this, that this was probably true, though there were at present far too few tiles in the mosaic for me to see the entire picture. At this time, I had little understanding of what purpose I was to serve. I had gained a sense of my own personal power through my experience in the hills on the previous day, and had been thrilled with the sensation and the quality of life pulsing through me so fiercely and so proudly. Now, I had this other piece to add to the picture. I did not know how these pieces fit together, but I reasoned that it might be many years down the road before I understood how the various fragments fit together in the mosaic of my life.

Jesus gathered us together, as he did the previous morning, in prayer and reflection. Though the air about us was quite brisk and chilly, once we joined together in prayer, I felt warmed and comfortable. When we were through with our prayer, I was very surprised when Jesus walked beside me, and said he would like me to go with him today. The others had already departed, and I had been moving slowly, with my usual early morning torpor. I was happier than words could express to hear him tell me this. We continued walking in a westerly direction. I was anxious and joyful at the same time, feeling completely unworthy to be in his solo company, yet also thinking that this was a special opportunity I would not have anticipated. As we walked, I remembered the dream I had in which Jesus and I had developed a special and intimate bond. My blood surged to think this might become a reality, and this walk might be the beginning of this linking.

I was a man who was never given to fearfulness of my surroundings, and yet the feeling I had in accompanying Jesus in the beginning of this walk was a sense of security and completeness I had never known. To be with him was to be in the presence of the divine. It was as if he were one with all of creation, for all of God's creatures seemed to respond to him in a singular fashion. As I walked with him now, it seemed that the air was clearer, the colors sharper, and each moment more distinctive and alive somehow. We walked with calm deliberation, and our conversation was casual and light to start. I sensed he wanted me to feel completely at ease, and that whatever serious discussion or experience we would have would occur at a later part of the day. I was grateful for this, and tried to tone down the awe I was feeling to a more manageable level.

At first, we walked a long while along the periphery of the Dead Sea. I barely noticed my surroundings, so caught up was I in the more than fortuitous opportunity to spend time alone with this man whom I was beginning to adore. I tried to balance my mind, for I was so prone to idolizing him, and I wanted to retain my objectivity despite the heightened emotions in my heart. We talked breezily of our various trades, his as a carpenter and mine as a fisherman, and of the joys and tribulations inherent in each. I was surprised to hear how much pleasure Jesus took in the physical act of creation, and the satisfaction he received from pouring his sweat, his muscles and his spirit into making even the simplest of furniture. I shared that I understood his pleasure in the physical toil, for in my own trade, I often came home physically weary and spent, yet satisfied on several levels for the work I had done. This was a side of this man I had not anticipated, for my focus with him was so much on the spiritual, that I imagined that the life of the body could not concern him much. I could not have been more wrong, as I was to find out over the years.

He described to me a cradle he had made while he was yet in his teens. He was making it for a Nazarene family that was expecting a child, and he was very fond of these people. He described to me the care he put into this cradle, how he took great pains to find the right wood, and how he took many hours to construct and carve this piece. All the time he was making the cradle, he was thinking of the infant who would sleep therein, and how he wanted to make this cradle so that the infant would be as comfortable as possible.

I listened to him as he spoke, and marveled that this great man would put such focus on something so seemingly mundane. He must have read my mind, for he told me that nothing that we do is unimportant, and the care we give to that which we are called upon to do, no matter how simple, is the way we best give glory to God. It is when we are fully present to the task at hand, he said, that we are sharing in God's presence, and allowing him to work through us.

I understood what he was saying to me mostly on a conceptual level. It made sense, but I did not really connect viscerally to this idea of combining spirituality and physicality. Then, suddenly I remembered my experience of the day before, in the hills. I told him about the lion, and how I shared in the combined sensation of the sensuality, sexuality and spirituality of that animal. I told him of the power I felt, and how enhanced was my ordinary consciousness. I asked Jesus if this were relevant to what he was telling me about our full presence in our activities.

"Exactly so," he said, smiling gently at me. "The lion does not consider that he is a lion, or if what he is doing is out of his higher or his lower nature. He simply exists, and lives fully present in his body and in what he is called upon to do. He does this with courage and with great majesty. He does not consider the opinions of others nor does he seek self-aggrandizement. He simply is what he is, and he is true to his own being."

I was grateful for this explanation, and marveled that the lessons of yesterday and today were dovetailing together so nicely. It was so easy to talk with Jesus. What he said always made so much sense to me! It was also so absorbing to be with him, that it was also easy to forget my hunger and my thirst.

We continued walking, and were silent for a time. We began walking away from the shore, still headed in a westerly direction. I was intensely curious as to why Jesus was accompanying me today. I assumed there must be some kind of reason, which I could not even begin to fathom. As if on cue, Jesus began speaking and telling me he had wanted us to have some time together today, and that he would want me to feel free to come to him any time I had questions or wanted to discuss something with him.

I could hardly contain my excitement at this, for to me it presaged a more personal kind of relationship between us, in which I was not just one of a group of students and disciples, but would have a closer relationship with him. I told him that I was honored, and that I would speak with him when the need arose.

He had more to say to me. There would be twelve of us around him. He said all were very carefully picked for the various qualities we could lend to his mission of spreading the word about God. This had been determined from a long time ago. What he wanted me to know now, he said, was that I had been handpicked to be in a special place next to him. He thought we would work extremely well together, and develop a special fondness for each other. This would mean that more would be asked of me, but he knew I was more than capable of taking on this responsibility. He asked me to be patient, to let time unfold the plan as it would, but hoped that I would feel comfortable to be open to this position next to him.

I was so dumbfounded that I was at a loss for words. My heart felt great joy and fear at the same time. Joy to contemplate the possibility of such an honored position; fear and terror that I might fail or disappoint him. I told him again how honored I felt, but also voiced my concerns that I might not be able to be all he needed me to be. He told me not to worry, that my resources were far more than I imagined, and that I had God as a partner in this venture and need not fear.

We sat and rested for a while, and the subject changed to far less weighty matters. By the time we were ready to turn back for the evening, I believed I would never again be the same John who left that morning. I cannot even remember what we discussed on that return walk, for my mind and my heart were so filled with what he had told me that morning. I prayed to God that He would give me strength, courage and purity to be the best partner I could be in this venture.

CHAPTER 10

WE SPENT ONE MORE FULL DAY IN THIS AREA before heading back to Galilee. Our nights were filled with prayer, and our day was spent in solitude, preparing for times to come.

That night, at the campsite, I felt comfortable for the first time to sit near Jesus. After what had happened during the day, it felt right that I would be nearer to him physically as well as spiritually and emotionally. From that time on, I assumed more and more a place by his side, where I felt very comfortable and protected. Jesus' energy field was large, so full of light and peace, that to stand or sit closely within it felt enormously comforting and even snug. Within it, I felt cared for, accepted, protected and always welcome. This first night, I felt these things to some extent. As time went on, the feelings grew deeper and I grew to trust them more. The only relationship I know to compare these feelings to would be that of a lover and his beloved. The physical embrace after lovemaking, full of peace and contentment and warmth, was like how it felt to be held within this energy field. I do not know how to describe it other than to say that there was always a place for me there. When it felt right to move into that space, I was soon to discover that I always felt welcomed in warmly.

I was sure that the others sensed a shift in my relationship with Jesus, especially after I caught James' eye, and saw him looking quizzically at me as I sat down next to Jesus for the second time that evening. I did not want to alienate others, or to be boastful in any way. For, after all, each of us had our own special relationship with Jesus.

After we were finished with our evening prayer, it got quite chilly. We bundled ourselves up, and thought of warmer times. Despite the

49

cold in my body, my mind was so excited with today's events that it took off on a life of its own imagining. Often, I forgot about the cold for long periods of time. I realized that my dream was coming true, exactly as it had foretold. I wondered how it happened that dreams had so much to teach. I remembered my mother's dream about Jesus taking both James and myself away. I also remembered my dream about the intense light, which I followed from before this life, down into this incarnation. As I thought about this latter dream, I realized that it had been predestined for me to have this opportunity to learn from and to follow Jesus. For many long moments I wondered about how this could be, and what was the nature of predestination. Also, and more importantly, there was the matter of Jesus, his predestined mission, and what he was here to do. I realized that I had many more questions than I had answers at this point. The youthful part of me wanted to know all about why he was on earth now, what would happen to him, and what would happen to us.

I was not a scholar, and yet I did know from what I had been learning, that the prophecies of old said the Messiah would come to teach of God and show God's ways, and that he would be scorned and slain by those who opposed him. It frightened me to consider this possibility. In my youthful naïveté I wondered if, given all his power, he could change the course of events so that this would not happen. I was beginning to be tremendously attached to Jesus, especially now that we were bonding on a completely different level. I could not tolerate the thought of losing him. I knew by now that I would be giving my heart to him completely and without reservation. This alone terrified me, not to mention that I might well lose him. I found myself thinking that if this horrible future were to have to pass, I hoped it would be many years from now, when we were much older, and having had the opportunity to experience many years together. In a way, I think I decided it made sense that Jesus would be around for many years to come, and I let the matter go at that.

I was having trouble staying focused on the mission I was here to help with, for I was finding that the dimension of our personal relationship was now taking on a new meaning. My heart fortunately was working on the same overall goals as my head, but I was a bit dazzled with the intensity of the feelings of my heart.

Next morning when I awoke, it was dawn, and the others were already stirring. I had slept next to Jesus that night, and I slept peacefully and deeply. I dreamt for some reason of my parents. They were telling me in the dream of a story of when I was a little boy, and had fallen and skinned one of my knees rather badly. I was crying, but also wanting to be brave, and did not seem able consistently to present myself in one or the other of these modes. I suppose I must have looked rather silly to my parents, who had commented to me at the time that I had the feelings of a little boy, but wanted to be brave like a man. This incident was one I had long ago forgotten. It seemed very strange that it would be coming up in a dream now, when so much was happening of a very different nature.

I got up and joined the others in a circle for our morning prayer. Today would be our last day here, and I was beginning to feel eager to get back to whatever the world had to offer us. Jesus led us in prayer, and asked God to prepare us today for the roles each of us would be playing, both individually and collectively. As our energies joined with the Divine, I reveled in the feeling of exhilaration that ensued, and thanked God for my special partnership.

In the moments of silence that followed, my dream of the night before came to my mind. I realized that those feelings of that little boy, of being so hurt and vulnerable yet wanting to be strong and brave, were like the feelings I had been having the night before after my experience during the day with Jesus. I felt incredibly vulnerable around him, and fearful of being hurt, and yet I wanted to be brave and strong, and to do whatever it was that would be asked of me as a man. I realized that maybe not that much had changed, after all, over the years.

On this day, I walked off more confidently on my own. It was not an eventful day, like the two preceding days had been, but was rather quiet and calm. I spent much time in prayer and meditation. I found a secluded place on a hill, overlooking the Sea, and asked God to fill me with the wisdom and the strength that I would need, when

I would need it. I felt a growing trust in my ability to connect with the divine within, and knew I would take this trust with me back to the world of civilization. As much as I wanted to know the details of what my role would be, it became clear to me during this meditation that it was not mine to know now. Rather, I would learn what I needed to know as it became necessary. Perhaps this deepening of this inner connection was what I needed to know about my role: that no matter what situation would arise, I would always have this ability to turn inside and to discover the manner in which I should act, and what it was I should say.

A strong breeze came up suddenly, seemingly out of nowhere. Somewhere in my psyche, the breeze served to me as reinforcement that what I had just been surmising was indeed true. The breeze was cooling and hot at the same time. I felt transported out of my body, and out of this time and place into a dimension where there was the certainty that all of this was taking place just as it should. My main task would be to remain present to it. I returned to my body and gave myself some minutes to adjust, before I got up and headed back for camp.

Once I was back at camp, I felt that I was now ready to leave. I had a much greater understanding of the forces that had brought me here, and though I did not know specifics about what was to unfold, I had a much better sense of my position in the drama. I felt very blessed, and held close to my heart this confidence and trust that had been put in me.

The evening went by quickly. I think we were all eager to get on our way, and especially to break the fast. The collective solemnity of our mood was now replaced by a much more light-hearted approach. We joked and bantered with each other. Our purpose had been achieved in coming to this region, and now we rested mentally before we would leave with a serious purpose early the next morning. Jesus was fairly quiet and smiled often, but seemed to be focused on a world beyond this one. I found myself often wondering where he went when he went away in this manner, and wondering what it would be like if I could accompany him on these journeys.

As was our custom, we closed for the evening with a prayer and meditation. Before I knew it, it was near dawn, and we were starting the day with another period of prayer. The feeling I had this morning was similar to the one I had that first day when I left home to follow Jesus: it was the feeling that things would be quite different now. There was an excitement and anticipation that come with knowing something momentous was happening, but not quite knowing what it was.

I was grateful for the cool of the morning for our hike. We walked briskly and energetically to warm up our chilled bodies. Jesus was especially quiet this morning. I longed to be one with him, to understand what he was thinking, feeling and planning. If this were adoration, then this is what I felt. I had never yearned to be so close to anyone. While the yearning was extremely strong, I also felt that these feelings were taboo somehow. I understand now that these feelings are like that of the lover wanting to be one with the beloved, and that these are perfectly natural wishes. In this case, however, the beloved was not the object of my physical lust, but rather of my desire to be one with this man who, to my mind, embodied perfection itself.

Simon Peter, who was now called simply Peter, was quite talkative this morning. He was eager to get back and check on his boats, and how his men were holding up. He was perhaps having a harder time than the rest of us in letting go of his old life, and felt he had to check back from time to time just to see how things were going without him. He was not quite yet accustomed to the idea that he might never return to his life as a fisherman, and it seemed he needed to maintain contact in this way. Jesus reassured him often that he was far more valuable, and would continue to be, in this work that he was now doing: the souls he would be helping to save were far more precious than any fish in the sea that were to be caught. Jesus wisely allowed Peter to disengage in his own way, in his own time, and made no demands on him. He knew, I am sure, that time would take care of this by itself.

The four days it took us to return to Galilee were mostly unremarkable in external events. We were exhausted by the time we stopped walking in the late afternoon. By the time we ate and prayed, we were more than ready for the rest that sleep would bring us. Occasionally we would come across people who had heard of Jesus, and we would stop and discuss God with them, or we would share a meal with them.

What was perhaps most significant during these days was the teachings Jesus was sharing with us on divining the energy field that is around each organic thing. He started us off with sensing energy. He had us feel the energy in a human hand or an animal, and then in a rock, a plant or some grains of soil. It was easy to feel the energy when he would place his hand on my forehead or on my arm, for he was a master transmitter of energy. He would transmit the energy at different registers, from much stronger to much weaker, so we would have the opportunity to become accustomed to what this felt like at the stronger and more obvious levels, before tuning in to the more subtle and less obvious. I was pleased he started us out at basic levels, because it never felt that he was moving beyond my ability to comprehend fully.

Next, he introduced us to the energy from each other. He had each of us touch one of the others and try to generate energy. The subject would tell the transmitter what he experienced, if anything. It was new to us to be trying to transmit, much less notice these energies. We had all seen Jesus heal, but I assumed this was an ability that was innate to him. What I was hearing Jesus say now, much to my surprise, was that healing and transmitting healing energies, were learned skills, just like carpentry or fishing, requiring training and practice to learn.

I practiced with James, and then with Jesus. I was able to perceive at a very low register the energies that James was sending. He, in turn, was able to experience slightly what I was directing. When I paired with Jesus, I was amazed at the different properties of the transmission that I was able to experience, from intensity of light and heat, to the quality of directedness (for example, the difference between a focused beam of energy to a more generalized and diffuse transmission of heat). When I commented on this, Jesus said it was very important to visualize in the mind's eye the type of healing energy one wishes to send.

The way he described it was thus: In order to pull down energy from above, that is, to gather in the divine energies, it is important to visualize the healing light and energy coming down from the heavens, in through the crown chakra at the top of the head, and in to the heart. He said it is very important to anchor this energy first in the heart before sending it out again, because then the energy is bathed in love and relatedness, and this prevents any abuses from the will or the intellect. Next, after the energy circulates throughout the heart, one focuses with the third eye chakra and directs the healing energy back out again in the form that the healer intuits is appropriate for a given condition or situation. He was very adamant that it is important that all of this be done consciously, and in a thinking manner. Though the healer is praying and allowing himself to be a channel for this energy, he emphasized that it is extremely important for the healer to direct this energy through conscious focusing and concentrating. The feet should be planted firmly on the ground, for this provides the grounding for the operation. Without this grounding, the healer would be much more apt to grow unfocused and to absorb into himself the negative energies of the one being healed.

I knew this was a simplification of the process, yet it gave me a good overall understanding of the mechanics of something I had always considered mystical and incomprehensible to the rational mind. Here, at least, I had a skeletal outline I could comprehend, and which did not overwhelm me with its complexity. I practiced these steps with Jesus, and then with Peter. I found I could begin to feel the flow of these energies as I consciously invoked them and began to direct them with my mind. Of course, when I was working with Jesus, I could feel the energies much more powerfully, for in his presence all of these higher vibrational energies were amplified, and felt much more clear and even tangible.

Jesus told us that after we were through with these energy transmissions, it was extremely important we then cleanse ourselves with whatever means felt appropriate or possible at the time. Sometimes we would feel the need to let go of the negative energy we had picked up; at these and other times we might feel the need to physically bathe or otherwise cleanse our body. We would often feel depleted, he said, after we had put out large amounts of energy, and in those cases it would be important to rest, eat nourishing food, and in some cases seek solitude. In all cases, he said it would be important to restore the visualization of a shroud of white light encasing us and protecting us. This would help to restore and cleanse us, and to replenish our energy and our light body.

This concept of the light body was one I had heard Jesus mention in passing up to this point. I had wondered what it was, but now I felt free to query him about it. It was a concept that would be very important to Jesus' teachings, but I had no idea at this point how important it would be. I asked him, on one of our evening stops: "Master, please tell us more about this idea of the light body. I do not understand what it is and how it is different from the energy field that surrounds the body at all times."

He explained that the light body is the sum total of the energy that forms the basis of the human body and its immediate energy field. It was very hard to grasp what he meant as he described the body as consisting of very rapidly moving particles of energy and light, that were clustered in such a density that the body only appeared to be solid. He said this light body had stored within it memories of various traumas and incidents that it had experienced. As one grew and progressed spiritually, the body became less dense, and clearer. The more tied to the earth, to greed, lust and other negative clinging emotions, the denser was the body, and the darker it became. Within this light body is contained the memory of the totality of one's experiences, thoughts and emotions. He would tune into this body in order to know what area or areas of a person needed healing.

For example, he told me that what he saw now in me was darkness at my right temple area, which he saw as a straining and as an area of tension. Although I had not been aware of this until he said it, I tuned into this area and realized that I was indeed quite tense there, for I was anxious that I was not capable of understanding this level of complex information. In fact, though I had not as yet developed a headache, I recognized the signs of one forming. I asked him how he would deal with this. He replied by touching this area of my head with his hand. I felt a buzzing in that area, and immediately felt relaxed. The tension in that area felt completely gone. I asked Jesus what he had done, and he said simply that he had done what he had just taught me to do. He saw the area of darkness at my temple, and transmitted a diffuse healing light, to break up the darkness and help it to disperse. That relieved the tension and left no traces of an incipient headache.

The lessons continued as we journeyed back to Galilee, on our rest periods. We were walking significant distances each day, and we were quite tired by the time evening came. I knew that the level of individual attention we were receiving would soon change. There would be many people clamoring to be around Jesus, and there would be more disciples. I tried to enjoy this time as much as I could, and absorb as much from Jesus as was possible.

CHAPTER II

By the time we returned to Galilee, it seemed there had been a distinct change in the level of public awareness of Jesus. Everywhere we went in the region, Jesus was recognized. People wanted to talk with him, to be healed or to have their relatives healed by him. We encountered many skeptics, but it seemed that, for whatever reasons, they asked as many if not more questions. In some ways, they seemed more ready to believe than I would have suspected: often they were looking to see an example of a healing so they could let go of their disbelief.

I knew it was important to Jesus that he finish gathering his disciples. I asked if he knew who he was going to select, and he said, somewhat enigmatically: "Those who will be with me have been so from the beginning. I only need now to request that they follow, and they will know this is their time."

I asked him what he would need of me now. He said he wanted us to continue with our lessons, and with practice. He would teach us when he could, but that the rest of us would need time to absorb and review what we were learning. He said he wanted us to grow more comfortable with each other, and in his absence, for he would not always be around to lead and inspire us. A part of me grew very alarmed by this, but then I comforted myself by telling myself that what he meant was that he would often be off in other places, and that he would want us to continue with his ministry while he was elsewhere. I imagined that I could grow more comfortable with these men, yet I could not imagine being comfortable in this work with Jesus gone for any more than a few days at a time. I realize now that I knew when he said this, that he was telling me much more than that he would be gone occasionally. However my mind drugged itself with the thought that he meant only that there would be occasional separations. How often as the months wore on I was to catch myself drugging myself with delusion around the subject of Jesus' departure. I loved this man more than I had ever loved anyone, and had given my heart over to him since the beginning of our trip to the Dead Sea.

I adored him beyond reason and beyond words. I felt completely loved in his presence, and completely understood. I truly believed he knew the darkest parts of my soul. In his knowing them and accepting them, he was able to give to me a sense of wholeness and completeness I had never before known. The depth of the love that was growing in me for Jesus often frightened me these days. It disquieted me that I could be so out of control of my feelings and emotions. I tried hard not to let any of this show, for I felt it was important to retain my composure, and not to be swept away with this inner tide. And yet, at times I felt overwhelmed, and did not know what to make of this growing passion that I felt. The following example illustrates what I have been trying to explain.

We had just finished eating our morning meal. Jesus was to be leaving soon to gather some of the other disciples. He was talking with Peter. I was daydreaming while I was watching him.

I was very aware of my sexuality, and of feeling heightened desire. As I watched Jesus, I realized that my love for him was complete: I adored him and the divine in him, and I was totally in awe of him. I was thinking how much I loved him, and how I would love to please him and love him however I could. I realized that this fleshly, sexually aroused part of me would love to give him physical pleasure and to be satisfied by him. I was quite surprised at myself, for I had never experienced these feelings for a man, but only towards women. I realized that my desire was a function of my passion and my adoration. My desire was strong, and its strength shocked me not a little bit.

I was startled out of my thoughts as I looked up, and realized he had read them. I was momentarily embarrassed, even mortified, but then I felt from him his complete acceptance of my feelings and of my love. I knew from this that it was acceptable for me to feel this way, and I felt no more shame. I knew we would not have a physical relationship, yet the fantasy of this complete love and of being physically loved and caressed by this man/God was rapturous.

In accepting me thus, I felt that he accepted me completely, without judgment. The passion I felt in my soul for him permeated my every cell and could not help but include my sexual feelings. How could I help but love him with every fiber of my being? And that definitely included my sexuality. I remembered the feelings I had in my encounter with the lion, and how, in my experience of its feelings, they were blended together in insurmountable majesty. The sexual was not separated out from the spiritual and the sensual: all of these energies had blended harmoniously, in a very natural and un-selfconscious manner. I tried to apply this to myself in the situation at hand. But it was mostly as I felt deep inside of me Jesus' acceptance of my feelings, that I could accept these feelings in myself. Without his acceptance, I would have judged and condemned myself. I did not tell anyone of this, however, for it was very private. It is only these many years later that I am comfortable writing of this experience.

My sexuality would prove to be a subject to be dealt with on many occasions. My drive was high, and I had no physical release for my passions. I was a young man, with a full complement of youthful energies. At times these sexual energies were so intense that I thought I would surely go mad. As an unmarried disciple of Jesus, I was not to have the sexual experiences of other men my age. It was only later on that I felt comfortable discussing this with Jesus, or with the others. At times during this early period, I could lose myself in prayer, meditation, or other spiritual work, but at other times, I was distressed that I could not let go of the feelings, which felt like they were driving me. At those times, I would absent myself from my brothers and relieve myself in order to be able to regain focus on the work before me.

With Jesus gone, probably for several days, we camped near the Sea of Galilee, and enjoyed the opportunity to do some fishing. It seemed like it had been a very long time since James, Peter, Andrew and I had made our living by fishing. I missed the natural rhythm of the fishing day, and James shared that he did also. We were changing with our new calling, yet so much was new and different that there were times when I found myself longing for the old and familiar. This time was helpful in that respect, and I felt grounded in something that I knew, something my muscles and instincts were deeply familiar with.

It was tempting to go back home for a few days, but it felt more important now to stay here with these men, and allow the experiences of the recent weeks to absorb into my consciousness. We practiced with each other in identifying energy fields and aspects of these fields. None of us were very good at it at this point, and we struggled with our learning. Jesus was a wonderful teacher, yet there was so much to learn. It seemed there would never be time to learn all he had to teach.

I was touched by Peter, who was such a large and burly man, and yet who tried in earnest to learn these lessons about these subtleties of energies and energy fields. One would never suspect from looking at him, that he had such sensitivities and spiritual passions. I doubt that anyone but Jesus could have inspired this in him. I had known him from our previous lives as fishermen. His crusty reputation was in many ways well deserved. He had always been good to me, though, but I was accustomed to his churlish manner, and had learned how to sidestep him when this was necessary. He could be very generous and caring; it seemed to depend on whatever mood he was in, or perhaps how he had done with fishing that day. Since he had been following Jesus, however, the darker side of his temperament had seemed to even out somewhat, and I found myself seeking out his company more than I might have thought I would.

James and Andrew liked each other a great deal, and formed a solid companionship. In many respects, their personalities were similar. Both were affable, good-natured men who took life as it came to them, and who were able to make themselves quickly at ease in new social situations. They did not take themselves too seriously, and as a result always had mental energy available to attend to others or to explore new situations. I admired their outgoing, relaxed natures, and sorely wished I could make myself as comfortable as they seemed to be.

Philip, Nathaniel and Thomas were each distinct individuals in their own right, yet for a number of reasons I had not taken the opportunity to get to know them well. During these few days, I had more time, and since Jesus was not there, I was not distracted. When Jesus was around, I tended to direct most of my energy and my focus towards him. We shared our perceptions about what we thought was happening in this very special time, and discussed how we came to first hear about Jesus and to meet him. We discussed that some day some of us might be called upon to write about the experiences that we were having, and to document what we knew about Jesus. This was a curious thought to me. It made perfect sense that a record would need to be kept, and who better to keep it than those of us who had actually known and journeyed with him.

I was surprised by how much I missed Jesus during these few days. We prayed together, ate together, and spent our days together. I had grown more accustomed than I realized to his presence. He added light amongst our midst. Even our prayers did not seem as powerful in his absence.

If I did not feel his presence amongst us then, while he was gone only in the nearby environs, I wondered how it would be on that day, however far removed, when he was literally gone from us. Within my mind, I heard very loudly and very clearly as I wondered thus: "I will be with you always. You will always be able to be in contact with me." I was startled by the clarity and by the strength of the words I heard reverberating within my head. I realized he knew my worries and my concerns, and that even now he was contacting me to reassure me that now as ever he would be able to be there for me and for us. I felt relieved, and even glad now for his current absence, for I had just learned something very valuable. There was no doubt in my mind but that the words I had just heard were directly from Jesus, and were not just a product of my vulnerable mental state. Obviously, he had been able to tune into my thoughts directly, and to respond to them with the reassurance that I had not previously known I needed. It was as if he were able to be there to meet my special needs almost as soon as I was able to articulate them, even in my thoughts. I was once more touched by the love he had to offer. Just as I so often felt adoration for him, I also felt very loved.

CHAPTER 12

MY DREAMING LIFE CONTINUED TO BRING ITSELF to my attention, often right upon awakening. Sometimes I would recall my dream later in the day, when something was said, or when some occurrence, smell or other sensate cue would remind me of what I had dreamt. While Jesus was away gathering disciples, the rest of us slept at a campsite. I often lay awake at night after the others had dozed off, staring up at the stars and fantasizing about what life might be like after Jesus returned, and once we resumed our ministry.

On this particular night, I had been wondering what miracles of healing I might be witness to, but also wondered about my friendship with Jesus and what the nature of that growing relationship with him would be. I reflected how his relationship to us as a group was special and very intimate. I had been deeply moved by the day we spent together at the Dead Sea, and was intensely curious about the direction our personal relationship would take. This was not something that I had discussed or would discuss with anyone else, and hence it took on even more of a charged nature for me. These were my musings before I slept.

In the middle of the night I woke up remembering very clearly the following dream:

> "I am in the middle of a garden, surrounded by everyone I have ever known and loved. I hear the sweetest music imaginable, and it is as if my heart responds to the sounds of the instruments. I am filled with a love such as I have never before felt. I feel satisfied and radiant with the glow of its energy. I know that this feeling is because of Jesus and what

he has taught me about the Kingdom within. He walks beside me, yet I know his presence is also within me, and is the love that I feel. It is no contradiction that he can be outside of me, yet within me at the same time.

Then he is gone, and I turn inside, and feel him in my heart. Each beat of my heart pulses out his love: I know with a complete certainty that he lives within me. No matter where I am, and no matter what body I am in, he will always be there with me, if only I tune in to him. That much I know is up to me.

I turn my attention once again outside of myself. Again, he is there, reaching out his hand to me. We will go walking, and I know that for the duration of this time, I will be able to bask in his individual attentions. I want to learn as much as I can and feel every bit of his energy that I can. I feel very blessed to be in this position. I am comfortable in the role of exchanging confidences with this man."

Despite the chill of the night, I woke up feeling thoroughly warmed by the energies circulating throughout my body during this dream. I felt that the walk he and I took in the dream was a familiar ritual. In my waking consciousness, I sensed that it was something that we had done on many occasions, and was very special to both of us. My critical consciousness told me it was presumptuous to assume this was special for Jesus too, yet if I stayed with the feelings in the dream, it felt very clear that we both cherished these times.

Morning brought with it a burst of activity. We somehow knew that Jesus would be back today, and wanted to be ready for him, for whatever he might want of us. We caught and cooked fish for our morning meal, and ate heartily. The atmosphere between us was full of expectancy. We wondered about the people Jesus would bring with him, and also about what we would be doing next. We had practiced our exercises with energy, and were ready to move on to further lessons. It was curious how we were beginning to get bored with each other, and restless. For myself, I was ready to get moving again, and wanting to go on to the next adventure, whatever it might be.

As I write these words now, many years later, I recognize the impatience of youth. Had I known then what I know now, I would not have been in such a hurry to meet the future. But, I was full of idealism and urgency, and felt I simply could not wait to be again with this man, and march into the next town or the next teaching and experience to the fullest what this life could offer me. I wanted with all of my heart to move into the spaces that only he could show me. I was very aware of the spaces within me that needed to be shown and to be taught. I had little if any sense of what I had to give to others. I was very much like a sponge at this point, and lived to absorb and to learn.

Peter was much older. I admired him and the sense of purpose he carried with him. It seemed that he had much better knowledge of himself and of the abilities he brought to bear on each situation. I liked his self-assurance, and I hoped that as time went on, I would find a sense of my own direction. Peter seemed very comfortable taking on the leadership role of this small group in Jesus' absence. Though he was a bit rough around the edges, and could be arrogant, with us he was gentle and circumspect, and had a disciplined manner about him when he pulled us together. He was clearly proud of the role he played with us, and we were glad to have him there. In ways he was like an older brother to me, and in ways like a father. His experience in the world seemed much greater than mine, and I sensed there was much to learn from him. I was learning that even when he was unsure about himself in a given situation, he proceeded to act as if he were sure about what he was doing, and the situation would usually work out quite well. My tendency would have been to be much more hesitant to act, so it was inspiring to observe this. I tried to incorporate this aspect of his style into my own, especially as time went on.

If there was anything lacking in my current experience, I would have to say it was the lack of feminine influence. I was around men all of the time, and the way we were together sometimes wore on me. I missed the softness and gentleness of my mother and sister, and I missed the tender smile of my neighbor. Jesus had much of the feminine within him, and this modified the way that we were as men together. However, these few days without him gave me the opportunity to focus more on this aspect of our experience. There was a certain roughness and demeanor about the group of us when together that was at times fine, but at other times could feel lacking in qualities that I could not define or articulate at the time, but certainly missed. We had all been accustomed to being around men a lot, but then we would go home, and we would have time with women as well. I do not know if the others felt as I did, but during these few days I was feeling this lack acutely.

In the groups that gathered around Jesus, and which were beginning to follow him from place to place, there were many women. It seemed as if it were easier for women to sense and trust the innate qualities that Jesus displayed. I suppose I should not have been surprised that when Jesus came back this time, there were women among the group. My surprise was not that I should see women around him, but that I had thought that the group of us who would be most closely associated with him would be composed strictly of men. In ways, I was shaken to see the women; in other ways, I felt glad for the chance to have more balance.

A group of about 25 to 30 people came back with him to our campsite around mid-morning. I was surprised and confused by the large number, as well as by the combination of sexes. I was soon to learn that the inner circle of followers would be far larger than I had realized, though the number 12 would still be the number of men at the core of this circle. Jesus had brought all of these people back to meet with us and to work with all of us. Among them were several more of the men who would continue with us wherever we went. James, Peter, Andrew and I went to catch more fish for the crowd, and were gone for several hours.

I grew distracted on the boat, and wondered what was calling my attention. I looked around and saw nothing unusual; then I heard a clear voice inside, saying to me: "You have been attentive to what I have asked of you. I ask of you now that you meet with me later tonight, after the others have gone to sleep. We have much to discuss, and I have need of you." The voice and the request were so clear, that no matter how I tried, I could not dismiss it as simply imagination, or as merely the product of a wish to have private time with my Master. I had heard his voice as clearly as if he had been standing next to me, talking directly to me. I was delighted with the request, and was very eager for nightfall so that I could spend this time with him.

The hours went by very slowly, and the day was full of introductions and sharing between these many people. Jesus talked to us as a group for a while, but made it clear to us that today was not to be a day in which we directly focused on him to give us knowledge; but, rather for us to share amongst ourselves. I enjoyed the company of women, and could relate directly to the kind of adoration they so readily gave over to him. They did not feel the need to hide that which the men, including myself, felt necessary to conceal. The looks they gave Jesus were more a direct expression of the total feeling of body and soul, whereas the men seemed more comfortable with intellect.

There was one woman to whom I seemed to gravitate more than the rest. It almost seemed that she could sense the feelings I held to myself so tightly. Without saying anything, she was able to help me feel accepted for them. No doubt she had the same feelings herself, and therefore was able to identify with me. I never had felt this transparent, or accepted for this side of me around any of the men except Jesus. With her, as with him, the clarity of their vision into me helped me to feel complete and whole. Our actual conversation was respectful and not personal, but it did seem that we were communicating on a whole other level while we talked. This woman's name was Martha. She seemed sure even at this point that she wanted to be where Jesus was, and that it was an important part of her destiny to follow him. I was extremely grateful for her presence, and looked forward to further contacts with her as time went on.

Martha asked me many questions about what I had seen and done so far. I told her of our recent trip to the Dead Sea, and said that it had been a very important time of learning, and of connecting with God. I said I had joined with Jesus relatively recently myself, that I had seen a number of healings, and that I was convinced that Jesus manifested God as he spoke and as he healed. I told her I did not have any doubts about the authority with which he spoke. Further, I said that we were extraordinarily fortunate to be born in this time, and to be selected to be in his presence during his lifetime and during his reign. I said the prophets had spoken of him for generations, and this time would be spoken of in the many generations to come.

We continued with this conversation until mid-afternoon, and then James came to get me and have me plan with him a fishing venture. We would be leaving the next day, and he wanted me to help him with pulling together food for the evening and morning. As we traveled, we knew that food would be provided for us, but in this site, he felt that we were able to, and should, provide fish. I agreed with him, and we occupied ourselves with this business. I was grateful for the diversion, for I was eager for the evening to come, and was glad to have work to do to help pass the time.

Over the course of the day, I often wondered what Jesus was doing, and frequently looked over in his direction. It appeared that he was worn out, and he seemed to be resting. People were innately respectful of his need, and though most were probably bursting to speak with him and spend more time with him, they left him alone. Peter discouraged people from approaching Jesus by his presence. Whether Jesus was praying, napping or meditating under that tree, I know not. Whatever it was, I knew that he was not in this world with us.

CHAPTER 13

THE EVENING COULD NOT COME QUICKLY ENOUGH FOR ME. I wondered often what was in store, and could not imagine what it could be. When I had heard Jesus' voice in my mind, it did not come with any kind of foreboding that would herald bad news, but rather, felt more positive, or at least neutral. I knew that with our journeying in the morning would come the public appearances and large crowds that had become such a regular part of Jesus' retinue. Martha had told me of several such crowds in the days Jesus was gone from us.

I lay down near Jesus as the group settled down for the night. I was anything but sleepy, as my excitement and curiosity had my body and mind in a state of alertness. When it came time to go, he signaled to me with a sound. We got up and commenced walking. It was not long before he began talking with me. It was by now cool and comfortable, and a very pleasant temperature for walking. The moon was almost full, and the moonlight helped us to find our way.

Jesus said he had asked me to come tonight because he was going to begin with me a new dimension of his teaching. He had talked with the group of us about dreams, and about the journey the spirit makes during the dreaming state. Now, he wanted to discuss the subject in more detail. This immediately piqued my curiosity, for I had been dreaming more vividly since he had entered my life, and the dreams had made quite an impression on me. One of the things that I remembered that he had taught was: "In dreams, we enter God's world. Through dreams, He enters ours." This had a significant impact on me, though I did not fully understand it.

Jesus told me how he and I would now begin spending time together at night, after we had gone to sleep, journeying together in our dreams. I did not know what he meant. He explained that the spirit leaves the body when we sleep, and that it is possible to make conscious journeys, alone or with others, to specific destinations or for specific purposes. He told me that at first I might be confused and not be clear about the state that I was in, but he would guide me, and I would gradually get to the point where I felt skilled in what I was doing. He told me many things that were possible in this state, that were not as easily done in the waking state. He told me that talking much about this now would not be nearly as useful as the experience. When we returned to our camp tonight, and slept, he would take me on the first of these, our night journeys.

I felt blessed to be singled out for the night journeys he was to take me on. The teachings for all of us about dreams during the day were absorbing and challenging, but had merely whetted my curiosity about dreams. We walked back, and I was so excited that I wondered how I would ever fall asleep. Yet I was exhausted, and before I knew it I was waking up inside my dream. I found myself in a bright sunny field beside my Master. The sense of him there beside me was strong, clear and vivid, and I knew immediately that although I was in a dream state, this was really his essence beside my own.

First, he took me to a very brightly lit place where the white light was all there was. I felt a great deal of love and divine presence here—it was exhilarating, but also very hard to bear. Somehow, I knew Jesus came here often. I knew more too—this was his home.

We traveled many places that night. It was almost like an overview, the purpose of which was to show me what was possible. We flew over towns and countrysides, and over distant lands I had never seen. He showed me the great mountains and the great seas and deserts. I was stunned and amazed to see how very immense the world was. Never before had I realized how small was my own world. He showed me how, when summoned, or needed, we could enter another's dream for the purpose of guidance or healing. He cautioned me to never do this without a very specific and clear purpose. He showed me how we could check on people to make sure they were safe: we briefly and respectfully visited his mother Mary as she lay sleeping. Then we went to a little boy who had been ill, and he showed me how he could do the same healing from this state as from the waking state.

I was awed and impressed by our journey. I felt well rested the next day, and was surprised at this. I hoped that this was to be one of many such night journeys and lessons. Jesus had said we would be journeying together at night now. After the adventures of last night, I felt my mind had been opened to a completely new dimension of experience and learning. I felt very limited compared to Jesus. Of course the comparison could only hurt me, for it was like comparing the finite with the infinite, or the mortal with the divine. I only knew that my gratitude was enormous for this marvelous opportunity that I had. I had no idea how I could be so blessed as to be so close to Jesus, and to have these intimate opportunities for further learning, but I was very appreciative that this had happened. I hoped I would be able to be worthy of the trust and the confidence placed in me. I prayed for this every evening before I went to sleep. I was always, from this time on, mindful of the responsibility I bore in this regard.

CHAPTER 14

THE DAYS BEGAN TO PASS MORE QUICKLY NOW. The initial period where everything was new was now over. Those days had flown by quickly in some ways, and yet since every moment tended to feel so charged and unique, they had also seemed long in that they seemed filled with so much of a new and extraordinary nature. The days of this next period continued in their extraordinary nature, but had some sense of familiarity and routine. It seemed that this kind of life would go on forever.

I grew to truly believe that Jesus was the Savior and the Messiah who had been prophesied since ancient times. He had been expected for such a long time; it was said that many previous generations had each expected and hoped he would be born into their time. Many had seen the emergence of men who claimed to be this Messiah. In more recent times, there had been a number of men who would individually arise, each with a small band of followers. These men would claim to work miracles and to be in special contact with God. Some of these appeared to have special powers; others seemed obvious fools or charlatans. Some were well meaning but deluded; others were no doubt mad. Though it would not be accurate to say that these would-be Messiahs were a truly familiar part of the landscape in these general times, there had been enough of them that it was a part of the texture of the landscape of our times.

Piety and religiosity were a natural part of the daily life of most of the citizens of our land. The spiritual nature of our people and of our times was intense, yet all too often the outer show and the political aspects of religion became highlighted, to the detriment of the actual religious or spiritual sentiments. The Sadducees and the Pharisees had their many differences over the letter of the law and the spirit of the law. For the most part, I had always tried to stay as uninvolved in this as possible. There were laws and rules that governed almost all aspects of our everyday lives. I had grown weary with all of the strictures one was supposed to follow.

Jesus was like a breath of fresh air to me in this regard. He taught that what was ultimately important was what was in one's heart and in one's soul, and that one's life should be a reflection of what one truly believes. When I was with him, I could feel that spirit was alive: what I was learning had nothing at all to do with the endless rules of daily conduct. The rules were suffocating. With this new expansive view of the world that Jesus showed, my vision was opening up into the infinite. I was beginning believe that there were no limits to what could be done, or learned, or given to others through love. There was joy in this new universe of expansiveness. Most of all, there was mercy, there was tenderness, and there was love. I was learning to feel and to react through my bodily senses, and was gaining a new sense of trust in what my heart said was right. I now experienced my soul as a real entity, whereas before it had been mostly a theoretical concept. When I searched inside for answers to my questions, it was into my soul that I looked.

The miracles of healing I had seen so far, the visions, and the incredible experiences I had been having, seemed to me proof of something miraculous that was occurring. It was clear to me that Jesus was able to see into my heart and into my mind, as well as into those of others, but these telepathic and healing abilities did not mean he was a Messiah. There were tales of many people over the centuries who had extraordinary abilities, and if it were just these aspects of him that I saw, I would surely not be able to say that I believed he was the man who had been sent by God to redeem the world.

In my heart and soul, I believed that Jesus was he whom God had sent. I asked myself at first many times a day if I really believed that this was who he was. There is a vast difference between an intellectual belief and a deeply held conviction of the soul. It was a long time after I began thinking that Jesus was the Messiah before I believed in the deepest recesses of my soul that he was. I cannot say at what point this happened, or even be sure that I accurately know where I was on this continuum at the point in time that I am currently describing in this writing. I do know, however, that I was definitely seated in many respects at the table of belief in the Messianic nature of Jesus at this point, and I was looking at the many aspects of what this meant.

With the wisdom of hindsight, I know now that I had many delusions and many misunderstandings about what it meant to say that Jesus was the Messiah, that he would deliver Israel from her enemies, and that he would rule on earth. But, lest I get too far ahead of myself in this story, I will say that at this time, I expected that in my lifetime, I would see the Kingdom of God established on earth, and its enemies overthrown. I believed these were the times of the beginning of Jesus' literal reign on earth, and I thought I would live to see him in the role of King. I was certainly not alone in these beliefs; the other disciples also had this quite literal view of the scriptures. Before we could arrive at the deeper layers of the truths in which we believed, we would have many layers of delusion and self-deception to work through.

Many were the whisperings about Jesus and the possible Messianic nature of his mission. Yet, it was now still early in his public ministry, and these things were not spoken aloud as much as were the tales of his healings, and of the miracle of the loaves at Cana. I know that for me, my transformation was a gradual one, marked at times by events that pushed me into various shifts. The time when I witnessed Jesus heal the old woman, and had the inner transformative experience of having the accumulation of muck around my heart removed, and my heart center opened, was one of those shifts. But as important as these shifts and my witnessing of the healings and miracles were, it was the nature of the loving relationship that was developing between myself and Jesus that was changing me and helping me to understand the nature of the Messianic role. This is very difficult for me to explain, as it is so intensely personal, as the relationship that each person has with Jesus is intensely personal and individualized.

By this time, I felt myself to be a very different person. I know that I was the same John, brother to James, son of Zebedee and Salome, yet in my very essence I felt that I was transforming. It was as if the consciousness that Jesus brought to bear in each situation was penetrating my very cells and changing them into something different, something lighter. My soul no longer seemed identical with my body. The dream state travels of the previous night had helped me, even on this first night journey, to have a much better sense of my essential spiritual nature. I saw my body more clearly as a garment to put on temporarily.

The adoration I felt for Jesus, and the love I felt from him for me, touched me in every part of my body and soul. It was his love alone, not the miracles, not the healings, not the powers and the supernatural abilities, that led me to know, in the core part of me, he was the Messiah. There is no way I know how to convey this clearly, for this love was so far beyond human love that to try to understand or convey this from the framework of human dimensions is to lose immeasurable meaning in the translation. I carried much of this around within myself, not knowing how to express it or what to express. Only when I was around Jesus did I feel truly connected to this love.

The healings he performed were an expression of this love that he gave with such abundance. I have seen in the course of my life many men who hold their loving nature closely in to themselves. They let those around them give them love, but act as if they felt that if they gave their love freely to those around them, they would be giving up something essential to them, and they would then lose something precious. Therefore, they guard it tightly, and hold on to it. What I have seen happen then is that it shrivels up inside of them, and their outer nature becomes coarse and dry, and without joy or fluidity. I observed in Jesus the opposite of this: he gave freely of his love. It was always replenished because the source of it was the universal God, and he did not claim it was his own. This love was like a fountain that would never run dry because the source was endless and eternal. It was not his own self, the personality of Jesus, which provided the perpetual divine connection. It was the anointed Christ self, the spirit that entered at his baptism, that linked him so perfectly with the divine. This he tried to convey to us in many ways over time. I was only beginning to understand.

If I had to sum up the essence of what I had learned up until now, so relatively early in my relationship with Jesus, it would be that I was learning self-sacrifice. This I mean not in the sense of being a martyr, but, rather, letting go of the personal self and surrendering to the higher self, or God. In this act of surrendering myself, I was learning, like an infant taking its first steps, how to walk in a completely new metaphor of understanding my relationship to the universe in which I lived. I felt very connected to this when I was with Jesus, especially in those precious moments when it had been just the two of us together. When I was away from him, I did not feel nearly so confident in this, much like an infant would easily falter when its mother's hand was no longer there to hold it up when it tried to take one of its first steps. When I was with him, I could easily connect with the love and the divine energy within him, and then I could feel that this was also within me. However, at this stage of my spiritual development, my ability to sustain this feeling very much depended on the presence of Jesus. I hoped to grow and be able to sustain much more of this when I was not around him, but now sometimes it seemed an impossible task. Then, I would remember that Jesus told me nothing is impossible for those who believe, and I would feel a bit more hopeful.

CHAPTER 15

WITH EACH PASSING DAY, THERE WERE NEW CHALLENGES to be met. At this stage of Jesus' ministry, there were many who doubted what he stood for. He was accused of charlatanism and deception with some frequency. This never worried him at all. It seemed that he was content to let his actions and their results speak for themselves, and to let people decide as they would, according to what they were able to perceive.

I, on the other hand, became angered and bothered by some of the comments I heard around me, and by some of the rumors I heard people spreading. At times, I felt consumed with indignation and other equally energy-wasting emotions. It was very hard for me to let go of my feelings about the accusations that were generated, despite my attempts to do so. James understood how I felt, but I think even he, who knew me so well, was puzzled by the fierceness of my feelings. One aspect that contributed to this ardor is that my loyalty to Jesus was well-established. I return to the lion metaphor in understanding this aspect of my nature. A lioness is fiercely protective of her young, and of her territory. I felt this same kind of fierce loyalty. It was an intimate part of my very being, as if this were somehow intertwined with my blood as it coursed through me. I struggled to keep my temper in check and to respond in appropriate ways. Perhaps there was more than a little bit of the hot bloodedness of my father Zebedee in me, after all. I did not like to admit this even to myself, but in this regard it seemed clearly true. Jesus teased James and me with the name "Sons of Thunder" because our father could be so fiery and cantankerous.

By day, we would often travel in the environs of the Sea of Galilee, where Jesus was firmly establishing his ministry. We did not always travel together as a group, but we often did. Sometimes Jesus would stay at Peter's home for the night; he seemed to feel very comfortable there. Wherever he went to speak, Jesus drew a crowd. Many people sought him out for healing. I never tired of watching him heal the deaf, the blind, the crippled and the lepers. I loved to watch their joy as they rejoiced in the feeling of freedom from the burdens that had oppressed them.

On a daily basis, we received our instructions. We were taught in a very methodical and even organized way about the workings of the spirit, and how to tap into God's energy, to channel it for good. What was seen in the healings and the miracles was indeed dramatic and startling, yet in private we were learning the mechanics of what we saw. It was understood that we would always carry this knowledge and that we would develop our skills. We knew we were to spread the message of God's love and plan for redemption.

We were all becoming more adept at reading the human energy field. We did not yet have the gifts of healing that were later to be bestowed on us, but we were in a preparatory stage. I was surprised by the many subtleties of the energy field. I had always thought of myself as a rather sensitive person, but now I often felt coarse and thick with built-up accumulations of time and experience that dramatically clouded my perceptions. I was like a child learning everything anew. I had to unlearn much of what I knew that got in my way.

Perhaps the best example of this unlearning and relearning process at this stage is as follows: I was returning from a long day in the public with Jesus and many of his disciples and followers. I was quite weary and hungry, and my mind was pointedly fixed on arriving at our home base, eating and resting. There were moments when I felt so tired that I could not imagine how I would make it another step, much less the distance yet to be traveled.

Jesus, as usual, was engaged in conversation with someone who was seeking some bit of wisdom from him. Nonetheless, I now became aware of him in my mind, and knew he was getting ready to talk to me. I suddenly felt infused with an energy that boosted me quite rapidly: I knew this energy would be present in abundance until we had reached our destination. I felt gratitude, and silently thanked him in my mind. I heard him respond to me: "John, you are weary in body and you now shall have the resources you need to get home. Remember always that God's resources never run dry. When you tire, open your connection to Him so he might fill you. I now provide you with the link; it is through me that you see Him. Remember this always. I will never leave you, and through me you shall always be linked to the eternal and the everlasting."

This lesson stayed with me very strongly. My perspective on my bodily fatigue was completely challenged by what had happened. I realized that my identification with my body had been complete, and now this assumption had been nullified. It was as if, at this point in time, I could now localize in my energy body the channel that Jesus was providing to God's abundant energy. I felt it and I saw it with my newly developing inner eye. I was convinced at a deep inner level that what I heard and felt was true, and that this connection would never be taken away from me.

The implications of this silent lesson would stay with me for my lifetime. I often returned in contemplation to these moments to understand a bit of the magnitude of what Jesus was bringing into the world. At my current advanced age, I still have trouble comprehending the magnitude of the incarnation, and I have spent my life pondering on what this meant. This seemingly little moment in time was incredibly transformative. It opened my inner eye into a new dimension of wonder, marvel and endless expansion of comprehension. Who would have known that out of my weariness would come such an important lesson? *It was this moment in which I first perceived, as a reality within my own energy field, the channel or pathway that Jesus brought to the world.*

From that moment on, a new relationship with God had been established firmly within me. This was a new testament and contract that was being made manifest in the world. Within me, I felt moved and stretched well beyond my ability to understand what this was, or how this was: I only knew that this was true, and that this work would change the earth forever.

CHAPTER 16

IT WAS INCREASINGLY DIFFICULT AS THE DAYS WENT ON to keep the personal aspects of what I was learning and discovering to myself. I knew there would be times for me to share, and I did share many things with James as well as some of the others, yet the very personal aspects of my relationship with Jesus I felt I had to keep to myself. I definitely did not want to seem boastful. I was very proud to have been selected for this role, yet it did not seem right that I would talk freely about that which the others had not been given. Because of this, much of this took on the guise of a deeply held and much treasured secret.

The others might sometimes have wondered how it was that I seemed to presume a special relationship with Jesus, by sleeping near him or walking near to him often, but I took great pains not to presume anything. Always I made sure that I was invited into these spaces before I stepped in. As time went by, I went into these spaces more and more often, and I knew I was welcomed there by the feeling I had when I entered. It was as if there was a special space there that was my own. When I entered that space, I felt more at home than I had ever felt anywhere.

These feelings developed over a long period, and intensified at different periods. After the initial dream-journeying experience, and the initial experience of the channel to God within my energy field, I felt my bond with Jesus had deepened significantly. I had fewer reservations than before about seeking out his company.

What I was also beginning to find, was that even though he might be elsewhere occupied with others, our minds could connect, and I received teaching on this level. I do not think this was a type of experience that was unique to me; in fact, in discussions with the others, I found that they all learned many lessons in this manner. A Master is able to conduct teachings on many levels and in different places at the same time. We all benefited from this on many occasions. I was beginning to learn that, if I wanted to learn or had questions, all I needed to do was to ask for what I needed. I always received some type of response. Sometimes a feeling, or knowledge overcame me; at other times, I would be directed to a certain place or to a certain person who might facilitate my learning.

My favorite kind of response was when I would shift into an altered state of consciousness. In this state, I was much more receptive to the importation of higher knowledge, and my mind received impressions of answers and teachings relating to that which I had asked. I grew to love these states. There was a kind of ecstasy in them, in which I would be transported out of my normal body consciousness, and set free from the fetters that normally tied me to earth. It was as if my mind and my spirit were set free, and I soared in these regions, as does an eagle on the wing. It was definitely intoxicating. Yet, I found that if I clung to the feeling of intoxication, I would lose the content I was receiving. I quickly learned to stay focused on the impressions themselves, rather than on the feelings that accompanied them.

There were days when I would not be focused on an inner direction at all. These tended to be the days when I accompanied Jesus as he traveled from village to village, healing the sick and infirm. On these days, I was sharply focused on what I observed him to be doing. It was as if I tried to memorize every detail of every move, so that I could recall it later and be able to incorporate it into my own developing work. I knew that it was not the details of healing that make it work, but rather the gift bestowed by the Holy Spirit. Nonetheless, I felt that the more I knew, the more accurately focused I could be in my work. There are many mechanical details to healing work, yet these details, all combined, do not add up to a healing. In my own insecurity about my capacities, and in my own need to incorporate all that I could from Jesus, I studied him extremely carefully. I listened to him very carefully as he talked to the crowds that gathered wherever he went. I tried to capture his words inside my memory so that I could bring them to mind whenever I needed them.

If I were to venture to give a general description of what I observed that was common to almost all of the many healings I witnessed, it would be as follows: what I always saw first was a request for healing. This is an extremely important point, and one that could easily be overlooked. This request to be healed, or to have a loved one healed, signified the readiness to give up that which was holding one back. I think all too often we accept our limitations as identical to our true nature, and forget they are only a limitation to the full expression of our true nature in all its glory. If I believe that my true, deepest self is without eyesight, then I do not seek beyond that which I think I know to be absolutely true. If I believe my true self is marred by the leperous sores that cover my body, then I do not seek to move beyond the hideousness and deformity that I believe is mine. When people heard that Jesus was able to perform the miracles that he did, their hope was restored in God and in the capacity of the human body to align with God's will. They were inspired with the belief, in a manner unprecedented in history, that God's will was for perfect health, and that this divine man could call upon God's power to set things right.

Secondly, one of the most important ingredients in the healings I witnessed was forgiveness. Jesus very frequently told those whom he healed that they were forgiven their mistakes, and that they should not repeat them. Forgiveness is a huge concept, one that could take up many volumes. The way Jesus discussed it in relation to these healings involved forgiveness of self for errors past, present and contemplated. Those infirmities that were present from birth tended to be carry-overs from past lives; past injuries that were not resolved and which repeated themselves in various ways until the soul was restored. Jesus said clearly on many occasions that *forgiveness was the shortest and most direct route to restitution of the soul's balanced nature.* He said that without it, our hearts grew hard, both towards ourselves, and towards others. From a hardened heart comes many errors of judgment. Forgiveness also included forgiveness of others, for the anger, wrath and darkness that we harbor inside of ourselves towards others can

84

poison our very souls, and make us susceptible to any manner of infirmities or injuries.

After a session of healing, Jesus often talked to us about what he saw in the energy fields of those he healed, and how a particular ailment came about. These sessions were extremely helpful, for they explained much about the particular symptom, or cluster of symptoms, which a particular person manifested. We grew to understand clearly how forgiveness of their transgressions would result in dissolution of the symptom that had arisen because of the feelings that lingered in the energy body. Of course, given that the healings Jesus performed grew to be so numerous, it would have been impossible for him to detail each one. However, when he did, the discussion was extraordinarily rewarding.

These comments were not often made to the person who was healed. Jesus' reasoning for this had to do with his explanation of faith, which he preferred to keep as simple as possible. Faith, he always told us, was the belief that the soul, through its belief in God, can restore the nature of man to its rightful perfection. This does not mean that man will easily be made perfect, for his faith is not perfect. However, if it were to be so, as with Jesus, then the divine would radiate out through him fully in every direction. Through the channel that Jesus provided in his incarnation, we could all participate in the path to divinity.

The third common ingredient to the healings I witnessed was a willingness to suspend disbelief on the part of the person requesting healing, and a willingness to surrender to the greater power that Jesus channeled through his body and soul. This receptivity to the seemingly impossible becoming possible facilitated the flow of the healing currents throughout the body and energy field, and enabled the transformative field to enlarge. The transformative field included the person being healed, Jesus, and the divine energy that he channeled through his being and into the other. He always explained to us that this tripartite interaction provided the basis of the healings he performed. He noted that it was not impossible to heal without the awareness of another, but that at some level there must be this receptivity or response to the healing process. He cautioned us, however, never to heal another without their asking us, for we must never enter their field that way without an invitation.

As we developed in our skills, we would be able to discern many things about others. He told us we must never let our curiosity lead us in places we did not belong or where we were not invited, for that would be an invasion of their boundaries, and an abuse of our power. The responsibility we would carry with us throughout our lives would increase as our abilities grew, for the greater the work of which we were capable, the greater the potential for a fall into darkness. We must always do what we did with prayer and recognition to the source of our energies, and with reverence and selflessness. Our works would be done for the glory of God, and to lead people to God only. Never must we let our work be done to bring glory to ourselves, or to win people over for personal reasons. He taught us to always ask ourselves why if we were going to perform healings of any nature. If we grew uncomfortable with ourselves as we tried to answer this question, then he advised us to consider this discomfort seriously.

This issue of healing was a multi-faceted one in other ways as well. Jesus recognized that others would be drawn to God much more easily if they saw miracles performed, but he did not want to be cast in the role of someone who performed tricks in order to convince people to have faith in God. There had been many tricksters before him, and would be many convincing ones after him. I have come to believe, as I have thought about this over the years, that he knew his words and his works would endure through the centuries, and that there was a delicate balance to be struck. Words alone carried down through the years might tend to fade, but the combination of words and deeds would bring more people into the realization of his divinity. His every deed was done with an eye to God's will and to bringing those who would listen over to God. He expected no less of us.

What I saw as I witnessed the many healings changed as my spiritual eye developed. I cannot even begin to describe the incomparable brightness that Jesus invoked around him from above, and extending down into the ground, when he prayed for God's help in a given healing. The energy field that was invoked would bear a resemblance to a triangular shape, the top point of which extended up to the heavens, and the bottom points of which extended down into the ground at points outside of Jesus and the person being healed. In the moments of healing, it was as if no force in the world, or perhaps from outside of this world, could penetrate into this energy field.

I have seen a number of healings performed by others since Jesus moved on, and I have performed them myself, but never have I seen anything like what he was able to do. If he needed a legion of angels, then they would be at his disposal. As my spiritual sight grew, I was moved in the core of me with the powers for good that I saw were at his command. This is something that can be described only very inadequately in words, but, to see this, to feel this, and to know what is involved, is to be changed forever.

CHAPTER 17

THE MANY EXTERNAL EVENTS OF JESUS' MINISTRY were very valuable to all of us who lived through those years with him. We knew they would be valuable to many people in years to come. The historical reality of Jesus and the manifestation of divinity in the flesh, or the incarnation, was a point in time once lived in the external world. The internal reality of the incarnation, the channel that was established by Jesus to be felt in the hearts of men everywhere, was one that would occur again and again as long as people believed, and sought to believe, in the divinity that was made manifest in the world.

In this manuscript, which I write to capture the experience of a very blessed and also very sorrowful lifetime, I seek to articulate the many feelings and experiences that transformed me personally. As I write, I have not decided what to do with these words. My feeling at this time is that I will continue to write, and to do so for myself, and that I will put away my manuscript in my heart. The history which others and I have recorded elsewhere of the external events is what is truly important. I hope and pray that those words will remain and will be handed down through the generations. *We were witnesses to a moment in time in which time was forever changed.* Because of this, the eternal is now present in every moment.

I have prayed over my writing. I write every night, assiduously and unflaggingly, because of my need to put down in words everything I have experienced. Perhaps most of this is vanity, because it is so personal and because it is so inconsequential compared to the reality Jesus brought with him. Nonetheless I, if only for myself, am obsessed with this need to write and to bring forth into my present, the reality I have experienced. I am now a lonely old man, one who finds no greater joy than a moonlit night with the stars shining brightly over my head. For, it is at these times that I feel closest to the man and to the God who was my closest friend, for a time, and for eternity.

At these times, I look up to the heavens, and I thank God for the love and the joy I have known. I thank him that I could be even a small part of this great work. I cry inside often for the personal loss, and after all these many years, tears still come to my eyes with great regularity. Many times I weep even now for the personal loss I have endured. I feel reluctant to even commit these words to paper, for then I have to admit them to myself, and it seems selfish. For, was there not great good news out of all of this, and was there not great joy and relief of suffering to be brought to the multitudes over the course of who knows how many hundreds or thousands of years? I feel immeasurably selfish and small when I consider my loss in the face of this. Did he not tell me that he would always be with me, and that all I would ever need do would be to call on him and he would be there, to talk with me, or to lend his grace to me, or to assist me with whatever I needed? Yes, he said all of these things. Yet, there are many times when my feeble human nature cannot or will not connect, leaving me feeling lost, desolate and inconsolable.

However, once again, I am far ahead of myself. It is as if I need to justify to myself the time and the energy I am putting into writing these words. I know I need to continue with this, to help me to remember all I have experienced, so that I might try to make the most sense out of it that I can. I feel compelled to do this. There are not many joys in my life today that are greater than writing at night, by candlelight, at my wooden table. Here, I can move deeply into my own soul and find him again who gave me so much more than he had to, he who gave the world love for which it was not yet ready.

CHAPTER 18

THE EVENINGS WERE OFTEN MY FAVORITE TIME WITH JESUS. These were often the times when there was the most opportunity for intimacy and sharing, when we did not have to share him with others who had need of him. He was a great storyteller, often telling us stories of the strange and marvelous things he saw and learned in his travels. Everywhere he went, when he met up with those who were spiritually advanced, they knew he was coming. They knew they had a special role in helping to prepare him for the ministry to come.

I remember Jesus saying that one of the things that dismayed him the most about some of these advanced travelers, was they became caught up in the psychic powers they acquired along the way. For them, the acquisition of powers became a goal in and of itself. He called this spiritual arrogance, and told us he found it everywhere among seekers who were not careful to acknowledge the source of their wisdom and their powers. What was unnerving, he said, was that so much energy went into cultivating psychic power. This emphasis often distracted people from the path upon which they had originally embarked. I suppose part of the purpose Jesus had in telling us about this on several occasions, was to warn us about the dangers inherent in the road we would be traveling. "For the glory of God, not for the glory of self," is a phrase from these those times that has always stayed with me.

He often repeated that we were to work with each other towards the same goal, and warned us not to be caught up in competition with each other. If I search my own heart carefully, I can still find those faults that I have tried hard to root out. For example, sometimes I looked at how both James and I, brothers and the closest of friends, were selected to be among the fortunate few. I would then invest it with the meaning that we were somehow different and special, and that our selection for discipleship had to do with something personal about us. I think now that the truth is more like we had been selected from eons before, and had been put into lifetime after lifetime where we received the appropriate training and circumstances to prepare us. Thus, it was not by my virtue nor his, but by higher design that we had been groomed for the position we were to take.

The dream I dreamt while I was at the Dead Sea often came back to me through the years. It was the one in which I was not yet born in this life, and felt irresistibly and inexorably drawn by the brightest of white lights into this life, as if I had no choice. The memory of this helped to keep me humble, for it was not for what I had done in this life that put me in this position, but rather it was the position in which I had been placed which prepared me for the work that had been assigned to me.

In these, my later years, by virtue of both choice and circumstance, I have become less of a man of action and far more of a man of reflection. Is it not true that I have much that is worthy to reflect upon? As I write about events that I remember, or time periods that left their mark, I often find myself digressing into reflections about where these events or circumstances led me as time went on. I have to laugh at myself, an old man who gets so lost in his reminiscing that he occasionally loses track of his thread...

The evenings were special in every way to me. Besides the more intimate group of us who were able to talk and learn and share our day's experiences, I grew to love the period of my sleep. As time went on, I more often adopted a place to sleep beside my Master. Eventually it was accepted that this was how it would be. No one knew about the journeys we took at night, not even James. It was understood that this was between Jesus and I, and that this was to be part of my preparation for times beyond when I would have need of this knowledge and these tools. At times, it was a hard secret to keep, because some of the adventures and lessons of the night before were so compelling and remarkable. Always, I knew it would be unwise to share this with the others, for it would only serve to foster contention and ill feelings. It was not that the others were not instructed in this night work; we all were. I was fortunate to be the most regular nighttime apprentice, making nighttime journeys with Jesus in order to learn all I could of these various worlds.

I loved what it was like in the morning when we awoke. We would lie facing each other. Often we awoke at the same time, just as dawn was breaking. We would look at each other, and a smile would break out on our faces. What a joy it was to wake up to his smiling face, and to have the shared memory of the work we had done at night. As we would fall asleep the night before, he would wrap us in a blanket of white divine light. Within it, I felt safe and secure, in a way I have never felt before or since. I can only approximate this feeling by comparing it to falling asleep in the arms of one's beloved, knowing that one loves and is loved, and that this bubble of love protects one from all harm and from all negative thoughts. I have never stopped missing this, and I have never, not even for one night, forgotten this.

There were many levels to my joy with this man/God, from the spiritual to the physical, to the mental and to the emotional. This of which I just spoke was at the emotional level: I was totally devoted to him, and gave my heart over to him completely. When later my heart was broken, it shattered completely. Although many years have passed, I have never completely recovered on this emotional level despite all of the wisdom, spirituality and healing that has been provided. I am embarrassed to admit this, even to myself, for I know this is not what he would have wanted. But I do not know how to heal my broken heart, and I have tried in every way I know. How closely my joy and my sorrow walk together! Perhaps if by writing, I am able to purge myself of some of my tears and my human heartbreak, then I will be able to carry the good news more joyfully and with less strain in my heart…

CHAPTER 19

ONE WARM MORNING WHEN WE GOT UP, I noticed that Jesus seemed preoccupied. He was often in other worlds, but there was a restlessness and a level of activity about him that made me wonder what was occurring. Whatever it was that was on his mind, he was not sharing it with me, and apparently not with anyone else, either. I had gotten so that I was very attuned to his moods, and I could not help but feel the agitation pulsing throughout myself as well. I knew that it did not feel comfortable, but all I could do was to wait. When he asked Peter, James and myself to accompany him, I was almost relieved for some movement into understanding whatever it was that was building up this tension. We walked into the hills, away from the Sea of Galilee.

We walked for what seemed like hours, and talked about various topics along the way. Nothing we discussed had the feeling of what I had been sensing about my friend and Master before we had left on this walk. I knew that whatever it was we had to discuss would be forthcoming, and there would be no hurrying him, for he would discuss it in his own time. I normally loved these long walks in the hills with Jesus, but today something felt very wrong.

He said he wanted to tell us something of the vision he had the previous night. Though he would not, even when pressed, give us the details, what he did tell us was, that within several years, this ministry as we knew it now would be over, and we would be on our own, scattered about, to continue the work we were doing.

In that time, nothing would be the same as it was now. We would be challenged, in ways we could not foresee, to continue. We would not have the same kind of access to him that we did now, and our faith would be tried in many ways. All of this sounded cryptic and mysterious. When we pressed him, what he told us then and later was that the scriptures must be fulfilled, and that he would do as he must for his Father.

Whenever I thought of the scriptures, and what they foretold of the Messiah, I focused, as did the others, on how he would bring with him the power to overturn all of his enemies, and that he would reign forever on earth. I thought that if anyone would try to hurt him in any way, he would simply use his power to conquer him or her, and move on in the same direction he had been pursuing. When Peter, James and I talked about this, it was clear that we all carried these same ideas. We did not want to believe, nor did we at the time have the capacity to believe, that our Master would be flagellated and crucified. If I can try to imagine myself, at that point in time, opening my mind to the idea of not having him around, and of witnessing him suffering such an excruciating and horrendous death, I do not know how I would have be able to contain all of this within me.

Even now, these many years later, as I was writing of this, I felt overcome by sleep at a relatively early hour of the evening, and could not see that I had any choice but to put my pen down and doze. When I awoke, I thought of continuing to write. Then, remembering my present subject matter, I felt as if drugged with the need to sleep. I understand now that this being overcome by sleep is my mind's attempt to protect it from more than it feels it can handle at any given time. If, even now, the truth feels almost too much to bear, then how much more so it must have felt then, when my attachment to Jesus was still alive at the level of day-to-day interaction and communion.

That day, we tried to give our friendship to Jesus in a way that the human part of him might have wanted. However, I was not able to see deeply into his own pain and dread, or to inquire further into what I sensed, because at my own personal level I was not able to process the information in any realistic way. I think this was true for James and Peter as well. We depended on Jesus so greatly. The thought of him not being there was inconceivable. I suppose he knew this. Perhaps that is why he tried to introduce us gradually to what would happen, and why he did not tell us the details of his dream. I suspect that it was probably a fairly clear depiction of what actually did happen, and that it shook him to the bone. There were few times when I saw him as agitated as I had seen him that morning. Later, I grew to recognize the restlessness.

He prepared us for what was to come over a long period, and at increasingly frequent intervals. This time particularly sticks in my mind because it was the first time, and because it left me with a gnawing feeling that all was not as I would have hoped for it to be. James and I discussed this later. We were both so clouded by our wishes, our needs, and our dependencies, that we could not let in the truth of what was being said to us. Of course, we did not recognize this at the time. Only the uncomfortable feelings that I recognize in retrospect told me, and James too (from what he later said to me), that we were suffering from blurred vision, and that our delusions were born out of our all-too human frailty.

Our return back to the others was very quiet. None of us seemed to have anything to say. This was an unusual state of affairs in and of itself, and I wondered about it a great deal. I did not know what to think, but I did feel more determined to make the most of the time I had left with him. If anything, I became more receptive than I had been previously. I was still, however, thinking in terms of having many more years in the ministry with Jesus. I had no idea how little time was left.

CHAPTER 20

APART FROM THE NIGHT AND THE LESSONS it brought, I most looked forward to our adventuring out into the countryside, with the attendant crowds, teachings and healings. I never knew what to expect next. The days never failed to bring with them moving experiences, and new lessons to be imprinted on my soul.

Usually, most of us came along on these occasions. Then, afterwards, we had the opportunity to discuss what had happened, and to make any observations or ask any questions about what we had seen and experienced. These sessions, which did not always occur on the same day as the public ministry, for a number of reasons, were always productive and thought provoking. It was within the context of this group learning that I received some of the richest spiritual direction.

There was a difference in his teaching now. It carried with it more of a subtle urgency. Though it had always been focused, now there was an even clearer focus. The shift very definitely was in the direction of each of us learning to stand and operate on our own. This shift took place in steps. The first step in this was very pointedly with Jesus teaching us how to support each other, and how to use group prayer to effect a healing, or to support the healer doing his work. I will elaborate on this later. First, I would like to include one of the precepts that always was taught, and later assumed to be axiomatic of the work we were to be doing in this area. It was that any healing work we would be doing was always to be done to help others for the glory of God. Never were we to do it for our personal or selfish reasons. We were never to set ourselves up as healers or miracle workers, for to do so would be to allow our energies to become so skewed that we would no longer be focused on God from whom everything came, but on ourselves and our abilities. We were warned repeatedly about the dangers of this.

There had been a man in the region, who had over the years been very good at a healing ministry. We were all aware of him because he had been in the public eye for a time. As he had savored his successes, he had gradually grown increasingly crazed. As he grew more incoherent, his abilities seemed to dry up. People had often wondered what happened to him, for at first he had seemed so genuinely gifted. His gift had turned into a tragedy in which he wandered around, filthy and lost in a world only he could understand, seemingly a lost soul. When last he had been seen, after a period of absence, he had only one eye. Where the other had been was now only a hollow socket, speaking to some horror he must have experienced. He had roamed about, silent, and always appearing to be searching for something that was far out of his reach. He had not been seen for a while, and it had been assumed that he was now dead, hopefully at last in a place where he could find peace.

Jesus talked to us of this man, using him as an example of what could happen if we appropriated the Lord's healing powers as our own. He said that the healing current did not stem from us. If we tried to channel this mighty river, not through us as in a natural flow, but into us that it might appear to be at our direction and belonging to us, then that current would flood and overwhelm our systems. The analogy was further developed as follows: if this current were allowed to flow in its natural course, then it is contained within the riverbanks. The land on either side of the river stays dry, but benefits from the water that flows through for life-giving purposes. But, if this flow were to be dammed up from its natural course, and diverted into a smaller manmade channel, it would quickly flow over the banks of the manmade channel. This would flood everything in sight, and drown the humans who were in its way. In this way, he said, the human voice that once was so tender and exquisite in this crazed man, had been drowned out by this river, which flooded his psyche as a result of his attempting to appropriate the divine energy as his own.

This made much sense to me. I had often puzzled over his fate, and had alternated between feeling pity and revulsion toward him. Yet, I remembered clearly the early days when he had done so much good for others. I had never understood the tragedy that had befallen him. Jesus had explained this sad fate in a way that was both easily understandable, and a supreme lesson and warning to every one of us.

"Always acknowledge the source," he repeatedly told us, "before, during and after each healing, or each time you teach in His name. If you do this, you will insure your success, and, you will avoid the psychic dangers that have befallen others along the way. Do not allow yourself to become puffed up by your successes, for they are not yours, but God's alone."

He was a perfect model for us in this regard. He began and ended each day, each ministry, and each healing, with a prayer of acknowledgment, and by asking for help. He would express gratitude for the help that was now given, or that was to be rendered. This model grew within us as a natural rhythm, as natural as the sleep-wake cycle that regulated our daily lives.

Jesus wanted us to witness the healings he performed, and to listen to the teachings, some of which we heard many times. He encouraged us to use both our physical and our spiritual eyes as we watched him. Often in our group discussions later, we would describe what we had seen and learned. In this way, we had the benefit not only of learning from him, but also of learning from each other. Each of us saw and perceived somewhat differently; the understanding that any one of us had added to and built upon our own. In this way, our individual visions were enriched and nourished by the collective vision. Even when Jesus was not with us on a given evening, we would still gather and discuss what we had seen and learned. We grew strong in trust and respect for each other.

The twelve of us who had been picked to be apprenticing to Jesus were now an established grouping. We were often joined by others. However, at this stage, the presence of others was not constant, and we had much time in relatively small groups, mostly during the evening. So it was we who reviewed the teachings and the healings. It seemed very important that we focus and concentrate as carefully as possible so that we might maximize each opportunity for learning. In the course of these evening discussions, we were also building a level of group support unlike anything I had ever known or have since known. We grew accustomed to the nuances of each other's behaviors and speech. We learned, repeatedly, how to surrender our personal needs and desires to the collective good.

This was accomplished at first through prayer, and through consciously asking that our will be surrendered to the will of God. It became clear in the group work, that unless we did this, there would be no possibility of the divine energies flowing freely and harmoniously through us, for our individual personalities and wills would be disruptive to a cohesive union.

I was tremendously impressed by the power of group prayer, and by the energy that was inevitably generated when we were all working together. Clearly, when Jesus was present, this energy was magnified to a much greater amount. Yet, even when he was not present, we would always picture and feel him within our midst. The clarity that resulted from this was impressive.

I do not mean to imply that it was always harmonious between us, for it was not. We were twelve very different individuals with distinct ways of looking at the world, and of dealing with people. At times there were heated discussions, but the atmosphere surrounding our purpose and our teacher was strong. We took great pains to not let our disagreements fester or build factions between us. Jesus let us work out our own problems. He rarely stepped in, other than to encourage us to resolve our differences, or to take time apart when that seemed necessary.

I was quiet, and definitely not of a gregarious nature. It was usually fairly easy for me to stay out of the disagreements that did disrupt, for I was not aspiring to a position of power within the group. Peter was clearly our leader when Jesus was not there. He was fair, and seemed to love the role and the responsibility. I was grateful he was there to take this on. My role within the group suited me perfectly.

The daydreamer-fantasizer side of me that had been part of my nature all my young life reveled in the spiritual work, and in the nighttime adventuring during the dreaming state. I was young, though not the youngest of the twelve, and I was content now to be able to act as a sponge, absorbing all that I could.

There were occasions when Jesus was asked to heal someone who was so ill, or who lived at such a distance, that they could not be brought to him for healing. On one such occasion, late one afternoon, we were all gathered in discussion under a tree. A woman came up who was obviously in great distress. She apologized for the intrusion. Her husband had been working in the field, and had cut himself very badly with a sharp instrument. He had lost a great deal of blood before she had been able to stop the blood loss with a tourniquet. Her fear was twofold; that he would die from the blood loss, as he was quite weak, or that, if he lived, he would lose his arm below the elbow. He was in great agony, she said, and she feared greatly for him. Was there anything that the Master could do to help him? Her husband had listened to Jesus talking only days before. As he lay there in his pool of blood, he asked her to run to Jesus, whom he knew was staying nearby, and to ask him for help.

Jesus smiled kindly at her, and told her to go back, and to be reassured that her husband would be well, and out of pain. She thanked him, with tears of gratitude in her eyes, and departed. Jesus immediately focused us on the situation. We all knew that this was to be a teaching situation, and we bowed our heads in prayer. I was excited, yet fearful. I had no doubt that this was well within Jesus' capability, but he was asking us to join as a group to heal. I did not know how this would go, as immediately I began doubting myself. He had no such doubts.

We formed into a circle, and he had us visualize the wounded man in our midst. I was shocked at how clearly I could see him. For a brief moment, I felt an agonizing pain in my left arm, below the elbow, which I did not feel I could tolerate. He told us that when we had the image clearly in our midst, to detach ourselves from any bodily pain we might have. This pain would, if it arose, let us know we were connected to the psyche of the wounded man. We were not to take it on ourselves, but were to ask God to lift the pain from us and from him. Otherwise, we would find ourselves completely depleted as healers.

Next, we listened as he led us in prayer, asking God to remove the injury and pain from this man, and to restore him to his natural state. Jesus asked God to forgive this man for the intense anger which he stored inside himself, and asked that this man be filled with a peace and forgiveness which would allow him to feel whole again. As he prayed, and we joined with him, to my amazement, I watched my visualization of the man change from a seriously wounded, very weak man in great pain, to a man who was looking, in amazement, at his intact arm.

This healing took perhaps a period of ten minutes from start to finish. It ended with a prayer of thanks for the healing that had occurred, and with thanks that we had the opportunity to be present, and to participate and learn from this episode. Our review of the episode took a much longer time. Jesus asked what we experienced. Each of us had similar experiences in our visualizations, in how the man looked, and how things changed as the healing proceeded. I was intensely curious about how Jesus knew about the anger, and how that tied in with the injury and the healing.

Instead of answering me directly, Jesus asked me to re-picture my initial visualization of the injured man. He asked all of us to do so, as he talked to me. I tuned in as best I could to the original picture. He then asked me to look in the man's energy field, and tell him what I saw. This was quite difficult, but as always when Jesus was there, I felt that my own sight was enhanced or somehow amplified by him. As I focused at this level, I saw a great deal of red surrounding this man. This red was not the bright red color of blood. A dark, murky, agitated red surrounded the man, and emanated out from him. It felt very uncomfortable, and I did not want to stay with this feeling for more than a few seconds. I described what I saw and felt.

Jesus told us that this was precisely what was around the man, and that the murky red energy I had seen was what identified the anger. "It was in this emotional state that he had his accident." The accident was really no more than the manifestation on the physical level of his anger at himself for having beaten his wife the night before. This amazed me, and yet made much sense to me. Now I understood the anger, and I understood how important forgiveness was to this particular healing. If he could not be forgiven for his sin, and if he could not forgive himself, the injury could not be healed.

"So," I asked, "in sending his wife to you then, he was asking, whether he knew it or not, for forgiveness for the harm he had done, and also for the physical healing?" The answer was yes, that he had on a deep level created the injury as an opportunity for the greater healing he needed. That was why he had immediately known to send his wife to Jesus, to effect the needed change.

This had been the first opportunity we had as a group to participate in a healing in this full of a manner. I was exhausted, excited, and glad to have been a part of it all.

CHAPTER 21

ONCE WE HAD FINISHED WITH THIS LESSON, I felt we had reached a new stage of our learning. Previously, we had been mostly observing and learning as much as we could, and had not been actively participating in the ministry. Though it still seemed that my knowledge was rudimentary at best, it was now time for us to begin participating more actively in the work that was to be done. My understanding was that not much was expected at this point, but we were to work with the ideas and skills we had been studying, and test them out. There would be a great deal of learning in this stage. Jesus compared it to how, as a young boy he spent many hours watching his father making furniture. There came a time when he was called upon to make his first piece, a simple chair. Though he had seen chairs made many times, when it was time for him to make one, it was all brand new. He had to re-learn the steps, in transferring them from the visual memory to his physical level.

Now, we were to be more active participants when it came to the healings that were requested. It was not the case that Jesus needed our help in order to perform any given healing, but our active prayerful support could make it easier for him by providing extra energy. Healing was extremely fatiguing, and we were taught that the group support helped to diminish this effect. Mainly, however, this participation would be a critical tool for our learning, as we would be able to witness, experience and contribute to the healing energies that would be used in any number of different situations.

It was sometimes more feasible to work this way in situations like the one which I have just described, in which an individual would come to Jesus for healing, in a more intimate setting. In these cases, whichever one of us who was there would work with Jesus in the healing. He would talk with us and offer suggestions, or instruct us during the healing. When we were in a larger crowd, and there were more demands placed on him, we were not able to receive any instruction, and sometimes we would not be close to Jesus to be able to participate as fully in the situation.

One of the aspects of learning healing that stands out the most for me now, is remembering how we were often told that the process of learning healing itself would bring us closer to God. I did not understand what Jesus meant by this at the time, but as time went on, I grew to understand that in order to become healers, we had to be healed of our own wounds in the process. Personal healing was a long, ongoing process, which was at times extremely painful. In order to channel the energies of God through a channel that was as clear as possible, I had to learn to tune into my own energies and clear the energies in my own energy field as much as possible. We worked regularly with each other on this, describing to each other what we saw in the other's field. Our initial work was to work with each other to clear any major disturbances, and to open up the chakras so that each one was fully functioning.

Our process of clearing out the auric field was often long and painful. We could begin the healing work without having to be completely clear, but Jesus emphasized that the clearer we became, the more proficient we would be as healers. We would take on less of other people's burdens if we were clear, and hence, more able to recognize the pain and illness as clearly belonging to the other without mixing it up with our own personal liabilities. As I cleared my own energies, I was astounded at the accumulation of emotional, physical and psychic debris just from this short lifetime. And then, there was the debris of the previous lifetimes. We dealt with those accumulations in very much the same manner. I was surprised at the memories that arose as we worked, and found there were several areas that were particularly problematic for me.

One of those was the heart area. It seems that I had been badly hurt on a number of occasions, and had built walls around my heart area in an attempt to seal me off from the experience of such a hurt again. As my heart had hardened, I had then in several lifetimes become that which I had abhorred, a person cut off from my feelings, who had treated my mates with callous disregard. Some further experiences of hurt had redeemed me in the sense that I was determined to be much more caring, and deliberately I chose to be much more careful in how I conducted my personal life. However, I had come into this life with a huge accumulation of pain and emotional clutter around my heart. It was this that the initiatory experience in the square those months ago had so swiftly and fiercely addressed. In that initiatory experience, described earlier, the many layers of accumulated psychic debris that had built up in my energy field around my heart had been suddenly wrenched off from my heart.

The work we were doing with each other, learning about the energy field and about auric field healing, was very detailed. It was always utterly absorbing and fascinating. We learned much on our own, by working with each other, and yet Jesus was often there to give us guidelines in doing the work. If a matter came up in the course of the work, then and only then would it be addressed. There was no particular order, but rather we were taught to respect the promptings of the Spirit in showing us what we needed to be shown, and how we needed to be taught. If a particular problem were pressing, then we would respect that level of urgency. Otherwise, it almost always happened that a certain aspect in the energy field would stand out by the strength of the impression that it made on the observer. Past life memories not infrequently came up as we worked with a symptom or with an affected area. However, we did not seek these out in and of themselves, but rather dealt with them only as they came up in connection with the area under concern. In this way, we did not allow ourselves to become distracted by digressions that might have taken us far from where we needed to be.

This work on ourselves formed a very important part of the preparation for doing the group support of the healing work that Jesus performed. At first, as we began to step out and participate on a group level in support of the healings, our role was very tentative and limited mostly to prayerful focus and support by invoking the divine light force. At this stage, we would attempt to stay focused on the person being healed. We would invoke healing energy to surround them with whatever was needed to perform the healing. It was very difficult at first to know whether I was really doing anything of value, or whether it was just my over-active imagination. I know that my having seen Jesus in such dramatic demonstrations of what he was teaching us to practice, made a big difference in the believability factor. This practicing stage was extremely helpful, for it was a time to explore without pressure, and a time to test out the limits of my novice status without fear of failure.

CHAPTER 22

IN ADDITION TO THOSE TIMES, ALMOST DAILY, when we worked with each other in viewing and working within energy fields, there were times when Jesus worked with us, both at a group and individual level. His timing always seemed to be perfect; he was always there with us to guide us at difficult points.

I welcomed the individual work; we all did. It was a time of great learning. These times always left me with a sense of being cleansed and purified. The feeling could be compared to how it feels to emerge after bathing, after one has been traveling by foot all day on a hot and dusty path.

I grew very familiar with the particular issues and blocks that regularly came up in the course of working with my energy field. I also grew to prefer doing this work at least several hours after a meal, for immediately after eating, my energies were tied up in the physical functions of digesting, and were not as free as at other times. Early morning seemed to be a good time for this work, as did late afternoon.

It is difficult to describe the process I went through in clearing and preparing my energy field. This process would never be finished, for there would always be new factors that would continue to affect us. I shudder to think what my energy field must have looked like before any of this work. I look at people everywhere, and read in their energy fields much pain, confusion, lack of clarity; and also uglier things, such as greed, avarice, envy, revenge, and utter disregard for anything not self-serving. If people only knew how much could be read about them without their ever having to speak a word! Our ignorance is protective in that sense, though in the times to come, we shall all be seen clearly.

The more I know about the energy I carry with me, and which naturally generates out from me (from us all), the more responsibility I carry for who I am. We send out messages from our field constantly, whether we are aware of it or not. These messages penetrate into the fields of others, and affect them. If I wish harm to someone, that energy carries directly to him or her, and lodges into any vulnerable place within his or her energy field, as well as within our own. Jesus taught us that we are accountable for our thoughts in this way, for every thought is a transmission of energy, just as every action is a transmission of energy. The more we advance, the more powerful our thoughts become, since the channel becomes more clear and we become more effective transmitters of energy. We were taught that, because of this, it is critical that we stay attuned and aligned to the divine will by means of frequent prayer and meditation. Our energy when unattuned and operating on its own becomes more potentially destructive than in someone who has not been schooled in these realities.

When this was explained, it made perfect sense to me. Previously, I would have thought that the need for prayer and attunement would be less for someone who is more advanced on the spiritual path, than for someone who is not spiritually inclined, because in that more advanced person the spiritual path is more firmly established. I think there is no better example of this danger, enormous responsibility, and potential destructiveness than Judas Iscariot. He was an initiate, well trained, who forgot his most basic lessons, and who would not allow the enormous responsibility to humble him. In his case, it was not the subtle energies that caused the problem, but rather that he forgot the source from whence came the new life that streamed through him, and he tried to appropriate it for his own. He ended up hanging himself from a tree, a victim of his own abuses.

The cornerstone of the energy work on ourselves was, first and last, attunement. This prepared the energy field with the highest level of vibrations so that whatever healing needed to be done would be done in the most efficient way. It also opened us up to releasing whatever negative energy we were holding onto. A lot of my work had to do with my heart area, as I have mentioned, but also there was quite a bit of work in opening all of the chakras. I had to learn how to keep my energy grounded, while at the same time doing the spiritual work. I learned that this was of particular importance because without grounding, there was the tendency to get lost in the other's energy. If that happened, there was a risk of taking on the other's pain or the other's problem. Then, the healer would help no one, and would endanger himself.

As we worked on each other, we worked mostly on disturbances in the energy field related to mental, emotional and spiritual issues. Sometimes these lodged in the body in the form of physical symptoms, but mostly with each other, we were dealing with a different order of symptoms than we would encounter in a public ministry. We knew this, and welcomed the opportunity to work in such a supportive setting, with these kinds of problems, before we would be put to the test around people who would be doubting and questioning us.

We learned how to protect the energy field from invasions from without. I was continually surprised at how much I learned about the many ways and methods we can be invaded from without, and weakened or hurt seriously. The biggest invasions, we learned, tended to come from those in one's immediate environment. We were warned to pick our living situations very carefully. If a person living in our home is someone full of venom and spite, the undercurrent that they generate, because invisible, can penetrate into our energy field on a constant and insidious basis, and weaken us without our ever knowing what is happening. This would be like a poison that invades the cells of the body, and causes a toxic reaction, but on a different level.

We were taught the warning signs of such an occurrence. This included a feeling of weakening or self-doubt when in the presence of someone, a feeling which did not feel a part of our nature when we are away from that person. We were taught that a person can have a seemingly positive nature, but still be sending out this kind of invasive negative quality under the surface. Another warning sign would be a feeling of dread, or of not wanting to go home, even without knowing exactly why. Though we were without homes of our own during

Jesus' ministry, we were taught the importance of a spiritually cleansed and comfortable home, where we could and did feel at our very best, and at our most attuned. We knew how to prepare a home, and how to pick a site that had the most positive energy field for our purposes.

As I read over my words, I realize it might seem that the main focus of our work was in the arena of healing. This is not the case, though certainly it was a critical part of the work. It is probably a far easier area to try to put into words than some of the other aspects of our study and initiation. However, learning about the energy field, learning how to clear it, and how to attune was of vital importance. It led naturally into the healing arena. Without our focus in this area, we could not effectively teach or carry on the work. We were taught that we must know from our own experience that which we were teaching. A mere carrying down of words would be like passing on an empty shell, devoid of its contents. The work for which we were being prepared was work of the heart and work of the spirit, and therefore our learning was in those realms.

Every day brought with it a new challenge, and new lessons. The human suffering we saw was immense. The roots of it were so deep that often it seemed unfathomable. When Jesus described to us what he could read about a person's history and current situation in their energy fields, I, as a neophyte, was amazed at what he knew. I also wondered if I could ever master even a fraction of the lessons he taught us. For example, he could look at a person, and tell us about their current emotional and physical health, any chronic conditions of any kind they might be coping with, any past lives that might be relevant to the current situation, and how these past lives were interweaving into the present. From there, he could tell us the challenges this person was facing in this lifetime, and where the current choices were taking this person in dealing with these challenges. We saw this energy field reading innumerable times. Each time, I was as impressed and amazed as in any previous time. Even though I was getting much better at reading energy fields, it still was the case that I was very much a beginner, and saw the fundamentals but little of the more intricate details.

Attunement to God, or lack thereof, was one of the factors that was more easily read in the aura. If a man were truly working on attunement to the divine, then there would be a lovely clarity about the aura, encircling that person in a bright light. Even though the energy field might have a number of different blocks and murky areas therein, such a man would have a radiance and a quality of being of one piece, or one mind. By contrast, someone who was not actively in a state of striving for this attunement, would have a lot more darkness and murkiness in the aura. He would send out emanations from different areas in the field, which would reflect the negative emotions that he was experiencing. Rage or intoxication distort the energy field completely. When in these states, a person's energy field becomes almost unrecognizable, compared to their normal field. I am perhaps oversimplifying the case to say that with a person who is actively working on his relationship to God, there is a quality of oneness and cohesiveness to their aura. With someone who is driven by his lower self, there is a quality of dividedness and fragmentation to the aura. Whatever emotions are being experienced in this person generate out, often from different areas of the field.

CHAPTER 23

I REMEMBER CLEARLY ONE DAY WHEN I FELT I was at a plateau with the energy work I was doing on myself. I was convincing myself that my limitations were so great that I would probably never be able to move on from this level at which I was now operating. I truly believed there was something innate to me that had set a boundary on the limits of my personal ability. This voice nagged at me despite the inspiring spiritual instruction I was receiving. I suppose that I needed to be jarred out of my negativity, but nothing could have prepared me for what then happened. If someone had asked me if I were feeling this way about myself, I would have denied it, out of lack of awareness that this belief system was working its way in and settling into my consciousness. In retrospect, however, I can see clearly that this had been happening for a while, and was at this point a limitation I had set up for myself.

Jesus asked me to walk with him into the hills. I eagerly consented to go. As I have said before, I loved our time together, and I felt very honored to be asked on this walk. Our nighttime journeys had continued, during which I learned a great deal. I was hoping we might now have an opportunity to discuss some of this. However, this was not the case; we were to have a meeting of another sort.

It was a beautiful afternoon, a perfect time to spend alone with Jesus. Much as the sun's rays were warming and soothing as they penetrated the cells of my body, so being around Jesus was warming and soothing as I experienced his perfect love absorbing into every area of my energy field. Being with him was always like this; the emanations of his love were so strong, pure and steady, that to be bathed in it was to experience paradise. I know no other words for it.

When we slept at night, we were wrapped and enclosed in the embrace of his energy field. Nothing ever felt so secure, so soothing or so loving as this.

After an hour's walk or so, we found a lovely spot to sit and rest. We made ourselves comfortable on the green hillside. There was a light breeze, which brushed our faces and our bodies so gently that it was as if it were talking to us, and welcoming us there. The moment was perfect. I said to myself that I would remember it forever. We sat quietly for a while, and enjoyed the peace and beauty the world was sharing with us at this moment. I loved this silence we shared together. It felt so full and so rich, that words would have been superfluous.

After a while of luxuriating in the day, I became aware that Jesus was now ready to talk with me about whatever was on his mind. I had been curious, but knew he would talk when he was ready. He had a smile on his face, and he looked at me, and gently chided me: "So then, John, you have come to the edges of your world and feel you will go no further?"

He was so direct with me, and so accurate. He put into words all that I had not been able to articulate for myself. I was unable to think of any way to respond. My jaw must have hung open. Then, I felt my defenses coming up, but knew immediately it would be better to remain silent than to offer up a feeble and defensive response.

He was warm and gentle with me. What he did then was to take me out far beyond my perceived limitations, to show me there truly were no limits to what spirit could do through me. I was afraid, I know it now, to allow myself to be too changed. The boundaries I had been setting up had been the defining edges of my fear. But how to explain what happened that day on the hillside? Even now, it is almost incomprehensible to me what I saw and experienced through him. I do not know how he did what he did, or how he opened my eyes and made me see, but somehow he did, and I was astounded.

I suppose we went out of our bodies, but, for all I know, we stayed still and watched the changing scenes in front of us. It was as if all my abilities were fully amplified for the time being; as if I were able to see and feel through his eyes, and see the world as he did, and do anything that he did. Somehow, he lent himself to me in those moments so I could, as he described it later, "experience the fullness of God as that experience is available to all who seek it."

I know that in many ways, even then, my experience must have been tuned down, for my vehicle was flawed and could not tolerate the intensity of the light he was able to carry. However, what I did experience was an ever-changing panorama in which I was taken to many of the situations I had already experienced with Jesus. I experienced them again, not in my body, but with his sight and with his intelligence. The doors of my perceptions were flung wide open. All was new to me, and I was exceedingly amazed at what I saw and felt.

I saw the blind man come up for healing, and I witnessed Jesus' consciousness as he scanned the energy field. I felt as he prayed, and as God worked through him to restore the vision. I experienced as the man was forgiven, and as the negative energy was dissolved in a bath of divine light. Time and time again, I experienced these healings. I felt what he felt, and I saw the world with cleansed sight. I experienced an attunement to God far beyond anything I had ever imagined.

We went to Cana, to the situation where he turned water into wine. He allowed me to experience his consciousness as he performed the miracle. In this situation, I perceived he was teaching me a deep mystery, in which, through baptism by water into the Spirit, one's essence becomes transformed into Spirit, represented by the wine.

The experience went on. Whether it took seconds or whether it took hours, I could not say. The learning was deep and transformative. I experienced his consciousness as he taught, and received his words directly from Spirit, without obstruction or intrusion. He took me to his consciousness on the day he first appeared in my life. I saw and felt clearly that the choice had long since been made, and that he had come directly to me simply because it was now time. This piece of the experience was particularly personally gratifying and fun.

He took me to times beyond this time, and gave me the eyes to see myself in different bodies in different times. With these eyes, I could clearly see the guiding light that would be with me and protect me in these incarnations. He showed me different abilities I would develop in these times. This was not greatly emphasized, and was like a side journey in the course of this experience.

The last portion was definitely back in my body. During this portion, the fullness of Spirit was upon me, as if he had temporarily joined me in my body. He had me scan over all the lessons I had been learning. To my amazement, for a few seconds, I was now a very advanced student who knew that God working through me would move me well beyond how I defined myself, and into spiritual abundance, the likes of which I never could have imagined. In those seconds, I knew with certainty that the Spirit working through me would work perfectly in whatever task it was called upon to do. I can only imagine that this momentary state of perfect attunement, lent to me in this experience by Jesus, must be the state in which he lived his life. If I had to compare my normal consciousness with that which I felt in these seconds, it would be like comparing the light of the smallest sliver of the crescent moon with the light of the moon at her fullest and most perfect. This state must be, I think in looking back upon it now, the state of perfect faith and attunement, where oneness with God is not only possible but also achieved.

When we were done, I was amazed and exhausted. I almost could not believe what I had experienced, but when I saw Jesus' smile, I knew that it had happened. I wanted to ask him a million questions, but I also knew that words could not contain any of this. I was humbled and stretched at the same time. I thought about what he had said to me before this experience had begun. I said to him that I supposed if I put myself aside, I still could grow and reach beyond the plateau on which I found myself. We both laughed. I was deeply grateful for this lesson at this time, and knew I would never forget it. The inspiration was now internalized, through the states he lent me. It seemed that new room had been opened up into which I could expand.

CHAPTER 24

I SPENT MANY DAYS AFTER THIS EXPERIENCE REFLECTING upon it. Indeed, the lessons it taught were ones that stayed with me for the rest of my life. There was so much to absorb from these moments. The more distance I got from it, the more it struck me how perfect this experience was for the state in which I had found myself. Looking back at it now, I think those moments gave me nourishment for a lifetime, for I have remembered this instruction in both good moments and bad. It has provided me with sustenance through some of my darkest hours, when I grew to doubt myself.

The absolute high point of the experience was when I shared Jesus' consciousness, when, for those moments, I felt I knew what it was like to have the consciousness of complete at-one-ment with God. If I had to pick the singular most transcendent moment of my lifetime, amongst all the many marvelous experiences I have gone through, this one was the most miraculous and the most astounding moment of consciousness I shall ever know.

It is true that later on in my life, when the spirit of the Holy Comforter was upon me and I was able to perform healings, I received the fullness of consciousness of Spirit upon me. However, these moments on the hillside were different. In them, I was blessed to know what it truly meant when Jesus said: "I and the Father are one." This had always been a mystery, but after this day, there was no longer any sense of mystery about it. I knew then what he meant, and was very blessed to have this experience of what it meant. I knew with certainty and beyond all doubt that he was God incarnate.

With this experience, everything had shifted for me. My experience of Jesus as God was now not merely a supposition, or a belief, or even a faith that what he said was true. I now had a profound inner knowing. I referred repeatedly to this state in my consciousness. This did not alter my relationship with him, as much as it deepened it. Because the memory of this state resided within me, I became even more than before concerned with my inner states of consciousness. There, and only there, was stored the most glorious, the most unbelievable and the most miraculous understanding of what and who Jesus was. It has taken me a long lifetime to even begin to understand the implications.

Words feel very inadequate to describe the indescribable immensity of this. I lay awake for all of that night, attempting to run through in my mind the entirety of the experience I had that day. Each time I went over the occurrences on that hillside, my mind seemed to fixate on this aspect of the experience. It seemed my mind was not large enough to contain all it had experienced. In many ways, I do think this is true. I have spent a lifetime trying to understand and to process the enormousness of the dispensation, and at this time, I still very much feel myself a neophyte. In that consciousness was contained complete clarity, strength, compassion; and also divine love, divine power, omniscience and omnipresence. I do not know how he was able to allow me to feel it without it being utterly unbearable for me, but somehow, for those moments, I knew that I was seeing and feeling as he saw and as he felt. The vision was exquisite and ineffable.

Of all the mysteries surrounding his existence, I think this one is the cornerstone, without an understanding of which a person cannot begin to comprehend the others. As I have said, I do not know myself how to totally grasp this mentally, even after all these years of pondering upon these questions. Gratefully, I do have the blessed memory of the experience. I remember the sense of knowing beyond doubt that through him the Word was made flesh.

My mind was reeling from the initiation. I could not let go of it for even a moment that first night. It was as if I had to understand the incomprehensible, but did not know how to approach it. How could this be? How could he be God? It did not make sense at all, and yet I had never in my life felt anything so real. I had known that he had great wisdom and great powers, but this was so far beyond anything I could have conceived in my mind that I continued to feel a kind of hopeless inadequacy as I contemplated. To say that he was the Messiah had not been hard for me recently, though I did not fully understand that of which I spoke. However, this was something very different, something radically different, something that challenged my notions of what was possible. I knew now that to think of him without understanding him as God incarnate was like tasting a wine that had been so oft diluted as to obscure any taste of the grape.

I strained to think of the implications of all of this. If God had become man, and was now living on earth, was this not a new moment in time, and would not time be changed forever? I had no idea how, but it seemed that this must be. At this point, I had no idea of the mysteries to come, so of course I could not imagine the impact as I turned it over in my mind, in an attempt to make sense or to discern any patterns in that which I saw and felt. I was still so stunned and impacted, that I could only endlessly review exactly what had happened, and wonder what more there was to know. I began to realize I could go no farther with this at present, and prayed to God to grant me the wisdom and the understanding that I would need to grapple with this.

As dawn broke, after having had wrestled with these issues all night, I finally had found a sense of peace with the previous day's impartings. What I did not know, I could not know now. Though it was not in my nature to let go of something like this without a struggle, I felt I had struggled all that I could or should. From now on out, I would need to trust that I would be shown what I needed to know, when I was ready to know. I knew that everything I saw of Jesus would now be changed. Because of this, a new dimension would be added to my perceptions and thoughts. I wondered if any of the others really knew. The more I thought about it, the more I doubted they did. Even Peter, who knew so much, and whom I admired immensely, probably did not have the experience of this. I felt immeasurably blessed and fortunate, and wondered if I were truly adequate to the task of working with that which was now before me.

My head felt filled and swollen almost to bursting, an experience that would repeat itself many times over the course of my long lifetime. This was the first time I had felt this way. I attributed this feeling to the sense that now I was a container for an experience of the infinite and the eternal: since I was definitely a finite container, I would feel stretched and swelled with that which was now inside of me. What was inside was no more me, than a container is identical with its contents. I knew that the light and the power that I felt were from God. They were a gift to remind me of Jesus' nature and to encourage me in my own growth and development.

CHAPTER 25

IT WAS NOW LIGHT, AND THE OTHERS WERE STIRRING. I felt like I had been working all night, even though I suppose I dozed off at times into a restless slumber. Everything was different now. From now on, it would be up to me to recognize in all that I saw and experienced of Jesus and his work, how the bare fact of the incarnation impacted on everything around him, and on all whom he touched.

If there were to be out of this time a single memory that I could say encapsulated how I was feeling about the inner shift I was experiencing, I would have to say that it was of the following event. What started out to be a very simple, even routine, morning was, in the event that followed, made into a symbol of a world that had changed in ways far beyond my comprehension. I wondered at the time if my relative youth prevented me from grasping the many ramifications of what I had been shown. I know now that the mystery of the incarnation is the deepest this earth has ever known, and that it is all but impenetrable by even the finest minds.

What happened was that I arose from my pallet, and busied myself with the morning's activities. After a while, we took time for prayer. I noticed that I felt unusually light-headed, which I attributed to the lack of sleep I had experienced the night before. In our silent prayers, I asked for understanding of the incarnation (though I did not have this word for it at the time), and I prayed that God would show me in simple, concrete ways that I would be sure to understand. I wanted mental pictures, symbols I could carry with me easily, rather than the burden of carrying extraordinarily complex concepts that could not easily be either called to mind or conveyed. I made this request, and after prayers were over, my mind turned to the activities that lay before us this day.

Peter wanted to journey to a neighboring town, where he had heard that people were clamoring to hear more of Jesus. Jesus was not opposed to the idea, and seemed to feel this would be a good direction for all of us to take this day. I was, because of the previous day's experience, in an overwhelmed state, and found myself with little or nothing to say. I was taking it all in. It was as if my entire body was adjusting to the implications of what I had learned, and needed time to re-settle itself. I envied Peter's self-assuredness and his gift of talking, especially now, when I was without words.

I stayed in this state throughout the morning. Though I listened to Jesus while he spoke to the people, I was busy processing everything through this new filter, and was preoccupied. James did not fail to kid me about this, for my intensity could pull me far inward even in the midst of a crowd. I was often the subject of his playful jabs. However, he seemed to sense I was even further away than usual. After a while, he left me to my own world. I had not told him about the previous day's experience, for I did not know how to begin to describe it.

Hours had passed since the morning prayers, for the sun was now in such a position where I could see it was early to mid-afternoon. People were pushing each other to get close to Jesus. Many had come, or were brought by others, for healing. I was watching, and offering my continual prayers of support as he worked, when suddenly, out of the corner of my left eye, I saw a young boy working his way through the crowd. He had dark hair and skin, and was quite thin, though not gaunt. I assumed he was pushing his way up to see Jesus, and thought nothing more of it. However, something about him kept pulling at my attention, and I kept returning my gaze to him. His eyes were clear and dark; in them was a clarity and a purity that struck me somewhere deep in my soul. He looked at me, and our eyes locked.

I cannot say how long we looked at each other thus, but the communication between us in those moments was astounding. I felt I could see to the bottom of his soul, and that, with his eyes, he could penetrate to the bottom of mine.

He came up to me slowly, and said to me; "I came here today to see for myself, for I have heard this man is from God, and what he teaches is from God. I see God in your eyes, and I know you have seen God. It is in this reflection of God that I have come home. This man Jesus could not be a mere man if this is what you have seen, and what I have seen in you."

With that, he moved closer to Jesus. I was left wondering and puzzling about this experience, and just what it was that this boy saw. I marveled at his easy acceptance of his experience; he did not question it or try to figure it out, but rather stated what he saw and felt, and acted out of this.

I recalled my prayer of the morning, in which I had asked for simplification of my understanding of yesterday's experience. I realized that this young boy, with his straightforward perception and acceptance that Jesus was God, was the answer to my prayer. For all the complicated workings of my intellect in trying to figure out how could this be so, and what does this mean, and what were the implications of this, and was I understanding accurately, this boy came to me with the simple gift of perceiving and knowing the miraculous and the unfathomable in a moment of time. He simply accepted and marveled, and moved on. What a beautiful gift he had in his unquestioning simplicity!

CHAPTER 26

AFTER THIS EXPERIENCE, I SETTLED DOWN INSIDE MYSELF somewhat, though the questions multiplied. Who was this boy? Was he an angel sent to teach me something so simple that my mind with all its fondness for complexity could just not fathom? What was it that he had been able to see in my eyes? What would it be like to look into someone's eyes, and to see in them that this person had seen God? There were no ready answers to my questions, but I knew this boy had taught me something very valuable.

Jesus taught that we are all God's children, and God is within us all. The fact of the incarnation was something else entirely. It was, and is, very difficult to sort out. I know what my experience was, and I know what I learned from this boy: I did find peace in experiencing this. Yet, my intellect continued to hunger to grasp how this could be, what it meant, and how this was different from what each of us had the potential to be and experience. I cannot say I have ever had a sense of mastery of this concept. I know what I felt in my soul, but what I search for in my mind, I cannot come to grips with.

A dream came to me during the days immediately following the experience with Jesus in the hills. It came as I was struggling with the concept and implications of the incarnation. I suppose it comes as close to elucidation of the concept as I could ever approximate. It started out with me being in the hills with Jesus on a beautiful day, as if we were back on that day when I experienced so much with him.

"I am so happy to be out in the hills with Jesus today. I know it is a very special day, one in which I will learn a great deal. Time passes very quickly. He teaches me lesson after lesson that I eagerly absorb.

Then, something very startling happens. I arise from where I have been sitting, and suddenly, without warning, I am soaring like an eagle over the hillsides. I feel ecstatic to be able to fly so effortlessly. Then, just as suddenly, it is nighttime and I am high in the sky. I discover that my nature is that I am a star, brilliant, hot and gaseous, blazing in the sky. Again, the scene changes, and I am back on earth; I am an ocean, cool, wet, salty and wild. I feel the enormous surges of energy within me.

I go through many changes in this way. Wherever I direct my consciousness, that I become, and I experience the essence of a tree or a mountain or an animal or a body of water. I know that what enables me to make these changes is that my essence is God, and that God knows and is known by all things, animate or inanimate. God is in everything.

I enter the consciousness of different people in this way, and I find in their natures a tremendous resistance to, and denial of these energies. I can sense how very far away they are in their being from expressing their divine nature. It is as if the very matter that makes up their bodies impedes the flow of divinity. Then, I am in Jesus' consciousness again, and I experience complete freedom from the limitations of matter. I feel once again that state of perfect attunement, and the sense of the eternal, the omnipresent and the omniscient that come with it. I am in a state of perfect awe as I pull away from this experience. I know that Jesus is God willed to be in human form, and the density of the matter that constitutes his body is very different than that which makes up the bodies of other humans.

I scan my experience of transformations, and realize each of my transmutations was a look into a different face of God. Each of these experiences presented a different facet of God's manifestation. The experience of Jesus was substantively different: it was a glimpse into the actual being and nature of God himself. He was God manifest, in his fullness and in his glory, and was all things within himself. He was the eagle, the ocean, the hillside and all living beings. He contained all of these things within him; all things were a part of him.

In this state of dream understanding, there were no contradictions. Everything made perfect sense. My understanding felt full and rich. I woke up with an enormous sense of satisfaction, not unlike that of a man who had just completed a most delicious and varied meal of many courses, which delighted all of the senses, and appealed to the intellect in its presentation."

When I awakened, it was with the sense that what I had just experienced was very real. In fact, it seemed every bit as real as the original experience I had on the hillside with Jesus. For a few moments, I pondered on the difference between the levels of reality in the dream state, and in the waking state. I mused that both are real, and was not sure if true levels of awareness were any different in either state.

I told Jesus about the dream later in the day. He smiled. He said he was glad I had found a richer understanding of the question with which I was struggling. He told me God had blessed me with a very beautiful set of images to enrich my comprehension.

"But," I asked him, "I do not understand what it meant when it said that the density of the matter which makes up your body is different than that of other humans."

We were walking around the edge of our camp now.

"Rest your hand on my shoulder," he told me.

I did not understand, but I did what he said. I put my left hand on his left shoulder, but to my amazement, it was as if there was no body there, and my hand just cut through where I saw his body to be. My hand fell back down to my side.

"But how did you do this?" I asked, incredulously.

"It is just a matter of where I will my consciousness to be," he said. "Try the same thing again."

I did. This time, my hand rested on his shoulder as if he were an ordinary human being. The look on my face must have been extremely puzzled, for he said to me, "John, for me it is only a matter of shifting vibrational rates. These I can shift at will. The higher levels are actually somewhat more comfortable for me. But for the purposes for which I am here, it is preferable that I be at the denser levels of vibration."

At an intuitional level, I grasped what he was telling me, but again, my intellect was struggling with what did not make sense to its narrow view of reality. He told me not to worry about this too much, that it would make much more sense later. He also said that if I observed carefully, I would learn to detect when he was changing vibratory rates, without having to touch him. In doing so, I would learn what purpose it served for him to do so. He said to look for these changes first in his energy field, and I would learn to recognize the signs.

That evening, I thought about the life I was leading now, and marveled at the adventure I was on. I thanked God for putting me in a position where I was so blessed. I could not even begin to imagine what I would be doing many years hence with all that I was learning. It was fun to try to imagine. In my imagination, I was always by Jesus' side, learning from him, and teaching and healing others with what he had taught me.

CHAPTER 27

IF I HAD MY LIFE TO DO OVER AGAIN, and could choose the events and people I would want to come into my life, I think I could not do any better than what God had in store for me. My youth and early middle age was full of events and action; my later age has been full of quiet time, both voluntary and coerced; time for reflection, time for teaching and writing. Most of all, of late I have made good use of the time to ponder the many mysteries to which I have been exposed. I do not believe any man has ever been given weightier and more substantial events and ideas to contemplate. I have tried to transmit, both orally and in writing, that which I have learned and been given.

Many of the teachings that were given to us were in the esoteric tradition. Many of these were not meant to be passed on to the general public. The fruits of these teachings, however, were meant to be shared. All of the healings and exorcisms, and many of the preachings that Jesus performed, and that later we did, were the result of a careful and disciplined schooling in esoteric as well as the more traditional teachings. We learned quite early on that the esoteric component of the teachings was the living, breathing part; the more traditional oral and written traditions could be passed on generally, and grasped in a general and literal manner by the public. Both were valid, and we learned a great respect for both sides of the teachings. However, we always gravitated to the esoteric tradition when we were alone, or in a small group with the Master. My particular nature was especially suited to the esoteric traditions, as I have alluded to in other parts of this manuscript. Of all the disciples, I was probably the one who most gravitated in this direction. The private meetings I had with Jesus did nothing to discourage me from this direction!

I was by now, a more confident young man. Nonetheless, I was always surprised when people sought me out, and showed respect for my words. My relationship with Jesus had thrust me into a very different position publicly, a position which many would have liked. I did not dwell on these thoughts, but did make these observations. The confidence into which Jesus had taken me, and the many hours we spent together, helped me to grow immeasurably. I now felt fully initiated into manhood and adulthood. I gained many skills for dealing with people. I learned much from Jesus about generosity and benevolence of heart. This, combined with the enormous amount of love and compassion that I was given, enabled me to be with people in a loving, grounded and connected manner.

Never was there a better teacher than the one I had. Always, I strove to be the best possible student I could be. Jesus was most patient with my many mistakes and failings. He was masterful in his corrections, helping me to learn from my mistakes. I was quite young when I started out with him, and perhaps had more than my share of youthful impetuosity, pride, and at times, ambition. I marvel sometimes at how patient he was with me, for I am sure I would not be able to extend my generosity and patience nearly so far. At times early on I had allowed my position to affect me in an adverse manner, and though I tried to let this not be so, there were times when I am sure I was more than a little difficult to endure. Unfortunately, my mother and my brother colluded with me in this, for James and I both shared an honored position. Fortunately, a bit of rebuking and some maturing was all that was needed. In time, the center of my concerns grew deeper and much farther away from worldly ambitions.

At times, early on, some people found me to be a bit remote and inaccessible: this is something I believe my early exposure to, and enchantment with, esoteric traditions, contributed to. This trait corrected itself naturally as I learned more, especially about healing. In healing, it is a mandate that the healer be intimately connected to, and related with, the person who is being healed. As I progressed in my training, there was a natural correction to the early one-sidedness. I bring up these shortcomings of mine now, for I do not wish to seem as if I am presenting myself in a one-sided light. I have struggled with my weaknesses, both in struggling to accept them and in struggling to correct them. There are many more I have not yet mentioned, but these are the main ones that come to mind that I became aware of, and struggled to change, in those early times.

CHAPTER 28

As THE DAYS AND THE MONTHS WORE ON, I grew more comfortable in my roles, in the private relationship I had with Jesus and those closest to him, and with those who sought him out and who were always around.

There was always a political aspect to our experiences in the towns and cities which we passed through. It amazed me how political the religious sects could be. An act of healing or love could have many political repercussions, especially if Jesus' words or actions were interpreted by others as violating one or the other of the extraordinary number of rules which characterized virtually every aspect of daily life of the Pharisees and the Sadducees. I was never particularly attuned to the political aspects of the culture around me, so where there were political repercussions, I had to exert mental energy to follow the twists and turns of the political reasoning that would follow.

The types of violations Jesus was accused of have been written about elsewhere, by myself and by others. Rather than repeating what has already been discussed, I will review some of my impressions of how decisions were made to break the letter of the law, in favor of going with the movement of spirit. Jesus was well aware of the number of laws that governed most of the aspects of daily life, and knew the infinitesimal details. He was also very familiar with the esoteric teachings of a number of traditions. He continually emphasized the importance of following the prompting of spirit. As a group, we often had discussions on how to know what would be the "right" thing to do if we had a choice between following the law and doing what might be asked of us at a given moment. This might be something such as breaking the law, by healing on a Sabbath. What we were taught, and what in my heart felt right to me, was to pray for the wisdom to do what was right, and to ask for guidance to lead us on the path we should go. It was understood that we were not to seek out ways to go against the prevailing cultural and religious constraints. However, if a situation presented itself to us, we were to turn to prayer if the way we should go did not feel clear to us.

In the highly politicized and highly regimented religious climate of the time, it was considered heresy to break, especially if in public, one of the many laws by which the people of the land measured their daily lives. If a blind man were to implore Jesus to heal him as we were walking by him on the Sabbath, the conventional religious wisdom said this man was tempting Jesus to sin. If Jesus were to heal the man's eyes, this would be seen as going against God's will. There was no flexibility in this perspective. As such, God's law seemed inflexible and rigid, without compassion for those in need. Jesus told us there was great wisdom in observing the Sabbath, for the peace and restoration of body, mind and spirit. However, if we stayed open to God's will for us, and if we listened carefully, we would be informed what would be appropriate in any given situation.

We saw him acting on this many times. It never failed to surprise me how greatly the zealots were enraged by these random acts of compassion. As I have detailed earlier, all of the disciples were trained to work in the human energy field. When we were moved by spirit to act, it had a very different feel to it than if we were acting out of our own personal will. We also observed, in watching Jesus, what it looked like in his energy field when he was healing or otherwise acting on the prompting of spirit, at a time when he was also breaking a law. One could then observe how light and almost fluid the movement of energy was through his body. There was no observable resistance or conflict in the energy field, and no dark pockets were created.

On the contrary, when I have had occasion to observe those who were breaking the law, ostensibly in the name of spirit, but more likely in the spirit of self-aggrandizement or self-promotion, the forces moving through the energy field would be very different. They would be full of conflicts. The energy moving through would not occur in a steady light flow that was characteristic of Jesus' energy field. Over time, I learned not only how to see these differences and personal motivations in a person's energy field, but if I closed my eyes I learned how to feel them, and, also (which might sound strange to someone who has not experienced this) to hear them. It did not matter which sensory modality was used; the same truths would come through nonetheless.

Perhaps one of the most memorable occasions where I witnessed both the breaking of the law, and the way in which Jesus responded to the commotion that this caused, was on a Sabbath. A woman brought her son, whom she felt was on the verge of dying, to the home where Jesus was staying. He had been suffering from an illness characterized by a very high fever. I happened to be there at the time. The woman was weeping and severely distraught, and had tried all the recommended remedies. When she had heard that Jesus was staying at a home in the town, she carried her son over. She was told at the door that it was the Sabbath, and she would have to wait until the morrow.

When Jesus heard the commotion at the door, he invited her in. It was one of the quickest healings I had seen him perform. The light flowing through his energy field was clear and bright. The young boy responded almost immediately by opening his eyes and offering a weak smile. The woman, realizing that her son would now truly be okay, was overjoyed. Jesus told her to take him home and to let him sleep, and that he would be fine by the next day.

After she had left with the boy, a heated discussion struck up. Certain of those people in the room were very concerned with how all of this looked, and insisted that no good could come of this kind of blatant disregard of the law. Their particular argument was not so much that it was wrong that the law was violated, for they saw the obvious benefit in the healing. They believed it was setting a bad precedent, in which people might feel justified in violating the law for whatever reasons they might imagine. They believed this would lead to a deterioration of the support Jesus was building. In addition, they thought a kind of anarchy might result in which people felt free to break whatever laws they chose.

Jesus listened to all of the arguments carefully, and then simply stated: "If I am to do the work of God, am I then to be hindered by the laws of men? Am I to worry in what I do about how others might possibly misconstrue my actions, and use that to justify their own, or am I to simply do what I know to be God's will? I must do what I am moved in my being to do, for not to do so would be going against God. I cannot worry about the rest." His argument was impeccable, and the discussion was ended.

I was not infrequently asked, by those who were upset when they had heard about Jesus' breaking of the law, just what this meant, and, if it were true, how this could be defensible. Our society and our culture were in many ways very restricted and regimented. This kind of freedom of action was very difficult for people to understand, for it was not something they knew in their everyday lives. I often used the example that I have just cited to explain to them what was occurring in these incidents. Sometimes this would be sufficient, but at other times a discussion ensued about how a man could claim to at all times know God's will. At these times, I had trouble articulating my deepest understanding beyond simply saying that Jesus remained in a state of constant prayer, and while in this state, he was receptive to hearing divine will. I did not wish to further aggravate an already inflamed situation by stating that he was God, for although my experience had certainly taught me this, Jesus was not making this claim in so many words. "I and the Father are one" was understood as more of a statement of constant attunement, and some of the cosmic implications of this were not understood until well after his death.

I found that being in the position of teaching, explaining and defending helped me to learn better what I was absorbing and learning. It was very difficult, especially in these earlier times, to express orally what I knew so clearly in my mind. As time went on, I became more comfortable in this medium. However, even now, I prefer the written word, and believe I can more powerfully express my thoughts and sentiments through my writing. I have often wished I could have gained much more of Jesus' natural gift for oratory. Though I have done much oral teaching over the many years of my life, I never believed I was as persuasive or as focused as when I wrote.

CHAPTER 29

THE MIDDLE PERIOD OF THE TIME I SPENT WITH JESUS while he was on earth was characterized by an increasing involvement with the greater numbers of people surrounding him in the outer world. At the same time, there was a significant deepening and strengthening of the level of understanding and skills in myself and the other disciples. I now considered myself more worthy of the nomenclature of disciple, in addition to the role of apprentice. My knowledge and skills had solidified enough such that I felt I had something to share with others as Jesus' emissary. I was no longer solely in the position of absorbing as much knowledge and as many skills as possible. I did, however, still feel dependent on Jesus as my Master and teacher, though he was pushing all of us out on our own more to gain confidence in ourselves, and in the abilities we had been developing. James and I continued to be the closest of friends. We eagerly shared with each other what we were learning, and worked very well together.

At an inner level, I always eagerly awaited my time with my Master. I was happy to be with him with the group, but my favorite times continued to be the quiet times we shared together. I always felt incredibly enriched by what he taught me then. When I was with him, it always felt that my attention and my ability to learn were greatly amplified beyond their normal state. Jesus' energy field was so great and so expansive, that it opened up and intensified the energy field of those who were within it. When I was close to him, the negative spaces in my energy field felt cleansed and cleared, and the positive spaces felt greatly amplified. My prayer felt more pure and much more focused, and my ability to think and meditate felt greatly expanded. It was literally as if being in this space near him had the effect of expanding my mind, and linking it directly to the mind of God in such a way that there could be no question of the linkage. As I have mentioned previously, these kinds of connections could and did occur at a distance as well, but when in close proximity to Jesus, this was a constant quality.

As much as one could become accustomed to the unusual, I suppose that by now I was little surprised by the many miraculous and spectacular events that he generated. Yet, perhaps the greatest miracles I was seeing were those in the movement of the human soul. I saw people transform right in front of him when they were healed of some long-standing debility, or when they apprehended his divinity at a deep soul level. I was so often moved to tears by what I saw, that I stopped trying to hide the tears as they flowed from my eyes.

I was especially moved when I saw those who had all but given up hope, when they were restored in their faith and their hopefulness. This happened on the most obvious levels when there were healings or exorcisms, for the change was always dramatic and the transformation was apparent to all. This happened on other levels as well. When Mary Magdalena was absolved of her sins, and Jesus prevented the crowd from stoning her by reminding them that they too had their many failings, the gratitude and the transformation in her spirit was radical and extremely moving to all of us who witnessed it. She became one of Jesus' most loyal and ardent supporters. Who can say in what manner her soul was touched by his recognition of her essential divinity, the divinity we all share. It was as if his forgiveness set her free and completely erased the darkness that had occluded her soul.

I witnessed many occasions when people who, when listening to Jesus, watching him heal, or in other ways benefiting by being in his presence, then seemed moved in powerful and deeply personal ways. Though I might not have known the exact manner of their experience, I knew from my own personal experience how he could move an individual at the deepest of levels, without appearing to the observer to be doing anything at all. The very witnessing of a healing or powerful oratory could be transformational.

Jesus was a very passionate man, in the most positive sense of the word. He helped me to see that my passions could be my allies, when they were channeled properly and with attention to the energy flow. Of the many passions that I saw in him, there were some with which I identified more closely than others. I suppose his belief in the inherent divinity of the human soul could be called a passionate belief, for nothing could have swayed him from this conviction. It was part of the very fiber of his being. This was one of the passions that I took some time to grow into, as my sight was so much more limited than his. It took many experiences of seeing profound transformations in people whom I would have called evil, before I began to glimpse the truth of his conviction.

For me, it was one thing to say in a very generalized, abstract way that "the kingdom of heaven is within you", and quite another thing to really believe and accept that a man who is malicious and evil in his actions truly has God inside of him. Jesus taught me that to harbor resentment or judgment towards one who has done wrong, was to afflict my own soul with a burden, for it tied up my own energy in the swirling darkness of a negativity. While I could grasp the concept, it was much harder to put into practice. My first lesson in this had been the one very early on when I had been carrying resentment against my mother, when he described to me the energy cloud that it created around me, and sent me home to work things through. However, to let go and forgive someone who deliberately wrought evil seemed much harder. It seemed that somewhere deep inside of me there was a need to have at least a few people onto whom I could place my anger and my venom. There always seemed to be those around who seemed to deserve it by the darkness of their actions.

One day when we were walking together, Jesus abruptly stopped and turned to look at me. I was a bit startled, not knowing what to expect. He said it was time we looked at the hatred I was storing up inside. At the time he said this, I had not a clue what he meant, but of course by now I accepted that he knew something which I did not know about myself. I prepared myself to take in something I knew might not feel altogether pleasant, but which would ultimately help me on my path. I asked him what he meant, and observed him as he scanned my energy field, and read from it to me.

It never failed to amaze me the details he could read in the colors, textures and movements in the energy field. I hated to be so transparent, and yet at the same time I rejoiced in the loving attention that never failed to bring me some needed healing. Even when I was the subject of a reading when I believed I would not be seen in a positive manner, I had an utter fascination with the process of the energy reading. I would tune in to my energy body, and observe how it felt when he was reading me. From this I would learn much about the process of reading energy fields. When I was being read correctly, as of course was always the case with Jesus, there was a resonance between what he would be telling me, and what I would feel in my own field. When we as disciples practiced amongst ourselves, and I was being read incorrectly, there would be a dissonance between my experiences of the energy scanning by the other, and between my own experiences of scanning my energy as it was being read.

In this particular case, though I was loath to admit it, Jesus' reading of me was consonant with my own scanning of my field. What he told me I knew, but also did not know in the sense that I really did not have consciousness of the deleteriousness of my own attitude. What he told me was a description of a series of resentments that I was holding against a variety of different people. Some were people who thought Jesus to be a fraud, and who openly spoke against him, sometimes telling what I thought to be the most horrible lies about him. Others were those who did deliberate evil, such as robbing, raping, or otherwise abusing an innocent victim. I know that when I had stored my feelings and attitudes in my consciousness, I felt entirely justified in my hatred and loathing for what these people had done. I saw myself as righteous in my feelings.

Jesus taught me on this day many things about the implications and ramifications of the negative energy I was storing. First, he taught me that the negative attitudes I generated out to these people only reinforced to them at a subtle level the self-definitions they already had of themselves. By my unconsciousness, I was actually fueling the very thing that I considered myself above. Secondly, he taught that in cutting myself off from the more human side of myself by my self-righteousness, I was forgetting that in less fortunate circumstances, I too could have been set off in a different direction. In that case, I would not want people to condemn me, but rather to send me prayers and energy to help me to rise above the state into which I had fallen.

I felt particularly humbled by this, for I immediately realized how many times he had been tolerant and accepting of my foolishness and my impetuosity, and when, instead of criticizing and condemning me, he had sent me energy and light to help enable me to rise above myself. He told me that in cutting myself off thus from my own human foibles, I was creating a split within my own self. In so doing, I denied my own darkness, and I would need to find others who could carry for me the weight of my own darkness. At some level, I instinctively understood this, though in some ways this felt too much for me to grasp. I would need to wrestle with this idea for some time before it became more consolidated in my consciousness. The essence of what he was saying was that in the attitudes I was carrying, I was furthering the problem that caused so much distaste in me. *If, however, I began to change my consciousness, I would be able to contribute something constructive to the situation.*

The obvious question at this point was how I could go about changing myself. It seemed easier to change myself on this particular issue, now that it was pointed out to me, than to change at those points when I seemed to adopt the attitudes that I did, in a very unaware fashion. However, even now, I thought, I was truly invested in the contempt I felt for these people, or, at the very least, for the actions of these people. Jesus seemed to catch my thought. He told me that this distinction between the actions of a person, and the essence of their being, was the clue that would help me in forgiveness. I could hate the sin, but love the sinner; that is, I could not like what they did or said, but I could remember the inherent divinity of their soul, and love the God within them. I could pray to God to enlighten them with His loving all-embracing energy. This made much sense to me. I am sure that it had been presented to me before, but on this occasion, it resonated clearly.

We did a meditation and prayer together, and worked on releasing the resentment I was harboring. We sent light and healing energy towards these people and towards these unhealed parts of myself. When we were finished, I felt cleansed and light, again almost as if I had taken a cool and refreshing bath after a long, hot dusty journey.

CHAPTER 30

AFTER THAT DAY, I STROVE MUCH HARDER to stay aware of the attitudes I formed and stored. I was surprised at the almost greedy attachment with which I tried to hold onto my negative judgments on people, and at the pleasure judging gave me. For a long time, I thought I must be unusual in this regard. However, I began to observe this trait in others, and was astounded at how easily judgments were made. It seemed difficult to extend true compassion, or to direct healing energy where it was needed. It seemed that we almost automatically function at the level of building ourselves up by putting others down. I grew very sensitized to the issue, and spent much time and energy observing how this manifested in one's energy field, and what kind of energy was directed outwards as a result. I was amazed to see how, in passing judgment, we link ourselves to that which we hate in an energetic connection, and thus become more connected to what we say we do not like in others.

Any time emotion passes between two people, or is directed from one person to another, a tendril of etheric energy is sent out and connects with the other. To observe this at the level of the energy field is fascinating, with all of the colors, shapes and textures that the energy connection can take on. A positive connection looks very different from a negative connection, and has a very different feel to it. A negative judgment often looks very dark and murky, and when sent, can lodge in any number of places in the other's etheric body. What happens then is that this negativity, once sent and received, becomes yet one more obstacle in the energy field of he who is judged against. It becomes that much harder for that person to strive to do right, or to do the right thing. The sender of the judgment is also then energetically linked by a negative connection, which pulls him down as well. This is perhaps oversimplified, but is the essence of what I repeatedly observed. If people are sending out negative energy towards me, that energy will have a negative impact on me at a subtle level, whether or not they or I have awareness of it. Unless I am trained to detect this, it will generally go unnoticed. As that negative energy lodges in me, it incorporates itself into my energy body, becomes part of me, and helps influence the manner in which I see myself.

As I continued to witness this process, again I was struck by my growing responsibility as I became more trained and sensitive to these subtle realities. If I am not aware of the forces I am generating, I cannot take full responsibility for them. As I become more aware, my task becomes more difficult. I must then assume a very different level of responsibility, for my thoughts and feelings, as well as for my actions.

I spent a considerable amount of time thinking about this, and discussing it with Jesus and with my brethren. As we traveled around the area with Jesus, I scanned his energy field frequently to watch how he dealt with this, and how he solved this for himself. I was fascinated and absorbed by how the entire process looked. For example, I will take the case of a man who was hurling out nasty epithets at Jesus. This occurred frequently, especially as time went on. I think that the natural instinct in a person would be to say something equally nasty back, or to at least think it, which, as I have been describing, effects a similar reaction on the subtle energy body level. What I saw repeatedly with Jesus was that, at a reflexive level, he surrendered his own ego and brought down light from above, through the crown of his head. As it passed through him, it cleared his own energy field, and forgiving and loving energy was sent out.

Though I have worked and worked on doing this myself, I have never been able to achieve that natural, reflexive ability to transmute negative energy in this way. With me, it takes time. I have more internal struggling, when I am able to do it, or when I remember to make the effort to do so. Jesus made this process look completely effortless. My best guess is that it was effortless for him, most of the time. His channel to divine energy was wide open, something which may happen for the rest of us, if we work tremendously hard at it, on rare occasions. I know this is true for me.

I do not know how it looks in my own energy field when I am struggling with transmuting my reflexive reactions to something someone has done that I perceive to be wrong, harmful or evil, but I do know the process I have learned over time to go through. It is a combination of what I have so carefully been taught, and what I have learned over many years of practice. I find it hard to isolate now what it must have been like for me then in this regard, though I do remember that at first I was quick to anger and judgment.

When I began to work on this process, since I wanted to be successful in handling this energy, I simply went the other way. I began to pretend to myself that I was not angry or judgmental, and tried to send out healing or loving feelings. As I look back on this stage now, I recognize how very tainted and tinged these transmissions must have been by the extremely raw nature of the negative feelings I was shoving out of the range of my awareness. Jesus and the others were very helpful in pointing this out, and how this looked in my energy field. I often got discouraged, and sometimes very frustrated.

It is very difficult to be read so clearly! I had no idea how very much I depended in my everyday life on being able to hide from others, and from myself as well, the truths of my feelings and my reactions to what went on around me. I think now, after many years of observation, that this is a general reality of the human condition. It is something we count on as we pass through our daily interactions. It is somewhat frightening to realize how very much can be seen by those who know how to see!

The process I go through now in attempting to transmute the negative energies I might direct towards another human being are, first, that I try to maintain a general openness to recognition of those times when I am in this state. I have found that this state is automatic, and is not easy to recognize when I am in the middle of it. A general prayerful openness to being guided to what I need to know is very helpful in this regard. In prayer, I refer to it as asking the Christ presence to remain with me at all times, and teach me what I need to know, when I need to know it. When I become aware I am reacting to a situation or a person in the way I have described, I keep in mind the picture that had been etched in my memory over numerous observations, of Jesus connecting with the flow of God energy, through the crown of his head.

When I pray, and visualize this inpouring of energy, I find that my angry energy grows calm and filled with light. Then, it changes into something altogether different, into a form of energy that now feels manageable and workable. By this time, usually only a matter of seconds, I feel that I have a much better conscious ability to work with my own energies, and to direct them in a manner appropriate and suitable to the situation. At this point, I am now over the most difficult part. I direct to the person or persons the kinds of energy I feel would be most helpful in the given situation. When this process works successfully, it is a wonderful feeling to be able to carry this through from start to finish.

I do not know how often I was successful at this, for clearly I do not know about the times when I never became aware of what it was I was doing. I have struggled with this process quite a bit over the years, and have had some considerable successes, even in some extremely difficult situations. The most difficult situation was, of course, with those who condemned Jesus and put him on the cross. I am sure I have never truly completed the internal work I have to do in this matter. However, this is a story for later.

My purpose here has mainly been to take a very important lesson, and to give a picture of the ways I have worked with it over time. In my youth, as I worked with Jesus, I had the belief that the hardest work in my learning process was to be had in those early years. I could not have been more wrong. I suppose that the largest impact of what I learned was felt at that time. However, little did I know that the application of the lessons would be a painstaking and arduous work, one which would never relent in the diligence with which I would need to apply myself. The day-to-day work I have done has rarely been easy, and has been a continual, ongoing process. The more I know about this work, the more responsibility for myself I need assume. This is not to say there was no room for gaiety or lightness; there was much of that. Yet, in my lifetime, this focus was clear: I needed to be a practitioner of that which I taught. I did not, and do not, believe my role was one that could be taken lightly.

CHAPTER 31

ONE CLEAR, SUNNY AFTERNOON, WE WERE RESTING in the shade of some trees after a mid-afternoon meal. I was startled out of my lethargic state by a shout of a woman running towards us from the west. I had grown somewhat accustomed to these sudden eruptions of need from someone, into those increasingly fewer moments we were able to take for rest. The woman, who appeared to be in her mid-twenties, ran towards us with her long skirt gathered in her hands so she could run faster. Her long dark hair flowed behind her as she ran. I scanned her energy field as she ran up towards us, and I saw the red and black of fear and terror dominating the upper half of her energy field. I always wished at these times that I was more skilled in this, for I knew Jesus would be able to look at her and read exactly what was happening and what he needed to do. Based on what I was able to read and decipher, I guessed that the problem involved a child, but I wondered, if that were the case, why she was not carrying him or her.

When she reached us, she immediately asked for the Master. He bade her come over to where he was resting under a tree. He let her tell her story, though I knew well that he had no need to do this. She was gasping and sobbing as she related that her mother had suddenly taken very ill, and the local physician had given her some potion that had not helped at all. She was extremely distressed, for if anything, her mother had taken a turn for the worse, and seemed in great pain. Her mother, who had been a stout woman for much of her adult life, and who did not move around with agility, was having a terrible time lately. Now, she was doubled over with pain and was having much difficulty breathing. Jesus began smiling as he listened to her.

His smile confused me. I thought perhaps he was smiling because he had already effected a healing on the woman, and was about to tell her about this. This was not the case. I listened as he told her not to worry, that there was no danger to the mother's life. He told the woman to go back, for her mother would need her help in taking care of the new baby boy.

The woman's eyes grew wide, and she said: "But this is impossible, my mother is past her childbearing time."

Jesus was warm and gentle with her. He said all was not as it seemed to be, and that her mother would truly be feeling a great deal better within hours.

I am not sure why this particular story, out of so many others, has stayed with me over the years. It was pleasant to have a crisis that turned out to be a blessing instead, to be sure, but there is more to it than that. The woman came back to us within several days to tell us the new baby boy was healthy, and both mother and son were doing well. The entire family had been astounded to learn the "problem" was in fact a delivery. All concerned had been quite relieved that mother's health had turned around so quickly. Because of the woman's normal large size, which had not appeared to change significantly during the pregnancy, no one had suspected the nature of the problem. All had assumed that she was beyond her childbearing time because of her age.

My read of the situation from the energy field, on that day when the woman originally came to Jesus, had been, as I mentioned, that a child was involved. However, I had erroneously assumed that the child was the woman's, and that the child was endangered. I took some time with Jesus afterwards to ask what he saw that told him the nature of the situation. What I learned was that, although we both started with the same general picture of the energy field, I saw only the grosser, more obvious features, whereas he read the linkages and lines of connection, and was able to trace them correctly. I wondered how the truth about the situation could be read in the aura of the woman seeking help, when she did not even know her mother was pregnant. The answer was one I had heard before in other contexts, but one with which I was still struggling. The answer was that through our connection to God, we are linked in our energy fields to the Higher Mind. Though a person may not be aware of something that is going on around them, the truth of the situation is carried in the etheric energy in the subtle bodies, in subliminal awareness. That truth is accessible by reading the energy field.

I imagine most people of my day would be surprised to learn there is a science and a method to the work that I and the others were trained to do, in discerning truth, and in healing. At this stage, I was comfortable reading the energy fields of others regarding their own illnesses. However, in a matter such as this one, reading in one person's field about someone else was much more difficult. There were more subtleties involved, and, for me at least, the forms and colors were not nearly as distinct and immediate as in the other kinds of reading.

I have used this example to illustrate another direction in which we were being taught to read the subtle energies. I found that learning to read the energy field was in many ways like learning to read, with a major difference: imagine that instead of learning to read in your own native language, you are learning to read in a foreign language which you are learning as you are learning to read. The complexities were enormous, and the possibilities of misinterpretation of data were great. We spent much time at first, as I have mentioned in an earlier chapter, simply describing to each other the that we saw, rather than trying to interpret it in any way. Only after the information was gathered and described, did we venture into the arena of interpreting. It was relatively simple to interpret moods by the colors that characterized the varying dispositions. Physical ailments or psychic blockages were identifiable first by location, and then by the colors that characterized them. It had not taken any of us long to see the actual energy field, once we knew what to look for, and had enough practice in thus doing.

Once my auric sight had begun opening, there were periods when it would tend to close off again. However, our training was so frequent, and often so intense and concentrated, that before too many months had passed, I found that my first view of a person would include the energy field. I grew to almost instinctively scan the energy field, much as one would with the physical eye scan the physical aspects of a person coming into view. The information that could be collected about a person with this additional perspective was extremely helpful, and could shed much light on the emotional, physical and spiritual constitution of the person at a given time.

The additional information that thus could be gathered about a person was not, by its very nature, information they would voluntarily give. We were instructed repeatedly to be very careful with the information we gathered. An enormous responsibility conveyed with the increased insight we now had into a person's nature. We were not to pry, no matter how tempting it might feel, to satisfy our curiosity. This maxim of respecting the other's boundaries in this way was made very clear to us. If we had a question in our own minds as to whether it would be appropriate to scan further into a particular place in the energy field, when someone was not asking us for help, the fact that we had the question was an indicator to us that we were not to go any further. If we were working with someone who was asking us for help, and this question came up, we were taught to respectfully scan that person's energy. We were to determine from the response that we felt from him or her at a subtle level whether or not it would be all right for us to proceed in this area of the psychic investigation.

If we were to go further into the energy field, after having obtained this permission, there would inevitably be areas which felt "closed" and which we were not to go into. These might be areas that the person was not yet ready to work with on any level, or these might be areas that they had decided they would not want to share with anyone, for any one of a number of reasons, often shame, guilt or fear. I knew from my own experience how difficult it could be to have someone, even someone I knew and trusted as much as Jesus, penetrate into those very personal spaces that I held closed off from the rest of the world. I could imagine how uncomfortable it might be for someone to have a stranger working in some of his or her most vulnerable spaces.

The symptoms of a physical illness very often tied in with spiritual and emotional issues, so that, in a given healing, it might be impossible and undesirable to separate out the different components. The many healings, which Jesus performed over the course of his ministry, were often dramatic physical healings. There were many times where there was a lot more involved. It would be left up to the person who had been healed to work with what came up from his soul in the aftermath of the actual physical healing.

What at first seemed to be the rare miracle of healing, soon grew to be commonplace in frequency, as more people learned of Jesus' great abilities and sought to be cured. The numbers of people who sought him out were great, and sometimes overwhelming. The great miracle of healing became to our eyes and ears a quite common event, something which came to seem as ordinary in its own way as catching fish had been for me in my previous lifetime. I do not mean in saying this to diminish in any way the very great and extraordinary work Jesus did in the healing ministry. What I do mean to say is we saw so much of it that the witnessing of the astonishing and the phenomenal became quite customary, and even routine. I never ceased to be amazed and impressed by the work Jesus did. I tried to take in whatever I could so I could learn as much as possible. Yet, what he did ceased to take me by surprise with the regularity that it had in the beginning.

One minor event that did surprise me during this general time occurred one evening after we had finished our evening meal. We were gathered together, talking about the day's events. As we sat, a dog wandered into our space and went directly up to Jesus. The dog then lay down at Jesus' feet, as if he had always known him. They seemed to carry on an unspoken communication between them. As Jesus stroked the animal's somewhat mangy fur, I could see energy lines being transmitted between the two. I was indeed curious as to what was transpiring, and watched them for a while. We continued our conversation, and after our evening prayer, eventually turned in for the night. I slept next to Jesus, and saw that the animal stayed close by him for the entire evening. In the morning, the animal arose early, and wandered off.

The next evening, he was back again, and once more, he left with the early morning light. This pattern repeated itself over several weeks. Jesus did not stay with us on each of those evenings, though he was with us on most of them. The dog came only on those nights when Jesus was there. I grew to look forward to the dog's appearance, and grew fond of him. One evening, the animal did not show up. From that time on, we saw no more of him. I queried Jesus about the dog, and about what had transpired. He commented that all living beings thirst for God, and this dog had a particular hunger, and had come to him to satisfy his need. When that was done, he moved on. I found this difficult to understand, but on another level, the level where so many unusual things were happening, it made sense. I wondered about that dog from time to time, and what happened to him. I supposed he lived an unusual life. I felt warmed by what I had seen.

CHAPTER 32

WE BEGAN SPENDING MORE TIME JOURNEYING from town to town to spread God's word, so people in many different places might see for themselves the heart and the fruits of the ministry. Sometimes our walks were long, hot and dusty; other times they were for shorter distances, and under better conditions. A crowd usually accompanied us on the journeys. Some people accompanied us almost everywhere.

I never tired of hearing Jesus talk, and of seeing him perform various kinds of healings. There was always so much going on, and often it was impossible to take everything in. I did not wish to miss anything though; it all felt so very important and so startlingly real, despite the otherworldly aspects of many of the phenomena.

In this manuscript, I have spoken less of what Jesus preached than of what he did and said privately; perhaps this reflects my personal bias on what I think is important for a document of this nature. What he said in public was not necessarily different than what he taught us privately, but it was more generalized and more aimed at opening up the public to the faith and the belief that lay inside them. With us, it was more a question of taking that faith and deepening it with regular practices and disciplines. The public and private sides to the teachings were different aspects of the same material, adjusted to the learning needs of those who were being taught. Jesus was very well aware that different individuals had very different ways of relating to the concepts he related. For the general public, he believed the simplest and most direct teachings were appropriate. Those who hungered for more were free to follow him, and learn from his more in-depth teachings. Many who followed were captivated by the man and his work, and wanted to witness as much as they could while the opportunity was present.

If there was a negative side to this period for me, it was that, from a selfish point of view, Jesus was so much in demand, and I had less personal time with him. Even at night, he often stayed in various people's homes, and the regular 24-hour rhythm I had grown accustomed to in his presence had changed to one that was less predictable. I counted myself blessed to have the amount of time with him that I did. No matter where he stayed at night, whether with us or with others, we nonetheless often met in the dream state to carry on his work, and to explore different areas needing attention.

My role in this dream state was mostly to witness and take in what was happening. I learned a great deal while in this dimension of reality. As I have said before, it seemed that more was possible in this state where the usual apparent laws that bind us can be suspended more easily. I learned more about healing; and of the various realms beyond our world where higher beings reside and do their work. I also traveled to times before and after our own, and alternately marveled and was saddened by what I saw. I saw joy and love that was brought into the world, and also saw cruelty and destruction which raged seemingly out of control for many epochs.

Perhaps what was most startling about scanning the passage of time was that the pace of the evolution of the human soul was so achingly slow. It seemed, as we crossed the many centuries, that the darkness grew brighter, with the light of God increasing only in very small increments. The bloodletting and the injustice done in the name of God were particularly frightening and gruesome. It weighed my heart down with sadness. The reason for seeing these things was to put the present time into perspective. I could not reconcile all of this, however, with my belief that Jesus would bring with him the Kingdom of God onto earth in this lifetime. It took me the passage of time and events, and the gaining of greater maturity before I would begin to accept that the time frame for the transformation was very different than I thought.

One of the most important lessons I learned through the work we did in the dream state was to identify myself more fully with the spirit body, which was, after all, the vehicle in which we moved while in this state. This disengagement from the physical body gave me much greater awareness of the actual scope of my energies, and lent to me a greater feeling of connectedness with the Divine. The physical body, while potentially a very powerful transmitter for these energies, also slows down the vibrational level of the higher energies in order to adapt them to the denser level of matter. In this slowing down of energies, a sense of limitation is felt which is not present in the dream body. In the dream body, freed from the limitations of the physical body, I explored the flexibility and the freedom of the higher self. Through careful guidance and a great deal of experience, I brought what I had learned from the dreaming state into the waking state. The ability of the spirit body to travel outside of the physical body, and to move freely into various locations, was one of the most valuable of lessons.

Among the places we visited while in the dream state was the angelic realm, which held great beauty and awe-inspiring power. This was the realm of the more highly evolved helper beings, who guide our lives on earth. They are responsible for carrying out missives from the highest levels of the spiritual hierarchy. To be in the presence of these beings was to be in a realm where there was no room for the impurities of the earth below. These beings were charged with the most important of works. It was their responsibility to inspire, direct, guide and protect through impression, in the manner they sensed their messages would be best received. I felt humbled in their company, yet given the company I had been keeping with Jesus, feeling humbled had become quite a familiar state of being to me.

I learned that dreams were one of the favorite vehicles of impression. Waking visions were also used for the more sensitive beings. Angelic visitations were common. Most of the time the person had no idea these were visitations, for the words of the angel came through someone who seemed quite ordinary. In these visitations, either the angel would materialize himself, or impress words and/or actions on another to whom the recipient of the desired message would be placed in close proximity. Direct impressions by angelic guides on the mind of the recipient were probably the most common form of guidance and inspiration. In these cases, the person who received an impression rarely would be aware that the source of the thought came anywhere from his own mind. Those who were more sensitive and more highly trained would often develop the ability to discern when the source of ideas was from angelic guidance. They were able to cultivate this so they could directly ask for messages or guidance from these sources.

I often wondered how much influence and how much of a role these beings played in the course of my development and my everyday life. I had grown accustomed to some degree to the idea that my thoughts and my life were not necessarily as much my own as I had always assumed. However, learning about these areas was not only puzzling, but also forced me to re-examine my own thinking processes, and the directions they took. When I asked about this in the dream state, I was told that it was often the case that I was "inspired" when I believed my ideas were pulling together well, and when I felt "pulled" in some direction of action or movement. Further, I was told that the more I would open myself to this, the more it would occur.

I learned that there were many angelic beings surrounding Jesus. They were there to support and learn from him (for he was of a much higher order than they), but also to love and to transmit what they could to those who sought to be near him.

I suppose that the hierarchical nature of the spiritual realms should not have surprised me; however, it was not something to which I had given much time or thought. It was beautiful and moving to see Jesus as King in the earthly realm, but also as King of the Heavens. (Whether those on earth recognized him as such was immaterial, though it was many years before I came to an acceptance of that!) I saw his role as King as more political, and wanted to see the whole of the earth's people as his subjects in a literal sense. The angelic beings were completely cognizant of their relationship to the "King". In this realm, he was accorded the recognition of who he truly was and all that he came on earth to be. There was no question about this. I found myself moved to tears about this on many occasions. The beauty and the truth of this blended very harmoniously. There was an indescribable heavenly sweetness in how it all combined. I wished so often that I could convey even a portion of what I saw in these worlds to the people of my homeland. I believed they would have been changed forever, if they could only have seen what I saw in these nocturnal experiences.

By day, I learned to discern at least a portion of the angelic presences surrounding Jesus. Sometimes it seemed by the size of the gathering that the entire heavenly host had come down to earth to witness and to celebrate what was happening in this most important of times. At times, I was so much in awe of the sheer beauty and power, and the coming together of so many divine elements, that I became overwhelmed to the point where I lost track of the actual physical events that occurred as Jesus ministered to the people.

These periods when I seemed so very far away did little to dissuade James' opinion of me as someone who had trouble staying earth-bound! There were times when he would ask me for my thoughts about something that had happened, or when he talked about something we had both witnessed on a given day. At those times, I would be at a loss to recall what he was talking about in any but the most vague and indefinite terms. Though he teased me about this, I think he knew on some level that I was not as completely absent as it seemed, but rather off in a different world. After all, he had seen these traits in me from when we were very young. There were times when I communicated to him what I saw, yet there were other times when I just simply let it be, for I did not have the words to express it. I was often overcome with emotion at these times, and did not have a language to go beyond that emotion to describe what that generated such intensities of feeling.

CHAPTER 33

IT IS MORE COMFORTABLE TO WRITE AS A HISTORIAN and as a documenter of the public ministry of Jesus, than to write in a journal about my personal memories and experiences. As I write the words in this volume, I tell myself repeatedly that I need do this only for myself, and that it is my option whether or not I will decide to reveal these words to the world. At this time, I cannot imagine releasing these words, for the experiences described herein are sometimes intensely personal. It is not my wont to share such times with another, especially another whom I do not know. Nonetheless, I feel that I have been instructed and guided to commit these words to paper. I have struggled over time with following this guidance. Writing in this manner has helped me to review my life and experiences, which has given me new perspective. It has also helped me to set my course for what remaining time I have. My fear in writing is that others would not understand, or that they would accuse me of an extravagant imagination. However, as I work with my fears, I realize that in the end, it does not matter at all, for I am doing this for myself, to make somehow more real that which I have known and passed through. If these words go with me to my grave, which surely could not be long from now, then I have gained from the gathering, and my efforts have not been lost or in vain.

I mention all of this, and herein give a hint at the great difficulty I have had in writing my story. What I am about to discuss is perhaps hardest of all to write. It is an experience I had when with Jesus, something we had many opportunities to discuss after the initial exchange. It makes some sense to me now, but it is something I have not discussed with another living soul. My secrecy has helped me to not think about what I have been told.

I remember the day vividly. We were staying on the shores of the Sea of Galilee. Many people were around. Mary, Jesus' mother, and Martha were there. Jesus asked me to accompany him on a walk into the hills. I anticipated the trip with eagerness. We brought with us wine and food. It was a beautiful sunny, breezy warm day— one of those perfect days. As we walked into the hills, we enjoyed the flowers of all colors that bloomed all over the hills. I knew instinctively that there was an important purpose for our time together that day, yet I could not imagine what it was. I was grateful for the time alone with him, as those special times had become more rare.

I did not know that the subject would be me, and especially I did not know it would be about me in a future lifetime. (This was to be the first of many conversations on the subject.) We sat on some rocks in a beautiful spot. The sun felt as if it was the warmth and light of God shining directly on us. There was a grand cosmic sense, as if all the angels were witnessing and blessing the moments. Jesus had a way of gathering this kind of dramatic intensity around him wherever he went.

When he first said I would be a woman in that lifetime, I was shocked. I felt with my inner vision down to my male gland and parts, and tried to imagine them replaced with a woman's. It felt so odd and foreign. As he began to tell me of the role she/I would play, it seemed so beautiful, yet also inconceivable. How could such power be rooted in a woman? He assured me the world several thousand years hence would be a very different place, and it would be a time when the power of the feminine would be in the ascendant. I was to anchor light somehow, through my human vehicle. I would be very beautiful and would be there to demonstrate that truth and beauty and love go together. My heart would show me the way I must go. I would be very reluctant at first, but as I grew more confident, I would step into the role assigned for me. My role would be in supporting his role. I would be very carefully prepared, in this lifetime, as well as in subsequent ones, and especially during that lifetime itself.

"But," I asked, " what about you, will you be there too?"

"No," he said, "not as you understand it, in a physical form. My Spirit will be manifesting all over the earth/cosmos at that time, and I will serve much better at that time in the higher realms."

Upon hearing this, I felt suddenly stricken and lost, for I could not imagine not having the living physical presence of this man/God to show me the way. He quickly reassured me he would always be with me, but it would be inspired guidance. I would need never fear that I would be alone, for I would only have to call on him and he would be there. He added that he knows well that I am extremely stubborn, and that he knows as does the Supreme God that I would never accept guidance from any other source other than the One: he would remain my anchor for as long as I needed him. This last point puzzled me, as I could never imagine not needing him.

As what he had been saying settled in, I felt great sadness. It was an awful longing, as if I were losing him forever, since only I would be in the flesh. Yet, I also felt peace in knowing we would be together forever on another level.

We talked for some time about this future time, and about other lifetimes in my future. There were several which particularly stood out, but this one, which he had brought me here to discuss, was the one we spent the bulk of our time discussing and examining.

We lay back on the hillside. He had me close my eyes, and he took me there with him. The times and the environment were indescribably different. It was very difficult to get oriented because of the extreme differences in culture, environment, dress, pace of life, and many other aspects of life. Yet, I saw her/me, and he showed me this woman at different stages of her life, in different places, and with different people. I was amazed at the freedoms a woman could have, and the degree of independence, autonomy and strength that would be accepted in a distant time. I saw how she wrestled tremendously in those times to find her way back to her core self. I saw how, once she began awakening, she found her way to the living Christ once again, as I had known him. I marveled to watch her and to attempt to grasp that this was me, just in a different body. She was an ordinary human being, like any other in many ways.

It was very hard to comprehend, not so much the concept, but that what I was seeing was also me. I was, despite all of my work on detaching my view of myself, my true spiritual self, from my physical self, much more attached to my current body than I had realized. Just seeing myself in this completely other, feminine vehicle was unsettling, and more than a little bit disorienting. I strove to place myself inside her thoughts and her body, so that I might understand what it was going to be like to be her. As I have mentioned, I had been on many astonishing and extraordinary journeys since the day I first made acquaintance with Jesus. However, this one, though less otherworldly than many of the others, was in a number of important ways, much more difficult to accept and fully grasp.

We spent several hours on that hillside, engaged in discussion and journeying through time. It was a very serious, yet profound and moving exchange. I was being prepared for what was to come, and many particulars were elaborated on in this dialogue. There were to be a number of conversations on the same subject to follow, this one being the initial outline and introduction. Most of what I was told I prefer to keep to myself. It is something highly personal and subject to my ability to actualize myself through a continuing connection with this man/God.

I will say, however, that one of the concepts I carried away with me from this afternoon on the hillside, was the concept of the light body. As I scan my body now, at the time of this writing, I can feel that it is made of light and very rapidly moving molecules. The light is energy, healing, illumination, protection and truth. It is as if my body is completely lit up—full of light. It seems to have no weight. I was left with the definite impression that one significant and focal aspect of the work I would be carrying out in that time would have to do with the light body.

I left the hillside that day with an altered perspective on myself. It is one thing to be outside of one's body and experience oneself in spirit, and quite another to travel into another time and to observe and experience oneself in another body. This was a very different body, in a very different time. The idea of carrying on this work in another time was not so difficult to grasp, but the idea of doing it without Jesus with me was very painful. Of course, at this point, I had little idea what the future held in store for me even within the lifetime I was currently experiencing. I had little difficulty with the idea of a woman of equal piety and spirituality as a man, for there were magnificent women close to me, such as Mary, Jesus' mother. However, the idea of a woman going out in the world, and having the drive and the outward-going nature to do such work, with the freedom and independence to do so, was completely alien. I could not imagine myself in a body without the physical aspects of me that felt so familiar and so masculine, such as my musculature and my deep voice, my beard, my body hair, and of course my male genitalia. However, even this physical part was easier to accept than to see myself in the role Jesus had shown me.

On this day, and on other days, I was shown a number of different lifetimes and different roles I would play, in bodies of both sexes. It was made clear to me that what I did with each of those opportunities would be up to me, for God gave us free will to do with our lives what we would. I was not surprised that on many occasions, I chose the religious and spiritual life. Given the experience I was having in this lifetime, it made sense that I would want to be in those experiences where I could use and develop the skills and abilities in the calling that felt most natural to me. I found it fascinating and absorbing to venture into these other times to discover not only what opportunities lay ahead for me, but also for the future of humankind. At other times, there were opportunities to explore the past. This was always very helpful in understanding the complexity of factors that contributed to the person I was today.

As we headed back toward the Sea of Galilee, my mind was racing with the import and the implications of what I had been shown. I had many questions about what would be, what I would need to know, and if I would be able to do what it was that seemed set out for me. I knew that in many ways it would be doing nothing more than following in Jesus' path, and continuing with him into another time and another aspect of our work together. When he told me about it in this way, it seemed simpler. I could accept that through him, I would be guided to where I must go. There would be many on the path, and I would not be alone. On the other hand, I did not want to imagine a time without his physical presence, and the enormous comfort that this brought me. His friendship, his pure faith and his unwavering support were something I knew could never be replaced by anyone I would ever know. I could not imagine ever completely relying on another human being, for the level of trust I had developed in him was so deep and so complete that I knew that no human being would ever be able to deserve such confidence.

What was clear was I would be thrust into such a different time and position from where I was currently, that I was stretched almost beyond my capacities to conceptualize what he showed me. I was growing accustomed to being pushed beyond my own ability to understand! The part of this that made me the happiest was that in this future time to which he was referring, I would still be drawing my spiritual nourishment and sustenance from him. This was a source on which I knew I could always depend. As difficult, as painful and as utterly unimaginable as it felt to walk on the earth without his physical presence nearby me to guide me, to light my way, and to love me, it was comforting to know he would be there in spirit whenever I needed to call on him. I think I would feel desolate to be on earth without any means of contact whatsoever.

I deeply valued the relationship I had with Jesus. I had grown to think of him as my life's blood, which pulsed through my veins and gave me life. He fed my heart what it needed to live and love. Part of me, the generous and giving part, wished that everyone could know Jesus as I knew him, so they might be enriched, enlivened and enlightened as I had been. A more selfish part of me rejoiced that no one knew many of the experiences that we shared. There were many things I would never tell, and there were others I would have wanted to, but the appropriate occasion or opportunity never arose. I shared much with my brother James, especially as time went on, but there was much even with him that I kept to myself. Often, I did not have the words.

After years of practice at writing and at expressing myself, I have become more articulate and better able to convey some of the experiences I have had that are ethereal, incorporeal, or abstract. This has taken much practice, and I am still quite inadequate at this, compared to how I would like to be.

CHAPTER 34

AMAZING THINGS CONTINUED TO HAPPEN during this period of the ministry. We were taught that we were the beginnings of a new church, and what we were learning would be transmitted to others, who would then pass it on through the generations. Much of what we taught was verbal, yet much of what we learned was, as I have pointed out in other places, very much on an experiential level. What stands out for me about learning experientially is that the learning is immediate, felt and perceived in both body and soul. This imprints what is learned in a permanent way not possible via the written or the spoken word. What I knew from Jesus, I knew in every cell of my body, and in my very soul. What he transmitted to me through some of the experiential means which I have described, was, I have no doubt, in some part of me to be known forever, never to be erased or completely forgotten, even over the span of many lifetimes.

I think it is a need for the human being to experience what is learned in order to fully assimilate it. I think this need explains why so many people sought to spend time around Jesus whenever they could. He offered to them so many valuable lessons not readily available elsewhere, and in an immediate and real fashion.

I have described elsewhere the feeling that I felt around him of feeling completely and fully loved. Feeling that love taught me much about the nature of love. When I was thus filled, I could much more easily radiate out love towards others. This was true for many people. Nothing could compare with being in his presence, and feeling completely understood and loved. His compassion was perfect, as his love was perfect. I can write about what I have learned and experienced about love, but the essence of what I learned cannot be adequately conveyed. If I were to attempt to describe in words the most exquisitely beautiful flower I ever saw, could I do it justice? Of course not, for the essence of that perfect beauty would be lost in the transmission. Many people had the opportunity to experience his love. I think that this, above all other reasons, is why so many chose to spend as much time as possible in his presence. All who opened themselves to this experience, and, on many occasions, those who were not necessarily open to this exposure, felt the love that radiated out from him for a great distance, in every direction.

Perhaps the greatest failings of the religions of the time in which we lived is that they were so given to outward shows of piety, and to endless legalisms and rules which governed every aspect of one's conduct. Those who "administered" the religion were part of a hierarchy that encouraged bewildering amounts of erudition and scholarship that, as far as I could see, had little or nothing to do with knowing the living God. Jesus was a complete departure from this pattern, for he taught, in his living presence as well as in his words, that God resided within and is accessible to all at an immediate and real personal level, without need of intercessionary aid. He taught that we should be guided in our affairs by the spirit of God, rather than by some highly complicated rule or formula stored away in a manuscript in a religious scholar's library. I will refrain myself here from expounding further on this, a subject for which I have strong feelings and great zeal, for I would be getting away from the point of this discussion, which is the immanent presence of love in Jesus.

I believe his mission was to teach love and forbearance, but most of all, love. The beauty of his love impressed itself on all of those who were fortunate enough to feel it, and to know it within themselves. It was in the very beauty of his love that one could discern truth of the highest nature. His love was perfect: in that perfect love was such exquisite beauty that the angels descended to earth to gather around him, and witness the truth he manifested. In the love that he manifested, for the first time in history, the fullness of the human capacity to love was realized, in a way glorious beyond imagining.

With Jesus, the old rules were no longer necessary. It was God that moved and guided him, and gave him his ultimate authority. The ability and capacity to love as fully as he did was one of the major aspects that differentiated him from other religious figures of the time. Although the healing part of his ministry was dramatic and extraordinary, it was merely one aspect of the love he came to manifest. All of his healing was done out of love: without that love, he would not have been able to accomplish what he did. It is true that he had absorbed and mastered many teachings and techniques, in order to be able to do that which he did. Yet, without his infinite capacity to love the finite and limited human being, with all his many faults and shortcomings, the healing could not have been done in such immense amounts.

There are many stories I could tell about love, and the power of love as I saw it both through my own eyes, and reflected through the eyes of others who had experiences relating to Jesus. It is very difficult to pick out any one above the others, for in each there is a lesson and a perfect manifestation of the divine, and of divine love. Given this introduction, I will relate one of my personal favorite stories, one that for some reason I often remember at night, when my mind is wandering and not focused on any particular thing. The story is brief, yet has never failed to move me as I recreate it in my mind.

This story came from an early time in the ministry, before throngs of people were often around, and when individuals had more access to Jesus. In the village where we were staying, a group of children was around Jesus. They delighted in playing around him, and in being in his presence. He was very kind, compassionate and gentle to them. It was easy for them to feel they were welcome in his presence, and they accepted his invitation quite naturally.

A young girl of 7 or 8, who had long dark hair and the prettiest dark brown eyes, came up to him and asked him simply, with the directness, simplicity and innocence that only a child can command: "Why is it that it feels so good to be close to you?"

He smiled. I witnessed his energy field enfold her in its loving embrace. He answered her that God wants her to know she is loved, and God rejoices when his children are happy. He sat her down on his lap, and she and he talked happily for a few moments while the others gathered around and listened. She wanted to know more about God. They talked briefly about God's loving nature. He told her that adults cherish children because in their loving natures they show God's love. She was so delighted both by her experience of his love, and by his words. I have often wondered what kind of impression and mark this simple encounter made on her life.

Behind and through all that he was, and all that he taught, was the motivating power of love. It was out of love that he came to this planet to teach, and it was love that generated all of the healing and teaching he did. However, to talk generally of love, and to feel love in the way he caused us to feel it, is quite a different thing. I can honestly say that his love so filled me from the times we had together, that throughout my life I have had within me the resources to give of my love to many. Had I never met him, I would not have been without my own loving resources, though in far lesser measure. Though my own family was a very loving family, the love he shared with me and with the world was much greater than the love we know in living in the world day-to-day. I saw on countless occasions how he literally radiated out love from his heart and from his very essence, and how that love warmed, lightened and healed everything it touched. I saw within his energy field how he generated this love.

It was always beautiful to watch as he drew down the divine light from above, through the crown of his head, and pulled it down into his heart. Then, from his heart, with the warmth of his humanness pulsing now through the divine light, the light issued forth brilliantly, toward the person or persons at whom it was now being directed. His hands became alive with the energy, and directed forth the most marvelous streams of loving and healing energy. I loved watching this at the energy level, for at this level one could discern the magic and the wonder of the marvelous energy transformations that were taking place. It was almost as if the very air that we breathe was transformed into a substance alive with God's love and power. The interplay of the colors and the energetic shapes was an exquisite unfolding in a divine pattern far beyond my comprehension, yet there for me to witness. I was fascinated and absorbed with this witnessing, and would have been content to watch this for hours at a time.

I have reviewed in my mind, both during the time of Jesus' ministry, and in the many years that have passed since then, whether I felt or thought there was a time when Jesus did not having a lovingness to his spirit, or if he treated someone unfairly. I have to honestly say no to both of these questions. There were times when I saw him angry, but this was not in a spirit of hate, but rather in upset at behavior that was exceedingly cruel, greedy or malicious. He never condemned the person, but only the behavior. He taught us to pray for the person at those moments, that they might be enlightened and surrounded by God's loving energy, and moved to the place of the higher good.

Much was asked of him during these years of his ministry, far more than an outsider could ever imagine. The sheer number of healings he performed was staggering. People also asked much of him out of their selfishness and greediness. He always saw through people and what motivated them, and did not pretend he did not see. I think people were sometimes frightened by how "seen" they were around him. He did what he felt moved to do, and would say no if he saw that people were attempting to use him to glorify themselves, and if there were no way to turn this situation around into a victory for God.

The religiosity and the piety of the day had little to do with love, and even less to do with warmth and compassion in relations between human beings. It was almost as if one's relationship with God and one's relationship with one's fellow human beings were in entirely separate realms. Before Jesus, God was seen as completely separate from man. He was seen in the religions of the day as remote and outside of man, inaccessible to all but the high priests. One's relationship with God was then, almost by definition, formal and distant, separated from the pulsing of the blood and emotions through one's body. There were many rules regulating one's conduct with fellow human beings, but, like God's strictures, these were determined by an outside source of authority. People were not taught to trust their inner divining, but rather to ask those in authority what they should do. Certain religious sects, notably the Essenes, taught very differently, and in almost a mystical way developed their inner senses and wisdom in a manner they felt to be harmonious with the divine. However, this was the exception of the time. Most believed that God and men were completely separate, and there was strictness and formality in God's dealings with man.

Then Jesus came, and turned all of this upside down. It was most difficult for the religious and political leaders of the time to accept or comprehend that in Jesus Christ, God was made incarnate in man. Here was a man of human flesh, in whom God resided, and who taught, in radical departure from the traditions of the time, that God was not separate from man, *and* that God was to be found within. Further, he taught that God's Kingdom would be found not by seeking out the priests, but by praying and sincerely turning within to find the answers. This core belief threatened the intricate and highly regimented religious structures of the time, which were competing for the "right" interpretation of God's laws and intent. The very authority on which these religious leaders based their claims was undermined by this new way of relating with God.

In this new model, any man or any woman could pray, seek and find answers on his or her own by searching within. Now that God was made flesh, many other questions came up that the leaders of the time were not equipped to deal with. For, if God were now immanent within man, then God had to now relate to man, and had to do so in a human way. No longer was God distant and remote, accessible only by the high elders. He was walking on earth and demonstrating the way that he related with man, and to man, was by loving man. This loving relatedness of God to man was obscured when the leaders grew anxious and threatened at the vision of their authority being stripped away. Those who claimed they were closest to God, and knew God's voice the best, could not hear the voice of God in the words and the works of Jesus. The irony in this was tragic.

I have had many years to spend thinking about God, and the many aspects of the message Jesus Christ brought to earth with him. The aspect I have been discussing, which has the strongest pull for me, is that Jesus altered forever the manner of our relationship with

God. He showed us that God's way of relating with us is through love, and not through excessive rules that regiment every aspect of our daily lives. Jesus showed us, in real and tangible ways, how God sought relationship with his children, how he loved all his offspring, and how he sought to demonstrate that love to them. It was as an expression of love that God sent his son to us, to demonstrate to us how love might be expressed, that it should be expressed, and that it was through the heart that God showed himself in relationships between people. Never has there walked someone on earth who was able to love in the ways Jesus was able to love. He was able to love his enemies, as he was able to love his friends. He was able to love those who could not find their way either to love themselves or to love anyone else. He was remarkably patient with the many shortcomings all of us exhibited.

Jesus spent many silent hours in prayer by himself. His loving nature was not without its struggles. Yet, always he prayed and surrendered his will to the divine, and was perfect in his ability to do so.

Sometimes, I fear, I became so absorbed and fascinated in observing the processes he went through, that I spent less time on my own work than I should have. I told myself at the time it was important to take in as much as I could, for who could know how much longer I would have to avail myself of this rarest of opportunities? I wanted to know everything about how he thought, felt and prayed, and how he handled the difficulties he felt within himself. It was tempting to think he held all the answers to the questions I would ever ask. I know he did not want me to be dependent on him in this manner, and I tried not to be. However, in my adoration of him I tended to lose myself in him and in his world, as I perceived he saw it. I was dazzled by him, and so loved him, that I wanted to breathe the air that he breathed, and walk on the paths he walked. When I observed in his energy field that he was working in a particular manner, such as sending out love to someone who was broken-hearted with grief, I would try to capture mentally the processes I observed. Then, I would try to imitate them so I would learn how to do what I saw him doing.

The nature of the love he expressed was the fullest possible expression of human love; it was divine love. He was not afraid to love, as the rest of us so often are. He did not love with expectations of anything to be given in return. He gave love simply because he was love, and to do anything else would be to go against his very nature. He did not hold back. Through prayer and meditation, he kept his energy field clear so that there were no obstacles that would block either the inflow or the outflow of love. His energy centers were perfectly clear. The energies flowed through him from above in the purest manner possible. The harmony in all of this is impossible to describe, yet is something I saw and felt on many occasions.

In my best moments, I do not think I could begin to approximate the love he gave. Yet, the recognition then, and the memory now, of that which he gave to others, inspires me to move constantly upwards in my consciousness, to aspire to the kind and quality of love which I saw him freely giving. He unblocked a part of me that had been blocked for many centuries. During his lifetime, I grew daring and generous with that love which I felt flowing through me. After he died, though I carried on with the ministry and the teachings he had given me, a very vital and passionate part of me had died. To this day, I do not think I have truly ever been able to heal that part of myself. I have given of myself unselfishly, yet there is a part of me that has not been able to give, perhaps most especially not to myself.

The memory of the love he gave, and the love he taught me to feel and to share, has stayed with me. I have tried in the ways I have known, to share it with the others who have crossed my path in these many years hence. I have done the best I have known how, but I am a vastly lesser light. There is no way to compare that which Jesus brought with him to this world, and that which I am trying in this manuscript and in my life, to pass on. He brought life, light and love with him in a vibrant and vital way that I hope will not be lost with the passage of generations. Perhaps the vibration he came in on will continue to radiate, but the aliveness of his presence, and the exquisite warmth of the gifts he brought cannot be conveyed except through direct personal experience. He assured me that there would be ample occasion for this personal experience because of the manner in which he would be working as time went on, and as people opened more to seeking this kind of direct experience with him.

As I write, my thoughts go in and out of the present, into the past, into the future, and back again. As I reread these words I put on to paper, I fear they may be confusing, but they represent the flow of my thoughts. My natural tendency has always been to reflect in this manner, something that was reinforced during the time I spent with Jesus. During that time, I often examined the past and the future, in addition to the present, in order to figure out what I needed to learn in order to maximize the role that I individually, and as part of a group, would be playing. If I tried, in this writing, to place the information into distinct time categories, I would get lost in this attempt, and I fear I would lose the flow of that which I am trying to communicate.

CHAPTER 35

THE HARDEST PART ABOUT BEING IN THE MINISTRY during this time was, for me, the lack of privacy that had become a regular feature. Of course, it is true that the point of the work was to bring God, and this new manner of relating with God, into the public eye. However, I was not accustomed to, nor did I ever grow to fully enjoy, the attention one gets when there are always numbers of people around. The size of our group depended on where we were staying. I was relieved when we were invited to stay at people's houses, for then there was some privacy. I was, and remain, a very private person, and had to make a number of adjustments in my personal space preferences in order to work in with the changing needs of our ministry.

There were often a number of women around, many of them attractive on both an inner and outer level. People told me that women often showed interest in me, but much of this occurred without my noticing. My focus was on Jesus, and on the studying and work to be done. There was not much of me left over to think about women. My feeling was there could not possibly be any greater love than the love I felt for this man. The love I felt for and from him was immense, and so satisfying that all my emotional, mental, physical and spiritual resources were directly centered on him. I was challenged to my capacities, and often beyond, by what I had taken on. I derived great pleasure from my tasks and my role.

I was happiest when closest to Jesus, or when involved in learning. By now, I was more comfortable taking steps on my own, and was more secure in my ability to meditate and tune in to the Godhead within. I felt more competent in working with the energy field, and was less afraid when I encountered the kinds of darkness that one can encounter when working with energy.

Mary Magdalena was one of Jesus' more ardent converts by this time, and was one of the women who was frequently around. Although her past troubled and frightened me, I could see that in her heart she had completely changed, and was not of the same nature as before. Her fervor and her devotion touched us all. From an energy field point of view, I could see many blocks and areas of trauma from her past. These began to clear as she continued to practice on her new spiritual path.

The transformations in her over time were fascinating to observe. Not only was there the initial healing and change of heart, but there was the ongoing, more systematic series of changes as she heeded her soul's new calling. I saw, in watching her, how a human being can really transform, and how long and arduous a path it can be to effect the changes after the initial decision has been made to move in a different direction. For all of the energy that she had previously invested into the artifices of physical love, she poured all of that plus much more into a newfound purity of love. She soaked up Jesus' every word. Because she felt she had so much farther to go than the others, she probably took in much more. We talked on many occasions. No one in Jesus' coterie outside of the group of disciples was more eager than she to give of themselves so completely in service.

What I could see, in thus observing Mary Magdelena, was that being touched by God in such a profound way provides the catalyst for change. However, great effort is required, on an ongoing basis, to surrender continually to the changes that are exacted of a student on the path. I related this to my own development. As I watched her, I looked at my own life since Jesus entered and bade me come with him. Constant hard work had been required of me to make the changes I had needed. The process was the giving over one's energy body, surrendering it to the will of God, and then providing the energy and the willingness to change so the restructuring can be done. I had learned that the work was constant and ongoing, with no fixed product to be achieved.

I saw Jesus apply constant effort into surrendering his own reactions to the will of God. He was such a perfect model in this regard, that sometimes I found relief in studying someone who had more of the same level of struggle I did. I found this in my brethren, and I found this in Mary. I took heart that it was not just me who had to work so hard to move forward in my development. Jesus made it look easy. He could, and, at times, did, amplify my energy so a given process would be easier for me to achieve. At other times, just having his energy focused on mine made it considerably easier for me to focus and work through the problem I was attempting to solve. In any case, when I was apart from Jesus, and when we were not connected on an energy level, I found myself having a more difficult time concentrating and working through whatever it was I happened to be attempting.

In addition to our morning prayer and meditation, we practiced an energy field clearing before we went out for the day, so we would be most receptive to the divine inflow, and also so we would be as clear as possible in what we transmitted. It was very energizing and powerful to do this work together, for the energy level when we worked together with Jesus in our midst was extremely high. There were other mornings when, paired off with someone, usually James, I felt enormously frustrated by the blockages and areas in my energy field that needed intensive concentration and work.

James and I worked together well on this kind of endeavor, for though we were very different personalities with very distinct styles of encountering the world, we had a similar history and vibratory rate, and understood each other very well. When we were doing the auric work on each other, it often happened that we ended up dealing with similar energy patterns. It was of great benefit to both of us to have this opportunity to learn more about the kinds of blockages and energy patterns we tended to create.

James was more open in general to people than I, something that reflected in his energy patterns. I had more defensive blockages, and tended to withdraw when threatened. He tended to become more expansive when threatened, and sought to link with other like-minded people. I know I was extraordinarily fortunate, not only because of my relationship with and proximity to Jesus, but also in that I had my brother with me on this mission. I could not have been more blessed in having loving people around me. Yet still I carried with me a pattern of fearing hurt from others. This was deeply rooted in me, to the point where my natural tendency was to shrink from contacts with strangers. With the increasing crowds we were dealing with on a regular basis, my natural instincts would have led me to withdraw off onto the side, and become as invisible as possible. This, however, was not to be my role: it used up every bit of my energy on these occasions to push myself to be in a more interactive and visible role.

I watched how Jesus dealt with the crowds who inevitably sought him out. I observed as he pulled himself together afterwards. He often restored himself by bathing, when possible, and by spending time in solitude, resting, praying and even sleeping. I cannot even begin to imagine how much energy the crowds drew off him, and I marveled that he was able to sustain the pace that he did. Of course, his source of energy was infinite, but he was clothed in a finite human body that had its limitations. At times, he ate great amounts of food; at other times, it seemed he barely needed food in order to sustain him. I compared myself with him endlessly, but this was like comparing the finite with the infinite. The gap between us seemed so large that the comparisons were a futile exercise. I would ask him how he could spend so much time giving to others, and in the enormous amounts he gave. His answer was a standard: "It is not me who gives, but the Father who gives through me. All I have to do is to be present, and this is the reason why I came."

He was amused by me, and teased me about my love of pulling back. He said I was running from the very thing for which I had come, and I made it hard on myself by my flight. I longed for the earlier days when I had so much more of him to myself, and had been so indulged by his attentions. I was like a lover impatiently waiting to be rejoined with his beloved, who could not be nearly as available as in the early days of the love affair. So, perhaps, in addition to my natural aversion to large crowds, and my private nature, there was the additional factor that a part of me resented the crowds, for they took away from my time with the man I loved the most. I did not allow myself to linger on these feelings, for I knew and accepted it was God's will that he share with as many as possible, yet the human side of me would have loved to have had more time with him whom I loved best.

James was a good model for me as I struggled with these issues. He was so good at being with people, even seeming to derive energy from this. He headed towards them, almost fearlessly, and seemed to know he could find his way through most situations. I found crowds to be draining. Until I got to know someone, I found it took a great deal of energy in order to relate with the person involved. I enjoyed those situations where I could spend private time with one person, and found I did best in these encounters. I also needed private time to myself, and tried to find at least a little of this on most days. James had the natural buoyancy of spirit that could withstand the idiosyncrasies of individual and group personalities. He could manage this with good cheer and optimism. I often tried to take on these traits. As time went on, I became more accomplished in these endeavors. James was a good teacher and a good friend to me in this regard, for he saw and supported me as I struggled with my own nature to become more than the self that I was.

As we paired off and did the energy work together, I learned a great deal from his energy patterns. It was somewhat reassuring to me to find that although he was able to that which was so painful and so difficult for me, he had a number of energy blockages of his own, which appeared to deal with similar issues, but which manifested in dissimilar ways. He said he was able to learn from me too. He regarded my ability to attune into another person's energy as a strength, and he thought I was a much better healer than he because of this. I do not know about this, but I do know we reinforced the best parts of one another. Our caring and respect for each other carried us through many difficult times. I could not have had a better brother and companion, and have been very grateful for this throughout the years. Our individual strengths were so different, and our bond was

177

so strong, that we were able to draw from each other's strengths, and to help to minimize each other's weaknesses.

CHAPTER 36

THE PUBLIC LIFE CONTINUED, IN MUCH THE SAME MANNER. Since this manuscript is of a personal nature, I am not repeating here many of the number of public incidents documented elsewhere. Much of what Jesus did will not be passed down, because it would take so many volumes, and the essence of what he wanted to be carried on, has been and will be transmitted. Any chronology that I might draw of my personal experience with Jesus is fuzzy at best, for it is difficult to draw a timeline of one's own learning and interior experiences.

Key in the teachings was that God was to be found inside of each person, and that Jesus provided the way and the pattern to allow the divinity to unfold from within. He said this in many different ways, and on many different occasions. Every person who was around him had a uniquely individual way of experiencing these truths, and each way was as valid as the other. As I have mentioned, my preferred manner of learning was experiential. I could learn far more from observing in his energy field how he worked with a given problem, and then attempting to replicate the same process myself, than I ever could have learned by listening to his words alone. Another individual might be so inspired by his words that a life-changing result would be promoted. Those who were healed were converted by the physical experience of the dramatic changes the spirit of God worked on their physical, emotional and spiritual bodies. As the miraculous became customary for us, I was often surprised by how little it took for some people to experience a conversion. Jesus called these people "those of great faith." Someone like me, who endlessly thought about everything and questioned so much, needed greater proof.

Jesus said an essential part to understanding God was to know that God was a living God, the spirit in all things that moved all things, and without which there would be no existence at all. To access this God, one only needed to turn within and seek the Kingdom of God. This God was an eternal God, a continual source, like a spring of clear water that would never run dry. A person might travel far from the source, but the spring would always be there upon his return. Nothing could ever take the spring away. No matter what errors an individual might have committed, if he or she should have a change of heart, and turn back towards the source, the clear cool water of the spring would always be available.

I was living in a time, and with a man, in the presence of whom the impossible became routinely possible, and the unimaginable was imagined and made real. Demons were thrown out, congenital blindness and deafness were cured, leprosy was healed, and the vilest of sinners were turned to God. Water was turned into wine, loaves were multiplied, and the dead were raised into the world of the living. All of this, and much more, was done in the name of God, and for the sake of love. There seemed to be nothing Jesus could not do. Yet, he said that those who followed in his footsteps would do all these things and more. This was inconceivable to me, but I had learned to suspend my judgment on such things.

Having seen all of this, I think that the most miraculous of his works was the healing of the human heart and spirit. This type of healing was not readily seen with the human eye. However, the changes that occurred in people who had been touched by him were so radical and dramatic that it was hard to believe these were the same people. In all truth, perhaps they were not, for an individual once touched and moved by the light and the love of God can never again be the same. Clearly I, in my own life, have been changed so dramatically that I cannot even begin to conceive what my life might have been like had I never known Jesus. Yet, since I know I came into my life specifically for this purpose, such a conjecture is a futile exercise.

Some of the most moving healings I witnessed include those in which Jesus touched the hardened heart, which then transformed into a warm and loving heart. Mary Magdelena is a good example of this. After her conversion, there was no one more loving and generous of heart and spirit than she. I have learned that a reformed sinner can be a far more loving and spiritual person than a person who has never experienced a departure from the path. Perhaps it is the recognition of how far astray one has gone that motivates a person to hold much more strongly to the path of righteousness, once found. I do not know about this, but I do know that some of Jesus' most loyal followers were those whose lives and whose behaviors had been directly affected by him. The human heart and mind are such delicate and intricate interweavings of factors, both light and dark, that he who does not seek to understand this is often deluded by a very skewed view of what he is and how he appears to others. Jesus had a gift for offering a mirror to all of us, so we saw ourselves more as we were, rather than as how we would have liked to have seen ourselves. At the same time he offered the mirror, he offered a healing touch, so that if we chose, we could move quickly out of our despair and into a position where we could begin to assume control over our lives. He frequently said, as he did with Mary Magdelena; "Go, and sin no more."

Mary told me that, at the moment when Jesus forgave her, she felt as if she had been cleansed down to her very soul. For the first time in her life, she felt as if she had been "completely seen," for the radiant soul she was, something she did not even know or believe about herself. The act of being seen in this way allowed her to see herself, and it was this "seeing" that was extraordinarily healing. This experience was so dramatically touching and life-affirming for her, that she could never forget it. It was the memory of that experience, she said, which helped her to get through her darkest moments, and to keep going through all of the many very difficult changes which she had to make. She said it was like being born at a completely different level of existence, one far more real and profound than anything else she had ever known. She further said it was as if she had been waiting her whole life for that moment. In that moment, her true essence and her true being were captured and presented to her in the most direct and restorative manner possible.

There were times when I saw the cruelest and the most evil of men, as we all do if we are out and about in the world, and keep our eyes open. I asked Jesus what made them so vile, and was there not anything he could do to at least prevent them from continuing to hurt others in the ways they did. To the first question, he told me there were many different reasons, and often this is the kind of actions and behavior they were taught as they were brought up in the world. But, and he was very clear on this point, no matter what we have experienced, no matter how horrible or how cruel, we have a choice as to how we act. No one else but us is ultimately responsible for our choices. For this, God holds us accountable. No matter what we do, or what we choose, we will have to meet ourselves, whether in this lifetime or in another. Jesus stressed that God is merciful, and God has compassion. However, it is not until we reach out and seek forgiveness, that the karmically generated reactions to our actions can be mediated and tempered. It is a universal law, he said, that we will and must meet ourselves through the mirrors the world around us provides to us. The more we recognize this, the more we will progress through our lifetimes.

The hardened of heart may need many lifetimes to move forward, and may even move further backward before they begin to learn the lessons they need to learn. That is why, he said, we must pray especially for these people, for they need our intercessory prayers to surround and help them seek the power of God. As for what he could do to help prevent them from hurting others, he said, when there were no direct actions we could take to prevent harm to another human being, we had to respect the free will of all individuals, no matter what we thought about what they were doing. He said he prayed for them, and held them in the divine light. However, unless they sought out help, he would not interfere, much as he would perform a healing only when there was a direct request for such assistance.

"For example," he said, "when I called you to follow me, though I knew it was your destiny to come with me, if you had resisted and said no, you would not come with me, I would not have in any way forced you against your will. You had to come because you wanted to follow me. I might have prayed that God's will be done, but I would not have enjoined you in such a matter. Your free will had to lead, no matter what I knew, or thought in the matter."

"But," I said, "I had come into this life to be with you. I remember this even in my dreams."

"Yes, this is true, yet still the choice was yours. You had to make it again at the time we met, even though you had already made a choice before you came into this life. There is always choice, and with that choice is the most serious of responsibilities."

This was new information to me. I had assumed, since I had made the choice before I incarnated to follow Jesus, that once the decision was made, there was no more choice in the matter. I had just learned this was not so, and that at every moment, I have the option to reaffirm my choice or to choose differently. I cannot see how I could have chosen differently, for it had felt to me at that first encounter that I had no choice. However, I was beginning to see that even following this feeling rather than resisting it, was a choice. What had seemed so simple was more complex than I thought.

For a long while, I reflected on this matter of free will and choice, in looking back at my own life, and at those of others. I marveled at the complexity of the mind and of the spirit. I realized I had taken a great deal for granted about the decisions and processes that had determined my own life. I recognized that no matter how much I had in recent years tried to open myself to being led by God, it was ultimately I who made the decision as to whether or not to go with where I felt I was being led.

This may seem rather simple, but it was a profound revelation to me. I had underestimated the number of choice points, and had made basic assumptions about my own mental and spiritual nature that simply were not true. This gave me a new and heightened appreciation for Jesus, because although he had a destiny to fulfill, it was up to him at each moment to choose whether or not to walk in those steps that would take him where he should go. I had often watched him as he struggled with various choices, but I do not think I had fully appreciated both the importance of, and the freedom inherent in, each choice. There were times when I felt swept along in a current that did not feel of my choosing. Whereas I do not deny there are powerful currents that can move us along in our lives, I was coming to a fuller appreciation of the power of my choice in attracting these currents, and in continuing to move along with them.

I have already discussed my difficulties in being with the groups of people who were by now frequently around, and how I had been wrestling with my own nature to acclimate to this. Now, with this teaching, I had another tool to use in my attempts to become more accustomed to a public life. I had been habituated to looking at my nature as simply a matter of "this is who I am." I began to recognize that with this definition, I limited myself to continue looking at myself in the same way as previously.

I took the new information on the power of choice at each step of the process, and began to see that at each choice moment, I had the power to reaffirm my sameness, or respond in a different manner. I could say to myself: "this is who I have been, yet I can be this also." Although this may seem like a small matter in comparison to others I have considered in this manuscript, it felt very big and very freeing. It gave me a tool with which I could make manageable changes, in small increments. I did not have to give up that self which I saw as constant and steady, but I could add on to it or alter it as I deemed fit. I did not have to be "this" or "that", but I could be "this" and try on a little bit of "that" too.

Of all the arenas in which I worked with this concept, it seemed to be most helpful in my dealings with people. Where I previously said to myself "I do not like crowds", I could alter my experience by saying "I have not liked crowds in the past, but in this case I might be able to enjoy speaking with these people." This way did not require a commitment to change what I perceived to be my basic nature, but did allow me the opportunity to discover a part of myself I did not know, and to explore this. Trying this, in combination with the energy work, and the continual inspiration provided by seeing Jesus work with people so regularly and so well, helped me to open my heart and my energy field to people. Much to my surprise, sometimes it even made my heart glad and filled me with renewed energy! I took this very slowly. It was at times a very painful process for me to let go of what was comfortable, and move towards what felt inherently threatening. To this day I would say I am much more content to be a private rather than a public person, yet I have found much fulfillment in sharing what I have learned with others, and in passing on the gifts of the Spirit that were so generously given to me. This is something that took years to develop, yet the seeds for it were sown in these early times.

Mary Magdelena was always an inspiration in this. If she had accepted that her former self was her basic nature, she would not have been able to make any of the many changes she made, both immediately and as the years went on. As I saw her change, she forced me to recognize the level of commitment required to move on the path we traveled. She helped me to appreciate the hours of often-painful hard work it took to stay aligned with the divine spirit. This was not an easy path, full only of healings, miracles and wonders, but was an extremely arduous journey into the depths and darkness of the soul.

At this stage, I was acquainted with some of the pitfalls within me. Though the most painful times were to come later, I already knew that being on the spiritual path was a long, complicated, and sometimes very painful process. This was far from the simple life I had envisioned for myself, fishing and with few concerns other than the daily life of the fisherman and the family man. Life was far more intricate and involved than I had ever imagined. The joy and the blessed delights were many, yet the price to pay was a dedication that exacted tremendous amounts of attention, energy and concentration, and a willingness to look much more honestly at myself than I would have otherwise been willing to do.

CHAPTER 37

IT HAS BEEN IMPORTANT FOR ME to include some of the difficulty of the work, for it would be tempting for me to look at this remarkable period and remember with longing only the glorious parts. Much pain and privation came later. By contrast, this was a much easier, more expansive, and pleasurable time. Yet, I force myself to recall the other side of these truths, which is that to be close with such a man was at times a very difficult task. For though he was enormously gentle and kind, through his eyes I could see the truth of myself. There was always much I saw that was not easy to see. He did not in any way intend to make it hard on those who loved him and who were close to him. In fact, his loving energetic embrace gave a buoyancy that helped suspend one in that vast difference of energy levels between his and the other's.

However, by his very nature, Jesus lived on such a high plane that it could be very difficult to attempt to remain attuned to a vibrational level so far beyond my own. I loved it, and tried to stay there for as long as I could, whenever I could. Despite his energy "assists", it could be very exhausting and painful to stay there for long. My adoration of him was such that I preferred to endure the exhaustion and the pain rather than miss out on the opportunity to be with him. Yet, I did notice the impulse to back off or to flee when I felt the challenge presented to me was too great. It seemed so easy for him to live in that state of constant grace and connection with God's will through surrender. For me, it was often hard work and struggle.

Did I ever rebel or truly run away from him or my commitment to following him? I think that I did in some ways, when I felt overwhelmed, or when I despaired of having enough energy or strength to continue on this arduous path. Though I never seriously considered leaving, there were times when I considered myself unworthy of receiving so much of his love. Sometimes I felt I might possibly not have the strength to carry out what was asked of me. Yet, deep in my heart, I knew he would never ask more of me than that of which I was capable. He also told me this. There were times when I did not pay attention as I should have, or when I did not give it my all. There were times when it felt too much, and I allowed the sweet heaviness of the unconsciousness of slumber to overtake me. I know he forgave me these things, yet it was harder to forgive them in myself.

He reminded me of the inherent resistance of the flesh of the human vehicle. He urged me to pray at those times when I felt weakened, and to ask God to enter in and strengthen me. This I did on many occasions, but this I did not always do. In living around such a man, there was not occasion to have the relative blissfulness of unawareness of what one was doing. It was as if there were always a presence that witnessed the truth of what was occurring, internally or externally; there was no escaping that witnessing. It was not a harsh or judgmental witnessing; nevertheless, it was a witnessing. For all of the healing potential this gave, there was also an inherent painfulness in this process. It was never easy.

A contradiction I cannot explain is that as difficult as this was, it was also easier to be around Jesus than to be around anyone else. There was no one who exuded more love, or who could make me feel more accepted for who I was. There was no one else whose energy was so positive, and who made me feel so light and energetic. The price this gift exacted was the price of significantly greater awareness. It is not for trivial reasons that we shroud ourselves with our delusions. We do so because the truth often feels too painful to bear.

When I looked at Jesus, and compared myself to him, I saw the vast distance between us of the one thing in life that mattered the most; soul development. The man Jesus, even before the Christhood descended upon him at his baptism, must have been far more developed than any of us could have ever hoped to aspire to in this lifetime, or in many lifetimes to come. Of course, he did not encourage such comparisons, and in fact, discouraged them. It was, however, one of my traits that I continually measured myself, using him as a standard. This doomed me from the start, for the temporal and the finite cannot be compared with the eternal and the infinite. Sometimes I think this was a self-punishment I inflicted upon myself for real or imagined sins. His message was one of forgiveness, forbearance and love. It was with difficulty that I would attempt to apply this message when I was operating in this mode. As I look back at that time, I see how I would sometimes trip over my own two feet in my attempts to learn faster, or to "catch up." Much of this eagerness was inherent in my relative youth, yet much was also owing to my passionate and sometimes impetuous nature.

I wanted to be all that he was, and, of course, I could not be. I studied him carefully, and was fiercely loyal to him. Never before or since have I felt, out of the depths of my soul, that which I felt for him. I would not have believed it possible to have such extraordinary stores of feeling as those he inspired in me. Sometimes just to be with him was sheer bliss, as if I were bathing in the radiance of his soul. And yet other times, as I have mentioned, it was much more difficult, for when with him I was face to face with all I would have liked to be, and was not. Of course, he did not do anything to make me feel inferior or insufficient; in fact, quite the contrary. With him, I felt much more closely in touch with the divinity that lay within me.

When I succumbed to my darker side, and stepped out of this state of grace, I focused on my limitations and shortcomings. If I were alone with him, he immediately knew when I made this shift. Sometimes he softly chided me for thinking I could make myself God by my own efforts. Of course, he was right.

I would then remember that the only way I had any hope of achieving the perfection he embodied was by taking the course opposite to the one I was attempting. The only way to move forward was to surrender to the spirit working through me. I had to give up all efforts except the one to release my own will, and surrender to God's will. When I did this, all seemed to be simple again, and I was released from my private despair. When I could remember this, I always felt much better.

There were many times when I could not remember this step. Perhaps this habit of comparing was my biggest indulgence in something that did not serve me well. It served as a positive when I looked at him as a model towards which I could aspire. This served to inspire and motivate me to continue on the path. But then, as I observed myself relative to his vibrational level, I saw so much I did not like, and the cycle might begin again.

It took me a long time to come to terms with this tendency, and to find a way to work with it. There were times when I felt jealousy and envy. I realized these feelings were provoked by the sense of my own tremendous inferiority. I did not begrudge Jesus anything he was or would be. It was simply that I did not always know how to handle all that he was. I would ache with pain sometimes as I watched him work; how I longed to be able to do and know a thousandth of what he did and knew! I was infinitely grateful to be so blessed as to be in his presence, but there could be a bittersweet quality to this. With James, or with Mary Magdalena, or the others, there was a partnership of equals working together and individually for a common goal. With Jesus, there was, of course, the working together for a common goal, but there was no equality. There was no way in which he did not outshine me. This was always extremely humbling, especially for a man such as myself who was accustomed to having many skills and attributes which others admired.

I felt his love always, and his deep caring. I have ultimately come to recognize that, in many ways, the sense of inferiority was also impersonal. It was nothing less than the inferiority that man will always feel before God. While the content of my feelings and reactions manifested as extremely personal thoughts and comparisons, I have come to the broader perspective and conclusion that it must have been a more universal and pervasive reaction, one that must surely have been evoked in all who were close to him.

Those who were not on a true spiritual path, and who came into close contact with him, could not but help be profoundly affected by these encounters. I have often wished I could be in the minds and hearts of those who opposed him, to understand what they thought they were opposing. My hypothesis, based on what I have learned about how energy works, both in myself and in others, is that the sense of inferiority grew too strong to bear. Rather than look within to find what was so uncomfortable, these people looked outside and did what they could in their minds and hearts to diminish him, so that they might feel greater.

I have thought about this often, in trying to understand the growing opposition to Jesus as he taught, healed and ministered. If in our hearts we do not accept God, we will always be severely threatened by those who are superior to us in whatever small or large ways. We must continually surrender ourselves to the divine intelligence, so vastly greater than ourselves, in order to accept that our unique gifts are divinely bestowed, and to understand our limitations. If we do not surrender to God's will, we will come to hate and envy those who seem to have more than we do. Jesus' gifts were from God, and were infinitely greater than those others had. How greatly he was hated and feared by those who felt threatened, and did not seek to understand him. As the years have gone by, I have come to feel compassion and forgiveness for these people, who, in their blind hatred, missed the greatest gift God ever gave to earth's people.

There were times when I wished he were not so perfect, or so good. I know now that I felt these things when I was not feeling comfortable with myself. I hoped he would not know that I sometimes had these feelings, but whenever I had this thought, I saw and felt his smile inside me, looking at me with acceptance and understanding of what I was feeling. There was never any place I could hide. Repeatedly, he helped me to realize there was no need to hide. He could love me for all that I was, and for all that I thought and felt. At that time, I thought no one else was feeling these things, and that something was uniquely lacking in me. As I matured and grew, my thoughts matured also, and I grew to recognize the universality of the reaction.

I wanted to offer him the perfect love that he offered me. Even in this I was frustrated, for my human love was far from perfect. I gave what I could, all my heart and soul knew how to offer. When I came to these dark spots, I would try to remember to turn them over to the light so they could be suffused with divine energy, to be diminished as they met with the light of day.

I think that this is what would happen when he would read my dark or jealous thoughts; he sent the light of his understanding and love to me, and they dissipated in the bath of his love. We would laugh about this side of me. When together we encountered it, we often dispersed it with a gentle laughter that contained within it his love and acceptance. With that love and acceptance, my own grew. He made me laugh at my overseriousness, and my attempts to be perfect not through prayer and infusion of the Divine, but through my own efforts. I could then accept the darkness within myself, for it was in this way forgiven. With this, I did not need to feel I had to hide it back in some remote corner of my soul. In thus allowing the darkness without judgment, and with love and acceptance, I became more whole.

There were times when I needed to pull away for a time, whether for a few hours, or even once or twice, for a few days. I did this in order to absorb and assimilate what I had learned, and to heal my feelings so I would be again at peace, no longer caught up in my feelings of deficiency. At times, when Jesus had to go off somewhere for a few days, I was relieved, not because I did not want to be with him, but because of the reflecting I needed to do. The breaks were restorative. I would eagerly anticipate the time when we were back together. He always allowed me the space I needed, and probably anticipated it before I did.

On one level, I hated that I needed the time. Nonetheless, I grew to accept and allow it, even though I felt I might miss something important. I wanted to be able to always be there with him, attentive and supportive, but this was not possible. I grew to recognize the natural rhythms of my own limitations. When I pushed against them, I became unbalanced. The time away always proved positive, and I came back to him with renewed and balanced energy. Meditation and prayer helped me in this regard, as did periods of solitude. The energy work that James and Mary did on me also helped. I knew Jesus was sending me prayerful energy as well to support me, but he was careful not to be fully present within me during those times, as he was at other times. The human in me could only tolerate so much of the divine. It was necessary to continually tune the instrument so that it could play the best tones possible.

CHAPTER 38

THE LIFE I LED WAS ONE OF CONTINUAL LESSONS and encounters with people from all walks of life. There were days when I felt so expanded that I could not stretch any further. Then, on the next day something else would happen, and I would be forced to move beyond the boundaries I thought defined my limitations.

For example, there was one particular day of healing in which the others and I participated energetically, in a support fashion, in a multitude of healings that Jesus performed on the sick and crippled. The day was exhausting, even though we had been taught to use the universal energy from the divine flowing through us as our source, rather than to tap into our own individual energies. I saw so many miracles on that day in Bethsaida, and was spent from the waves of emotion that swept over me as I felt the relief, joy and great gratitude of those who had been healed.

It seemed that a massive transformation was taking place in the world; a world which would never be the same again now that God had walked on the earth and allowed his presence to be felt, and his healing miracles to be wrought. I marveled at the holy miracle of what I had seen and felt, as person after person was relieved of the most disabling and cruel of infirmities.

In my energy body, I lay down on the earth and wept, overcome with the beauty and the power of what I had witnessed. Never before or since, I mused, would such greatness, tenderness and poignancy be witnessed on the earth. I felt sorrow that all the peoples of the earth could not witness the great joy and great blessings that had been bestowed on the needy and the previously unfortunate today. On this day, I vowed I would chronicle these events, so that a record might be kept and handed down through the generations of the wonders that one man, perfectly surrendered to God, might bring to the world. It was my hope that the generations to come might know what he brought and gave to all of us who were fortunate enough to live in this blessed time.

I saw so much on that day. It seemed my mind had expanded in every direction as far as the human mind could possibly go. I was exhausted, and looked forward to the soundest of sleeps, so all levels of me could rest from the stretching they had just experienced. The world had been so full of miracles on this day, and I imagined there should be a trumpet playing in the angelic realms that signaled to everyone, in all the far corners of the earth, what had happened.

When we gathered back at our campsite, activity was going on around us as if it had been a normal day. Fish were being cleaned, and food and drink were being served to those who had been out on the mission. The sheer normalcy of the activities was striking, in contrast to what I had just experienced. It helped to ground me, but my mind had trouble staying present in the excited conversation that ensued. In my mind, I was back among the crowd, witnessing and feeling the tremendous surges of energy that were flowing both to create the healings, and also as a result of them. My heart had never felt so moved, or so expanded, as I felt the tremendous joy and relief of so many souls now freed up within their physical bodies.

The collective experience of being moved into a new realm where spirit was everywhere present on this piece of earth where we gathered was palpable. We had witnessed and experienced a joy and an ecstasy of spirit that I was certain had never before been experienced on earth. I wondered how much more of this was to come. I envisioned a future where this kind of experience was more commonplace, and where people interacted harmoniously in accordance with the Spirit inside of them.

The energy and loudness of the conversation around me as we ate kept bringing me back to the people around me, who were sharing what they had seen with those who had not attended. I was acutely aware that Jesus had gone off alone. All of us knew to let him be, especially after a day like this, for we knew he was exhausted, and needed solitude and time to replenish his soul. He gave so much, more than had ever been given. I marveled that he was still walking. I felt my complete insignificance in comparison, and thanked God for allowing me to be a part of what had happened on this day.

We turned in early, and I lay close to Jesus. I basked in his energy field, and felt welcomed and embraced by his love. There was nowhere I felt more comfortable, or more at home, than embraced in his energy in this manner. It was like being in heaven on earth; my entire being luxuriated in the extraordinary energy flowing from this man. I would like to think that the human part of him enjoyed my presence and the love I sent to him, though I know this could never in any way match that which he was sending me. I quickly drifted off to sleep, completely spent from the events of the day.

When I awoke before dawn, it was with the most incredible dream I could ever imagine. In the dream, I was going through time, passing through as if a visitor into a new town or village. With each place and time I visited, I felt the energy of the people there, and I read the energy fields. At first, it was very saddening how much darkness and ugliness I saw and felt. It was thus many times. There was light, which I recognized as the Spirit that Christ brought in with him to the world. This light was isolated at first, and surrounded by the darkness of the lower urges of the human spirit. As time passed, the darkness became more dangerous and more ominous. However, at the same time, the light was growing brighter, and began to expand into more of the energy fields that were present. For a time, the light seemed to retreat into isolated areas of the world. I was puzzled greatly by this.

Yet, as I moved on in my dream, I saw the light spreading, and I heard the beginnings of a chorus of the most exquisite song I could ever imagine. It was as if the notes in the light of the energy fields of these isolated human beings began to resonate in the energy field of the universe. These notes then began to resonate with each other. Slowly, over many years, the notes and the light grew majestic in strength and in beauty, and carried with them great truth and great power.

I remember thinking within the dream that the effect of the notes and the light on the people of earth was much like what I had experienced on that day in Bethsaida. I felt the collective movement growing in intensity and in purpose. At the end of the dream, I was overcome with joy at the surety of the knowledge that one day all of the earth would be joined in the spirit of love, beauty and light that Jesus had been sent to bring.

I woke up in waves of ecstasy and in tears of joy. Surely there could be no better future for mankind than that which I had just experienced. I had no doubt that what I had just envisioned was the way of the plan. I was overcome with joy that the beauty and joy I had known on the previous day would one day be a part of the collective experience of mankind.

CHAPTER 39

PETER HAD A WONDERFUL, OUTREACHING, AGGRESSIVE STYLE. He saw no limitations whatsoever to the good work that could be done. His fervor was so great that he at times had an almost frenzied quality to him. I admired the way he had of striving to realize his dreams, even though at times I thought he pushed harder than was necessary or desirable. Still, he was "bitten" by the love of the work and the message, and no one could fault him for that. He was an excellent organizer. Jesus had chosen well in picking him to take a leadership position. Peter was also a terrific motivator, and people listened to him when he spoke. He spoke with an inner authority, the authority of trusting the voice of the divine as it spoke through him. People recognized this, and respected it. Where I dreamt of the future and worked quietly to help these dreams to be realized, Peter went after the future with the certainty and forceful energy of a man driven by a vision. When he moved, it was as if he left a strong energy in his wake that drew people in, and led them to follow him out of curiosity as to what would happen next.

I loved Peter very much, and grew to admire him more than ever during this period. Since he was significantly older, he was like an older, wiser, and worldlier brother. He was a fiery soul, and his fire sparked motivation and drive in me. I needed this sometimes, for I think, if on my own, I could live forever in the life of the mind and the body without moving outward into an ongoing world of interaction and action.

One day, after a difficult discussion with some brethren, Peter took me aside. In an uncharacteristic move, he asked me to accompany him on a visit he was planning on making to a village woman who had asked to speak with him. I was glad for the opportunity to be with him, and to wander off from our temporary home. We departed after our afternoon meal. The woman was the wife of a wealthy community leader, and was afraid to be seen in public with us, for fear of recriminations from a disapproving husband and others who were associated with him. She had many questions for us, for her curiosity had been greatly stirred by the stories she had heard of Jesus and his ministry. Peter was a distant relation of hers. She had contacted him through her cousin, and asked him to come by while he was in town.

Peter was patient with her as he answered her questions about the ministry and about Jesus, and about what had led him to follow Jesus. She had been skeptical about the stories she had heard. Her husband was overtly negative about Jesus. She had for a while deferred to his judgment and not pursued her interest in finding out more about this man whom people were talking about so much. Then, she heard that Peter was one of Jesus' inner circle, and her interest was piqued. She relayed to us how one night, after she had been thinking quite a bit about what she had heard about Jesus, she had a dream.

In this dream, she was wandering about in the marketplace. She felt lonely, she said, and everywhere she turned, there was darkness and desolation. She could not find anyone she knew. All of the familiar places, from the market, to the streets, and to the temple, seemed shrouded in a darkness that made her feel uneasy. Then, as she proceeded, she saw a light in the distance. It felt warm and safe to her, and she went towards this light. As she went on, the light grew brighter and brighter. Many people were also drawn to this light.

Within the radiance of this light, she grew to feel more radiant herself. She became aware that her heart, instead of feeling the emptiness she had known it to have been feeling for quite some time, felt open, and filled with love and caring. She was aware of a similar energy exuding from the others who drew near to the source of the light. It was as if they were all drawn together by the force of a love unlike anything she had ever known. As she arrived near enough to the light to see the source, she saw Jesus standing in the midst of many children, telling them a story about God, who sent him to them to teach them about how they should be with each other, and how they should pray every day to be united with God in their hearts.

She was moved to tears in this scene, and woke up with tears streaming down her face. It was at this point she decided to contact Peter, to learn what he knew. She knew she could no longer deny the yearnings of her mind and spirit to understand more about Jesus.

After Rachel told us her story, we spent several hours talking with her. We encouraged her to come and see for herself what Jesus was offering to the world. Peter was, as usual, impassioned. He told her that her dream was her call to come see for herself. He guessed that her world felt dark, dreary and lifeless, and that she yearned to be drawn out of herself, and into the world of the divine and the spiritual. He told her of his own calling to follow Jesus, and said that each is called in his own way. In his case, he said, he was asked to give up everything and to follow, but this was not true for everyone. He thought she was being led, in a gentle way, to explore that which was being offered to her. It was her choice whether to stay in the darkness, or to come and witness the divine light that Jesus was offering to her and to all of us to light our paths.

This presented a serious conflict for Rachel, whose loyalties were torn between her husband and what was stirring inside her. We spent some time talking about this, for in these days it was considered a wife's duty to obey her husband. We all agreed, however, where there was a choice between the calling of true spirit and the calling of men's laws or customs, it was important to follow spirit as long as this harmed no one. In this instance, it seemed that her following spirit would open her, and hence, her family, to a greater love than could now be imagined. This could benefit everyone in the end, even if in the short term some conflicts were created. Since Rachel's husband was so often occupied with community affairs, it would be relatively easy for her to slip off unobserved to hear Jesus talk. She could then make up her own mind, and no longer have to rely on the reports of those around her. At the very least, it could settle her mind on some of the questions that had been brought up. She might learn a great deal from the experience, and, an even more positive outcome could happen. Rachel concluded we were right, and said she would find the soonest available opportunity to hear and observe Jesus.

Before she would let us go, she had her servant bring to us the finest food and drink. Though it had not been long since we had eaten, we enjoyed the sumptuousness of what she offered. We partook lightly. While we did, she asked more questions about what we had seen and learned, and what we thought about Jesus. I loved her curiosity and her passion to discover the truth. We answered her questions as best as we could. As we left, Peter commented that he thought, with time, she could become an extremely valuable ally to our work. He was sure she would follow up with a visit to one of Jesus' public ministries in the near future.

We tarried on our way home. It was dusk. The sky was a luminescent pink, and the air was crisp and clear. We discussed the importance of the kind of individual work we had just done, and how it was fulfilling to us on an individual level. The mass healings and the ministering that took place in large groups were gratifying, and always moving. However, in the informal atmosphere we had just experienced, we had the opportunity to express ourselves individually as well. Peter had enjoyed this experience, especially since he was related to Rachel, and since it was through this connection that she found a way to inquire about Jesus. I have mentioned previously how I tried to emulate parts of Peter's outgoing style. On this occasion, I sensed he admired my ease in interacting with individuals, for, in this setting with Rachel, the conversation had flowed easily between her and me. He was a bit brusque and aggressive, and tended to dominate, whereas I was more adept at encouraging a back-and-forth exchange of words.

On our way home, Peter was animated, and full of energy and ideas about the times to come. He was bursting with concepts of communities based on Jesus' teachings, and of governments that would have Jesus at their head. It was hard not to become swept up in the enthusiasm of his visions for the future, and in the boldness of the plan that he saw. Peter was extremely charismatic when he was at his best, and on this evening, he was definitely at his best. He foresaw a time when each of the twelve would be responsible for going to distant towns and countries, and establishing communities of the Way in each of these places. He believed, as did the rest of us, that Jesus would rule on earth in our lifetimes, and we would be directly involved in establishing the groundwork for the communities which would inaugurate heaven on earth.

The others and I had general ideas of what the future had in store; Peter had the most imaginative way of concretizing the ideas, giving them a shape and a form, and grounding them into reality and daily life. He was convincing and persuasive in his ideas. I agreed that the forms of which he spoke were the forms the future would take. The others became similarly convinced, and we grew to have very comparable projections of the future. Jesus did not deal in these specifics, but that did not stop us from trying to fill in the missing pieces. Before long, I found that we had quite a picture painted of life in the future.

I enjoyed listening to Peter as he went on about the different aspects of the changing world order. I delighted in the obvious thought and attention he gave to detail as he described changes in the political, economic, social and religious spheres. The way his mind worked fascinated me. I found him to be a refreshing change of pace, even though that pace tended to be exhausting sometimes.

As we neared our campsite, the tone of the conversation turned more personal, and we slowed our steps even more. Peter wondered what I saw for my own personal future, apart from the work I would be carrying out. Did I want to marry and have children? Did I have other personal dreams? He had known my family for years, and had seen me growing up. He was, he said, an older man, who had lived some of his dreams, but I had been involved in this from such a young age, and was there anything in addition I wanted for myself?

It seemed almost a betrayal to consider what he said, for my mind had centered so exclusively on Jesus and the work, that I had barely considered myself apart from this world. True, I was a young man with a young man's desires, which sometimes grew very strong within me. Yet, for the most part, I considered these as something I must put away so that I could focus my full attention on the many wondrous things happening around me. However, I had to admit to myself, and to Peter, that I hoped I would have the time and the opportunity, within the framework of my mission, to some day have a family of my own. I could not foresee this happening any time soon. I wanted now to spend every possible moment with Jesus in the ministry, learning and absorbing as much as I could. I thought that a family would only take away from this.

Besides, I thought to myself, I cannot imagine ever being as close to a woman, no matter how wonderful and loving she might be, as I felt to Jesus. In that sense, I felt spiritually married to him, and I did not know if there would ever be room in my soul for another kind of marriage. I could not imagine preferring to sleep in the company of a woman to preferring to sleep next to Jesus. It was unfathomable that I would choose to give up the world of wonders I lived in, to be with a woman, no matter how beautiful in spirit and pure of heart she might be. Peter said that the joys of married life were plenty, and he missed the company of his wife and family, but he could certainly understand how a young man in my position would want to postpone marriage in order to experience these opportunities.

I asked Peter why he was asking these things of me. He said he was merely wondering, for he felt blessed to have had the opportunity to have a family. He knew my family, and the great emphasis they placed on family life. He guessed I might not have entirely given up hope of having a family of my own. I admitted to him that it felt very strange indeed to seriously consider these things at present, for it seemed the world I lived in had changed so very fast. So much was continuing to happen, that to think of something so rooted as a family did not seem consistent with any conceivable lifestyle I might have.

CHAPTER 40

AFTER WE ARRIVED BACK AT THE CAMPSITE, I found that Peter's questions had stirred up many questions inside me. I had to admit a strong part of me had always longed for a family of my own. Yet, once I had begun following Jesus, I had put that part of me aside, and barely allowed myself to consider the possibility that some day I might have my own family. If I were a woman, I would say I was completely in love with Jesus, but, as a man, I did not know quite how to label or classify my feelings. The extraordinarily strong feelings I had for Jesus did in many ways preclude the possibility of any other primary relationship, because of my desire to spend every moment possible with him, living with him, loving with him, and learning from him.

I found, as I thought more about what Peter had asked me, that I could not entertain at this stage the thought of a marital relationship that would take up much of my time and energy, and draw me away from Jesus. It seemed to me there was no choice at this point. I am sure Jesus would have wanted me to feel free to follow any inner directives I might have in regards to these choices, but for me, the choice was already made. I did spend some time this evening, however, and in the days that followed, considering the possibility that at some time in the future there might be the opportunity for me to wed and have children of my own. It gave me joy to contemplate that this opportunity might not be closed off to me forever. Yet, when I considered the circumstances under which I might feel free to make the time and energy needed for a wife and family, I could not imagine such a time.

In my fantasies of the world to come, I imagined a linking of communities in Christ all over the many countries. I could see myself living in such a community with a wife who believed in Jesus' work as I did. I wanted to live close to him always. Yet, in these moments of imagining, a dark disturbing cloud would flow through my mind when I thought of always living in close proximity to Jesus. The image felt full of foreboding. I had been well trained in paying attention to these images flowing through the mind, but this one so terrified me that I dared not follow it and allow it to open itself to me. Instead, as I thought about the possibility of married life within a Christian community, and saw and felt this darkness and this fear, I pushed it aside. I told myself that the love that I knew with Jesus felt too good to be true, and because it was so good, I was experiencing natural fears that it could not last. I convinced myself that these fears formed the basis of the feelings of foreboding. It seemed very logical and well reasoned, and to some extent, I suppose I convinced myself that I had no need to worry events would take a turn for the worse.

Politically, however, there were a number of rumblings, for Jesus was beginning to be perceived as a major threat to the priesthood, and to the authority of both the local and the centralized government. I did not take this particularly seriously, for, I reasoned that Jesus had it within his power to handle these threats. In my belief system, as I have mentioned, he would become ruler over all the earth. I envisioned this in a very political and concrete manner.

I enjoyed trying to think of the qualities I would want to find in a woman I would want to marry. Many women, beautiful both in body and in spirit, surrounded me on a daily basis. However, none of them moved me in my soul, except Mary, Jesus' mother. She seemed the epitome of everything I could ever hope to find in a woman. She was beautiful in every way. In her presence, one could feel the presence of God manifesting through her. She was one of the holy ones, and I had enormous respect for her. She was unlike any other. I loved her tremendously, and felt great warmth for her. I loved being around her. It was my special pleasure on those occasions when I accompanied Jesus to her home, to be able to hear her talk of his childhood, and to see the tremendous pride she had in him, and the awe and reverence which they held for each other.

There were no women in my own age group who moved me in my depths. Mary Magdelena was my good friend, and as I have mentioned, I grew to have tremendous respect for her. We nurtured each other as we developed on our paths. I did not consider her beyond a friend, though I did find her extremely beautiful, and even more so as she matured spiritually. Because of her past, many of the disciples were afraid of her, and kept a respectful distance. I did this at first, but she sought me out and took me into her confidence. As time went on, I outgrew my wariness as I learned and sensed the depth of the transformation she had undergone. If ever a person was reborn completely in this life, it was she. I watched as the dark residues of her former life burned off and were replaced by a spirituality and a devotion to God that was matched by very few. The transformation was startling and complete. If a comparison were made between her energy field during the time when the people wanted to stone her, and then after several years of following Jesus, one would not be able to identify that these energy fields belonged to the same person.

One thing was clear to me in the musings I had at this time about the future possibility of being married and having a family; I believed it extremely important for us to make our spirituality and our beliefs at the center of our lives. I believed that with God at the center, we would stay focused on whatever we would need to be focused on. With the inexhaustible supply of God's love, the love between the family members could not help but be endless and ever flowing. There would be the inevitable difficulties, but with love as a base and as a motivator for working them out, I believed no obstacle would be insurmountable. My own family had been a tremendous model in this regard. I thought it was not just a coincidence that two brothers, James and myself, had been picked to follow Jesus, having come from the strong, God-centered loving family that we had.

I wanted to know a full love that included physical love as one of its expressions. I imagined that great joy could be gained in this expression of the body and soul, when such was done in love and in tenderness. I had great abundance of physical drive, and had been working very hard to learn to channel these energies into the prayer and healing work we were doing.

Since Jesus was my model in so many ways, and because he had chosen not to mate, I wondered if this were an indicator that this was the "highest" and the best path to take. Did this enable him to stay more focused on God, and on the mission for which he had come? Would mating with a woman distract me from my work, and would it make me less clear, or less able to heal? Would it take away from my vital energies, or was it possible it might enhance them? I remembered Jesus told me once, completely without judgment, but with a warm and teasing tone in his voice, that I would most likely fare best if I married, because of the tremendous sexual urges I had, and because it took so much of my energy to control them. At the time, I completely agreed with him, though I knew it would be a long while before I would be ready to take on the responsibilities of a family.

As I thought about his statement, I wondered if it were a deficiency in me that I would need to be married in order to cope in the best manner possible with my sexuality. Did this mean I was flawed, and that if I were more fully developed, I would not need to marry?

Jesus' response to me when I had asked him that question was that my passion and my ardor were what made me the perfect choice for a disciple. He said there was no shame in wanting to have, or even in needing to have, a full expression of the human body in all of its dimensions. Again, he cautioned me against comparing myself with him, for I would always fall short in these mental contests, and not learn anything positive about myself in the process. He said I would best serve God by being the best John I could be, in the fullest possible expression of my own soul. It would be a betrayal of my deepest self to try to be as someone else. The divine shone uniquely through each soul. He spoke of Peter, and how uniquely wonderful a soul he was, and likewise how I was. However, if I were to try to be Peter, I would inevitably fail myself, by failing to be myself. When seen in this light, this made perfect sense to me.

As I came back again in my mind to the conversation with Peter that had started me on this particular sequence of thought, I returned to the original question he posed. I felt more accepting of myself as I was, including my high sexual desire, and accepted the likelihood I would be a much happier person in the long run if I were to marry and have a family. However, in the short term, I wanted to be with Jesus whenever I could. For now, I would continue to put my personal desires of the body aside. I would pray to God, and trust that whatever should happen to me would be best, and in alignment with His will for me.

I was tired of thinking about my life, and eagerly went to join some of the others in an animated discussion about some events that had transpired in a neighboring village. When I finally lay down my head to rest that night, I was at peace, and looking forward to what the morrow would bring.

CHAPTER 41

THE LUXURY OF INTROSPECTIVE TIME was quickly to be replaced by a very active, bustling journey into a number of villages and cities. I would soon be looking back at the recent relative lull in activity, and wondering how times could change so very quickly. There was little warning that we would be moving on, though we had become accustomed to that. There was no anticipating that this time we would be gone more than several months.

Jesus told us over supper one night that we would be traveling on the morrow. He did not know how long we would be gone, but he expected we would not be back for at least a month. We would be head first to Ephraim, and eventually would go to Jerusalem, where we would be meeting with some of those who had expressed an interest in setting up an area there from which to carry out the work. I was ready and eager for an adventure. Most of the others seemed to be feeling this way as well, judging by their reactions to the news. The camp was humming that night. We had to force ourselves to lie down to sleep, in order to be well rested for the next day's journey.

There had been many people around Jesus that evening. I had grown annoyed, for I knew he needed his rest, and, I had strongly hoped that we might have at least a brief time to talk before we slept. This was not to be; nonetheless, I lay down beside him and was warmed by his loving energetic embrace. There seemed to be little or no transition time until I entered the sleep state. Once in that state, I soon woke up into a scene in which Jesus and I were walking in the mountains, in one of our favorite spots. It was sunny, warm and beautiful.

I was always glad for the special intimacy and teachings that these nighttime adventures provided. I could fill volumes with the details of these journeys, of which I have tried to memorize the details. I cannot say that the waking adventures were necessarily any more important, dramatic or informative than the nighttime ones. It is simply that since the daytime ones are the ones that are shared collectively by the world, they meet a more general consensus as to what constitutes reality. This will be generally true in my recording as well, though I hold in my mind many events from the night that are as memorable and impactful as the daytime events.

I could always tell when Jesus had something on his mind that he wanted to talk about, for there was a sense about his energy field that was almost like a pregnancy come to full term. Any attempt to initiate conversation at those times on another subject would feel like an intrusion or interruption. This was one of those times. I had learned to keep my silence, contain my anxiety, and wait until he was ready to speak. I waited as he prayed and asked for the right words. I knew that whatever this thing was, it was serious indeed. There was often little discernible difference between these night discussions and the daytime ones, and prayer in this state was no different than prayer in the waking state.

Jesus started by calling me in the endearing name that he used for me, which has no adequate translation into this language. This both warmed me, as it always did, and frightened me, for I had a sudden chilling sense that I would not always be hearing this. What then ensued between us, I will attempt to describe in the most articulate manner possible. This will be very difficult to do, for this was not one of our usual discussions, and the entire exchange occurred on the energetic level.

First, he looked into my eyes, and I looked back into his. From this point, we began an exchange of information, concepts, feelings, and future historical happenings that remained wordless and virtually formless. Nonetheless, I felt as if I had gone into his mind-space, and had seen what was to come for him, for me, and for all of us. It was not that I saw pictures, or that I heard words: it was that I felt energy pictures and patterns. I perceived a time, not too far away, when he would be gone from me and from us, when my first reaction would be to sink into complete and utter despair at the loss of him. Then, his energy came back for a time, and gave us comfort, but then his immediacy was gone again, and it was all I could do to keep from completely dying inside. For most of me, dying was all I wanted to do. Yet, at some level he was there to sustain me, even though I could not always sense his presence.

The core of the message was that there was great hope. However, I had the most terrible time connecting with it, even though in my intellect and my voice I could express what I was longing for but could not truly find. Next, we scanned the energy of thousands of years. We searched humanity for what lay deeply buried and locked inside. *It seemed, as our energy field expanded outward through time, that the difficulty I was experiencing with my personal loss, despair and subsequent desire to shut down completely, was also the difficulty of many generations.* I knew that I had to fight for the truths I knew, despite the personal pain I would have to endure. It was not that I alone had the secret, for everyone did, within himself or herself. It was that I was given a greater connection through the gift of this greatest of friendships. This connection gave me a responsibility that I could not deny, now or ever.

I went through such a mixture of joy and despair and hope and sadness during this experience, that even within this sleep state, I felt exhausted and numbed. Despite this, I attuned to Jesus, and felt his great sadness as well. This, perhaps more than my personal sadness and sense of loss, broke my heart.

Sensing this, Jesus pulled energy down from above. We were lifted with a buoyancy and hope that provided the fuel for the entire mission on which he was embarked. We were joined for some moments in ecstasy. In this ecstasy, we were at one with God and the universe. We knew that all that happened was meant to be, in the greater service of the ultimate reunion of all that is with God. In this wholeness, which has always existed and always will exist, we were one with

God in joy and in purpose. All pain and suffering dissolved in the ultimate reunion with the One.

I woke up in the middle of the night from this experience. I sat up, and looked around me at the still, sleeping bodies of Jesus and the others. I could not comprehend on an intellectual level what I had just experienced, for I had no idea of the details of that which was to come. I only knew that I would suffer great loss, and that Jesus would not be with us for much longer, in the way he was with us today. My sorrow at losing him would be as great a year from now as 40 years from now. I preferred to think that the change would occur at some time in the farther-off future.

Whenever this would happen, I knew that I would be in for a great sorrow, and a great deal of adjustment. I would need to learn to call upon my inner resources in a manner that I did not need to do in these current times. My heart pounded with anxiety and with pain at the thought of losing my dearest friend, now or ever. For a time, I despaired of ever being able to endure such a loss. Yet I knew that whatever would happen, he was preparing me. He was giving me the direct knowledge that I would survive, and that I would need to be there for others, in order to help them survive their losses as well. I tried to remember the feeling of the bliss that I had experienced with him in the dream state, to calm myself down. It was several hours before the pounding in my chest began to calm, and before I was able to fall back into sleep again.

CHAPTER 42

WE AROSE EARLY, AND GATHERED THOSE THINGS we needed to take with us. I brought my journal with me, as it was my intention to keep a record of those events, whether in the awake or sleep state, which struck me as having importance. Jesus seemed to have been up earlier than any of us. When our eyes met, the events of the night before came back to me as strongly as if we were living through them again. He sent me courage and strength, which buoyed me. I remembered the despair, and when I did, it was difficult to move beyond those feelings. I registered in my mind that this was one reason why this experience was shared with me when it was; if he must go, then I would have much work inside myself to do to arrive at the strength and balance I would need in order to best serve those who would be counting on me. I did not like to think about this, and was glad to busy myself with the tasks around me. This helped me to clear my mind of those deep and dreadful feelings I had experienced. I knew I would be back to them soon enough, but now I made extra effort to focus on the work that needed to be done, and on the people who surrounded me.

I sought out James when it came time to begin walking. I knew from experience that many would be seeking to surround Jesus, and talk with him as we journeyed. I did not want to join in the crowd pressing around him. I always felt at home with James, and it was comforting that he knew me so well. We could talk as we walked, or not; it did not matter, for the level of comfort and connection between us was high, and we did not need to have a verbal exchange. However, today James was unusually ebullient, and I was glad both for his company and his conversation. As different as we were in our individual personalities, inside ourselves we were like pieces of the same soul.

If he guessed that I was distressed on this day, he did not say, yet I felt in his energy and in his conversation a brother's helping hand. I appreciated this aspect of him, for he was a very giving soul, and today I needed him badly. I was not yet ready to share with him what I had experienced. I had not yet digested it myself, and I was not sure I could give words to it, even if I had been ready to try. As I think about it now, I am sure he must have read the dark feelings in my energy field, for by now, we were quite skilled at doing this with one another. We had been taught well, however; and if we read a protectiveness or a boundary around areas in the field, we knew to respect these boundaries until such time as the person was prepared to share or open up these areas for exploration. James' energy field was quite clear on this day, and I rejoiced for him that he could be feeling so light.

James was optimistic about this mission, and had an air of positive expectancy about him. He talked about the many people we would gather in our midst over the course of the next few months. He had much excitement about the impact Jesus would have. As he talked about Jesus establishing dominion over the peoples of the earth, and establishing a new order, I found myself questioning what this meant. I wondered if we would see this brought to fruition in the manner in which I had always assumed it would be.

I brought this up to James, and asked him if he thought there might be any other way in which this new order might be established, other than by Jesus literally being a physical king in our time. He seemed a bit shocked, and asked what would prompt me to ask such a question. He had respect for my ideas, as I did for his, so he did not dismiss me lightly as being foolish. I told him I was not sure yet what I meant, but a part of me was beginning to wonder if we were not short-sighted in how we saw the fulfillment of the prophecies, and if there were not other ways Jesus might establish his kingdom on earth. Of course, I was beginning to re-visit the information in the light of what I had experienced the night before, and what Jesus had told us earlier. I had no clear ideas as yet, and found myself unwilling to let go of the old conceptions. James attempted to probe me for a while, but was unsuccessful, for, after all, I was not yet ready or willing to probe these ideas myself.

As an old man writing this now, remembering what it felt like to have the foundations of my mind-set begin to shake loose, I can look back and see the tenacity and the desperation with which I tried to hold on to my old ideas. Nevertheless, I felt the old structure crumbling in my mind. At a very deep level, I was terrified beyond my conscious ability to recognize, that all would be changing, in a way I did not want and did not expect. In this talk with James, I felt the first rumblings of the devastation that would manifest itself at Gethsemane.

When James and I could go no further with this conversation, we fell into silence. Since we were so attuned to each other, I knew my spoken thoughts had opened up a pathway in his mind he now could not close, and he was attempting to go further with these ideas in his mind. I could feel him at the edge of my experience from the previous night, but I would not open up to let him in. I myself was too afraid to open that up, and consider the possibilities. I recognized that this would take me some adjustment time, and I would need to rethink the future traveling that Jesus had taken me on, in light of what I had learned last night.

The present, the near future and the distant future would all be very different than what I had assumed. I now knew this with a certainty. I could not imagine how the times would be different, and I did not wish to imagine how. However, I did know that my mind, which had expanded so much on so many occasions, had a very significant amount of expanding yet to do on this particular subject. I prayed a silent prayer that I would be given the strength, wisdom and courage to open myself to that which I would need to know, and to be able to handle that which would be coming.

What I wanted most was reassurance that I was mistaken, and that all would be as I had previously thought. Deep inside, I knew this reassurance was not forthcoming. I felt myself going into deep and despairing feelings. I countered these with the thought that all would be according to God's will, and my plan, compared with the wisdom of God's, would be hopelessly inadequate. I told myself that I needed to trust all would work out as it was meant to be. Yet, the thought of living life without this man whom I had grown to love and on whom I had grown to depend, sent my emotions into a panic and deep sorrow. He was God, after all. How could he die, or leave this earth, especially so soon after he had begun his mission. None of this made any sense at all. I became lost somewhere in my own thought processes. My normally clear mind became blurry. I was glad when I heard from others in the group that we were nearing a place where we would rest, and have some nourishment.

It was beginning to get hot, and a break from the walking and the hot sun was most welcome. There were not many trees in this area, but we found one, and sat in the shade it provided. We had a meal of bread, dried fish, dried fruits and wine. After all the walking, I was very hungry, and the food tasted quite good. I did not count how many people had come along with us on this trip, but my estimate is there were about 75 of us. Maybe two-thirds were men, and a third were women. It was considered quite radical by the customs of this time for women to be traveling thus, and I admired their courage in breaking away from the norm. Many of them endured censure from their families or neighbors for coming with us, and not just a few of them had been called bewitched. There had been times when my own mother had accompanied us, and it had pained me to hear the kinds of reproaches and condemnations she had received. She and my father, Zebedee, had grown quite fond of Jesus, and were devoted to him. As time went on, they came to visit him more frequently, and invited him to the house to dine and rest.

Because of the heat of the day, we decided to remain here for several hours before attempting to move on. There would be time for discussion and for naps, should anyone care to take advantage of the opportunity. I observed the large group, with its many different characters, and the various activities in which they participated. It seemed so long ago now, since those early days when there were just a few of us with Jesus, and when he spent so many hours teaching us.

In many ways, I still longed for those days. They were much more simple, and it was wonderful to have so much of Jesus' direct attention. But, I told myself, I was extremely fortunate to have had this time at all, and now it is time he is shared with the world. I knew this was how it must and should be, yet it was difficult to let go of the many special private times with him. I was more than grateful for the time we were able to find now, and I felt blessed that we shared nighttime journeys so frequently.

My heart felt like it beat in its proper rhythm when I was with Jesus. When I was not with him, my heart felt a deep longing, as if it missed beats. The truth and the love he brought to me filled my heart, and gave to my life a cadence and music I had never felt or heard before. In these moments before I dozed, my eyes misted with the love from my heart, and the sense of overwhelming joy I felt in being lucky enough to be who I was and where I was at this point in history.

CHAPTER 43

THE AFTERNOON REST FROM JOURNEYING WAS TO TURN into an afternoon and evening of rest for the majority of the group. At some point during the early part of our break, Peter, James and I were sitting near Jesus. He let us know that he wanted us to follow him. Others wanted to come too, but he told them this was a private matter, and he wanted to have some time alone with us. I rejoiced at the opportunity to have time with Jesus in the smaller, more intimate company that the four of us provided, but intuitively I knew I would not be happy with all that I would be learning.

It was extremely hot, but as we climbed up into the hills, the temperature grew cooler. A steady breeze was blowing that buffeted us and somehow seemed to carry us on the wings on spirit. I knew from the feel of this wind, that this was no ordinary wind. It was almost as if it were the very breath of God, present among us not only in the form of Jesus but in the form of this animate, intelligent spirit-breath. I had never before perceived a breeze in this manner, and I knew that whatever would be coming to us would be utterly profound and beyond doubt the word and will of God. It seemed that each of us felt this profoundly, for we grew silent as we climbed. Even Peter had nothing to say. Whatever this intelligence was to bring to us, we knew in the deepest levels of our being that we were in the presence of the most holy. I was in awe, waiting for the message that was in store for us. I remembered the story of Moses on the mountaintop, receiving the Ten Commandments, and I received in my mind that this occasion would be similarly momentous.

Jesus signaled to us to wait, while he climbed to the top of the mountain. We were accustomed to his going off alone to make special prayers to God, and we knew the energy on a mountaintop was much more conducive to communication with the divine than in most places. This was especially true on this mountain, long considered sacred, where one could go to seek truth and supplicate God, especially in the most dire and critical of circumstances. All we could do was to wait, and support him with our prayers, which we did. We had learned this practice very early on. We knew the power of group prayer was very effective at garnering the divine forces to work together towards a common goal.

The three of us wondered aloud why we were here, and what was happening. The air felt as charged as did the wind. I could not take my eyes off Jesus as he ascended to the top of the mountain and began praying. I was astounded as I watched the light body around him expand in all directions to an enormous extent. His field, normally extremely expansive, was now far larger than I had ever seen it.

I remember that I was to the right of the three of us, with James to my immediate left, and Peter on the other side of him. There was a large boulder to my right, on which I was leaning. All of a sudden, it was as if the heavens opened up, and light poured down upon Jesus, in an almost blinding intensity. I was completely entranced. I heard the most beautiful music imaginable, and I watched Jesus draped in light and divinity itself. His presence was completely transformed by the light pouring down and shining through him. Suddenly, around him I saw a man whom I somehow knew to be Elijah, and another whom I knew to be Moses. When I saw Moses I was surprised, but not completely surprised, because of the musings I had about him only a little while before.

I was overcome by the momentousness of what I was witnessing, even though I did not yet understand what was happening, or why. Jesus' face shone with a radiance that was beyond this world, as he talked with Moses and Elijah. Then, suddenly the figures of Elijah and Moses were gone, and Jesus alone was standing there. I felt that I had been transported into another dimension entirely. In this dimension, time and space did not exist, and planning was done here to map out the ways these Beings could help bring God to the souls of men on earth. There had been so much exchanged between Jesus, Elijah and Moses on an energetic level, a great deal of which I could not understand. I felt privileged to be a witness, and was glad Jesus wanted that it be so. I could barely focus on the words that were spoken, for my attention was on this incredible energetic exchange.

Then, all of the forces once more gathered together. There was a large bright cloud above us that radiated a light far brighter than that which would normally be from the sun. The cloud parted, and I heard clearly the words: "Behold my Son, in whom I am well pleased. Hear him well."

I could not say whether I heard these words with my outer or inner ear, but we all heard them spoken just the same. For a time, eternity was made manifest in the present. We witnessed the oneness of the Divine, from the Absolute to the divine made flesh who was on this mountaintop with us. We were all wrapped in transcendence, I know not for how long. I will never forget the beauty and the power of that experience. I was in total awe.

As the transcendence of the experience subsided, I gradually came back into the experience of being a man on earth. I would have loved to stay with the beauty and love and power of what I had seen. As the experience ebbed, there were questions to be asked and meanings to be found. Some of the meanings I can only surmise in retrospect, but much was said as we descended. Jesus told us to tell no one of what we had experienced, until the Son was raised from the dead. We fell quiet for a while. Peter quoted from the prophecies and asked why scripture said that first Elijah must come. Jesus responded that Elijah had already come; he had not been recognized, and he had suffered much, and been killed. We knew what he meant was that Elijah and John the Baptist were the same soul, and that John was the reincarnation of Elijah. He further said the Son would also suffer at the hands of men.

I was not alone in not wanting to think about, or ask about those matters pertaining to the Son being killed, and being raised from the dead. These matters were so tremendously frightening to us, for none of us could imagine life without our Master. What we did not know, we could imagine in a manner that felt safest to us. I did not understand this about myself, or about the others at the time, for I was locked into my fear. Now, as I look back, I can understand the patterns. I can see how the three of us reacted in similar ways, on many occasions, when it came to coping with these matters. Mentally and spiritually, I consider myself now and then to be a strong man. However, when it came to my love for this man who was my Master and who had all of my heart, I was weak. I did not wish to know the truth, for in the deepest parts of me, I did not think I could bear it.

Soon after this, Jesus took the twelve of us aside, and began to tell us that when we went into Jerusalem he would be sentenced to death and crucified, and that three days later he would rise from the dead. Inside I was reeling, for I remembered my dream in which I was taught that one day he would not be with us any more. Again, I did not wish to know further, and wanted to think there was a significant amount of time ahead that I would have to spend with my Master. I noted that the others did not ask any further about this momentous information. We fell silent. None of us could have wanted to know. What I focused on here was that he would rise again, and that meant, to my mind, he would then be with us again.

The events on the mountaintop marked a definite shift in Jesus' mission. I say this after having reflected on the events leading up to the mountaintop experience, and on those afterward. There are thoughts I have on this that I feel I must add here, even though it may take away from the linear flow of the telling of the story. First, I would like to say, that after this event, there was a quickening in the preparations for what was coming. It seemed that this event lent clear focus to Jesus of what he had left to do, and of what was coming. He told us directly what was coming, though we would not hear, and he told us of many other things that would be happening as time went on. He tried to make more time for teaching us, and we felt his presence with us much more strongly. Second, I think the mountaintop experience was for Jesus a preparation, and a gathering of divine power and strength for what was to come. My conjecture is that part of what was discussed between him, Elijah and Moses on that mountaintop had to do with what was to come. From that point on, he had a much sharper focus, and a different kind of directedness than he had demonstrated previously. I think this event came to charge him with all of the energy of the new covenant he would be creating between God and man, and to signal him the time had come when he would bring this covenant directly to earth. He never told me this, but I have searched in my mind over the years to discover the meanings in this wondrous event, and this is the conclusion to which I have come. After this, all had changed inalterably, and for always.

I can only imagine that Jesus, knowing the mission he had ahead of him, would have needed all of the heavenly power and strength possible. A meeting with other Masters, one who had set up the first covenant, and the other who had foretold the coming of the new contract over several lifetimes, could have helped set out for him the specifics of the events to follow. It could also have helped to provide him with courage in the charge he was undertaking. I have wished a hundred times over that I could have heard what had been exchanged between them, yet I know the level of planning which was being undertaken was so far beyond my human comprehension that much of it would have been lost on me. I feel awed in attempting to comprehend the level of intelligence at which these greatest of spirits were operating, and consider myself fortunate to have been able to witness this exchange between the Divine Absolute, and these three greatest of messengers.

Though I did not have all of the information then that I do now, I knew life would now be very different, and that in this tremendous occurrence lay the unfolding of something very new and significantly altered from what any of us had known before. For after all, when Moses received the tablets on the mountaintop, did this not herald a completely new agreement between God and man? I knew at this time of no such new agreement, yet I was left to speculate on what would be coming as a result of this encounter. It was difficult to keep an incident of such magnitude to myself, even though by this point I had significant experience in keeping major experiences within me. There was not much opportunity at this time to speak with James or

Peter privately about what had happened. I would have liked very much to have had time to discuss this with them, and to speculate on the importance of the mountaintop experience. I suspected that each of us had a need to keep this information to ourselves, so as to begin to digest this overwhelming experience, which in many ways spoke for itself. The experience was so transcendent, and so moving and powerful, that beyond an actual description of the events, words were woefully inadequate to describe what transpired. Words were made for humans, to describe human experiences. This experience was not of the human realm. My experience of it was a human experience, but what I witnessed was a completely different realm of experience. What Jesus received in that experience could only be sensed, but not known. Even if he had wished to share with me the details, I do not think this could be done orally, but perhaps only by experiential sharing, as we had done on the hillside so long ago.

CHAPTER 44

POLITICS WOULD NOW BEGIN TO PLAY a much greater role in our collective energy field. As the days of this trip went on, I was startled to find that in many places, the impact of what Jesus was doing and saying was having quite an unexpected effect on people. Instead of focusing on the work, and on the miracles that God was creating, rumors were circulating about the political desires Jesus had. People said he was trying to build up his power base so he could overtake both the political and the religious structures, and replace them with his own. Rumor had it that he was already calling himself King, and that the momentum around him in this matter was building.

It is true that the disciples had these hopes for the future, but I was very clear in my own mind and heart that Jesus held no ambition for these things. He wanted only to share with as many people as possible the wonders of God. Perhaps we were ambitious for him, in our great eagerness to have the Kingdom of God established on earth. In my naïveté, I saw the mass conversion of souls as a reality that could come about relatively quickly, though I knew from times when I sat down with Jesus and scanned the future, that there would be many dark times yet to come on earth over thousands of years. However, I saw these as periods of backsliding, after a period in which God's kingdom was established and Jesus reigned as king. In my eyes, he could do anything he willed. However, I was not willing or able to recognize that the one thing he could not, or perhaps more accurately, would not do, was to interfere with the free will of the human beings who peopled the earth.

It was upsetting to hear these rumors. I asked Jesus what he thought of them and what he planned to do about them. I found him particularly cryptic in this matter, for he said people would say and think what they would, and the course of history could not be changed by anything he might say on this matter. When I asked what he meant, he said only that great fear lies in the hearts of men, and that at this point in history, man was choosing fear and the tangible over love and the intangible. I shivered inside, remembering for some reason the recent experience we had shared in our dreaming. I remembered losing him and how desolate I felt, and yet I knew that what was happening was all part of the Plan.

He could not concern himself with politics and earthly power, he said. He had much more important concerns to attend to. In his view, if he could restore one soul, that was much more important than any political victory he could imagine. I see all of this now as politics nonetheless: what I see as I look back, with all the perspective that time, pain and suffering can offer, is that Jesus was a consummate politician, but of a completely different order than any politician to which I had been exposed. He was a radical politician, but rather than being a politician interested in earthly power, he was a politician of the heart, and a politician of the soul. His focus was absolute in this.

I think the greatest misunderstandings around him and about him were in the failure of people to understand this fundamental fact. This is why he came, and the purpose to which he was completely committed: to show people the way to love through their hearts, and through this, to lead them back to God through their individual souls. It sounds so very simple, yet is so incredibly complex. Without this love that he gave so freely, and which he taught people to give, there was no way back to God. Perhaps he was so threatening to the religious leaders of the time, because, for whatever reasons, they had failed to grasp this, and did not teach this. He shook the very foundation on which they structured themselves.

We now found ourselves in a situation where increasing divisiveness surrounded us, the very opposite of what we were trying to accomplish. I think it disturbed Jesus much less than it disturbed me, for he had a much better understanding of the overall picture. I had envisioned that he would unite people of all persuasions under one God. Though that was to happen, it would happen much later. However, at this time, factions were created that angrily denounced his work and his teachings, something that utterly confused and baffled me.

My idealism led me to believe that if people were simply shown the truth, they would feel and know it. I believed they would inevitably respond positively to this, especially if that truth were as profound and as powerful as the truth Jesus demonstrated in his life and works. It is true that at this point, I had seen the destructive power of greed and envy, but I had no idea of the scope and vastness of darkness that could lie in the hearts of men. I wanted to believe in the better nature of mankind, and I still do, but at this time, I greatly underestimated the power of darkness and how strongly men could react when they felt threatened.

Extraordinary people surrounded me personally, on a daily basis. This cushioned and sheltered me from an awareness of what lay out in the world. Some of the older disciples were much more aware than I of the evil that lay out there, but I was recruited at such a young age, and my life had been such a good one until then, that I maintained with me an innocence that probably still has not yet been fully shaken. I was teased about it on occasion, but was also told that it was a quality that was refreshing. Whatever it was, there was little I could do about it. I think Jesus found this side of me endearing, though I have to wonder how a man with his enormous breadth of understanding could not also find it at times amusing, in his loving way.

What I am attempting to depict is a self-portrait that explains why it took me so long to comprehend the political machinations going on around us. I found myself not understanding, and startled and shocked as I saw the harsh, unrelenting darkness in the energy fields of some of the people we were encountering. This was different than in previous times, when the darkness in the energy fields was personal to the people who carried it. Now, I could see that the darkness was directed at us, and especially at Jesus, and the aim was to hurt or to destroy. We had practiced building shields of light around us so invading, destructive forces could not harm us. Now, I found that I built and rebuilt my shield at least several times daily. The need felt much greater. There were often times now when I would feel dark, invading energy from a distance, and when I would have no clear idea from whom it was coming, or for which particular reason. It was clear only that the intent was to harm. I would watch Jesus, and attempt to identify the dark, harmful energy that was sent his way. I was amazed, startled and saddened by the tremendous quantities. His energy field was huge and brilliant on any given day, and yet I began noticing that he was now invoking quite a bit more of protective forces, and that there was much more of a shielding effect around him.

We all found ourselves individually doing this shielding almost automatically. At some point we discussed it, and found we were all feeling tremendous need in this area. It was frightening. I think we wanted to feel invincible, but we were feeling anything but that. It seemed that as we brought with us forces for good and for love and for healing into the world, we appeared to somehow stir up opposing forces of evil, hate and destruction. Part of me had little comprehension of how the light and love that Jesus brought could stir up so much darkness and enmity, and then I remembered how difficult it was even for me sometimes to be around him because of the feelings of inferiority and incompetence that were stirred up in me. This recollection helped me to be compassionate, for it was only because of our deep trust and friendship that I was able to recognize these feelings as my own, and not caused by him somehow. I realized that for others, this might not be true; envy might easily overtake them like a poison, until they were in its grip and possessed by the vision that he was the darkness or the enemy, when that darkness was truly within their own souls.

It was possible in this way for me to understand up to a point the undifferentiated darkness that I felt being directed at us. What I had substantial difficulty with was in understanding some of the vileness and directed evil that was sent in our direction. It was as if there was no light within it at all. Although I was trained to send light to it and permeate it with light, the intensity of the nefariousness was something I had the greatest of difficulty in understanding.

At times, I turned to my friend Mary Magdelena for help in understanding, for of all of those whom I knew, she knew best the dark side of life. Her insight and understanding in this area were unsurpassed. She helped me to see so very much. She knew far more than the others the extreme dangerousness of those people who are so identified with their own powers that they forget and deny the true source. I must admit that I took her warnings too lightly, as did many of the others. She knew never to underestimate the power of an opponent, a lesson I had not yet learned. My innocence and idealism had not yet been penetrated deeply enough by the cruel experiences that life can bring. As a result, I listened to her, but did not really hear or understand. Both she and Jesus' mother had a keen understanding of the dire seriousness of the forces that had been set into motion.

I understand now, with the wisdom that comes with age, that women have such keen protective instincts because of the need for these in bearing and nurturing children. They seem in general to sense a threat to those whom they love significantly in advance of men. Men are trained to be in charge, and like to think there is nothing they cannot handle. I would not like to think this would be operative for me in the spiritual realm as well, but I think it is, as follows: even though I was not a soldier in the physical sense of the word, I saw myself as a soldier of Christ. I thought that with his love, his presence and his power, we could conquer all evil. I believed that as good spiritual soldiers, we would overcome all threats by love and spiritual will, and establish the kingdom of heaven on earth. I did not want to sense a real threat, and therefore I did not. My recent dream experience with Jesus had informed me there would be major shifts, yet I still was not expecting sudden violent changes. I did not want to hear what I was hearing and perceiving from these various sources. After all, I reasoned, God is with us and not with the opposition, so how could any real harm come? The women were much more realistic, as I think they are in general. Because of their relative position in society, they are more perpetually poised for those radical events, which can take so much away from them, and against which they can feel so powerless.

If I could go back now to this time, and change myself in accordance with the knowledge I have gained, I would like to think I would put more of my mental energy into dispelling the illusions and denials I was building up around myself. Yes, I have forgiven myself for my human frailties, but I do wish I had somehow had the strength to fully face the reality of what was beginning to come in to my awareness, and into our collective reality, so strongly. I would have liked to have been strong enough to be more fully conscious of what was transpiring. I think this would have made me a better friend to my dearest friend. I do not shed tears easily in most matters, but in this, I have grieved many times over for my failings, for I was not he who I would have wished myself to be.

These were my inner realities of these times. Much of this journey was a blur, as I was overwhelmed by the new information coming in from so many different areas. My focus became internal, as I tried to sort out the many different avenues that were presenting themselves. I will attempt, however, to depart from this inner region somewhat, so I can describe some of the events that were occurring. Many of these events have been well documented, and I will attempt to fill in some of the gaps that remain.

CHAPTER 45

WE STAYED IN VARIOUS TOWNS AND VILLAGES along the way. We traveled much more slowly now. With so many more people along with us, there were many more needs to be attended to within our larger group. At times, some of us would go ahead of the others, in order to find suitable places where we could stay. In many ways, this was an excuse to break away from the slow pace of the group, for Jesus could have easily scanned ahead, and found a site. I enjoyed breaking away sometimes, for I had such great abundance of energy that it was difficult to remain at the slower pace of the group.

Jesus seemed more worn down than I had seen him, which concerned me. He always had much to attend to, and there were always many people asking much of him. James, Peter and I, in particular, were very concerned that he have opportunity for restoration on all levels of his being. We made sure he had time to be alone after the evening meal, if he so chose, whether to rest or to wander off on his own. The need others had for him seemed never-ending. We had come to realize that the world had so many sorrows that his physical vehicle could not possibly ever begin to meet all of the needs that were presented to him.

We spoke with him, and offered to help him in this. He readily agreed. Previously, there had been more opportunity for rest and privacy, but now everything had changed, and the demands on him had become tremendous. He was very good at taking the time he needed for himself, yet I think he was glad we offered to take on the role of gatekeepers. He was very clear with us that soon he would be taking time to be with the twelve, and that he had some further teachings he wanted to share with us on this trip. I looked forward to this, for

I missed the small group work we had done so much of in earlier times.

We continued to pray together in the morning soon after we woke up, and to center ourselves in God's will for us. As I have mentioned, I loved working in meditation and prayer in such a large group, for the energy and love and light that so many people could invoke was truly awe-inspiring. These morning sessions would energize me for the day to come. Jesus had always led these before, but more and more now, he was asking us to lead the group. He said he wanted us to grow comfortable in these leadership roles, and it did not matter whether or not he was leading, because God would come through all those who called on Him.

When I took my turns in leading, I was always amazed how, when I opened myself to be led by God, I was always inspired and moved by words that seemed to flow out of my connection with Jesus' spirit. It was not that he gave me the words directly, as if by verbatim telepathy. The process was first that I would tune inside to listen to God's voice and I would connect with Jesus as intercessionary. Once I made that connection with the Spirit of God, the words that needed to be said unfolded. Only sometimes in this particular process did I hear Jesus' voice. These occasions tended to be for special reasons, or because of a supplication on my part for help. I felt he was deliberately holding back more now, so we would learn to work the process for ourselves, and grow to feel much more familiar and skilled with it.

The responsibility felt enormous, for there were so many people now. When they looked to me for spiritual direction, I had to keep reminding myself that if I were not up to this, Jesus would never have entrusted this special responsibility to myself or to the others. These experiences were to prove to be a turning point, both in my ability to work with larger groups and in my comfort level in front of a number of people. I had never realized how easy it could be, for when I truly invoked and felt filled with the Spirit of God, my words flowed and my work was clear. Of course, the group I was working with was entirely sympathetic and harmonious to our purpose, which made my work easier.

It did not escape me that more responsibilities were being handed over to the rest of us, at a time when I was receiving such an influx of information about major changes up ahead. I do not know how much information others were receiving, but I do know that the entire group appeared to be making a transition in its energies. This was happening in ways both subtle and not subtle. It was not something that was often verbalized, but it was more like it was an operative group assumption that was not necessarily based on anything consciously realized. I found it quite easy to fall into the new patterning. It did not feel abrupt or dissonant.

One afternoon, many of the group was resting. Jesus and a number of the inner circle walked into a small village. There was nowhere we could go now where we were not known. In most places, his arrival was greeted by a charge of excitement and positive expectation. (His hometown of Nazareth was one of the major exceptions to this general rule, but that is another matter entirely.) I remember walking into the town, and through an uncrowded street. An old man who was sitting down on a stone or a bin of some kind greeted us. He had a cane beside him, and his dry, lined face was framed with a long gray and white beard. Apparently, he knew exactly who Jesus was as soon as he saw him, and he pushed himself to stand up to properly honor his arrival.

Jesus spoke to him, saying, "Why have you feared God's punishment and wrath for so long? It is your own wrath upon yourself that has punished you, and surely this has crippled you more than your injuries. You are forgiven. Punish yourself no longer, and walk in peace and without pain for the rest of your days."

The man tested his previously crippled right leg, and finding that he could now walk on it, fell down weeping at Jesus' feet, and blessed him.

Jesus spoke, saying: "Bless not me, but the One who is in me and who works through me, and who will be with you also."

This event has stood out in my mind, not because it was unusual, for I had seen many thousands of these kinds of healings. It stands out because of the discussion later generated out of this event. At the time of the healing, I watched carefully the energy fields, both of this man and of Jesus. There was significant darkness around the man's leg and heart. When I tried to read the energy, I felt a block, and knew from experience that this block meant this man did not want the information to be accessed. I asked Jesus about the healing. Had he too been met with the same blocking, and if so, how had he worked with it so to obtain the information that he did?

I do not remember his exact words, but the gist of what was said was that he had an instantaneous reading of the man when he saw him, and all was given to him. It was on this that he moved, and spoke. Jesus said that since the man wanted privacy around his past, he could not speak of what he learned, except to say the man was crippled by guilt and by rage at himself, and did not know how to move past it. My question had to do with how I would work with this kind of situation, if I were not allowed access inside the darkness, and if a "knowing" were not given to me. The answer was simple, but also complicated.

I was told that I had learned to recognize how to read guilt and self-rage in the energy field. I knew that whenever I saw this, the work to be done would be in the area of letting go and forgiveness. This in itself would suffice, even if the person to be healed did not know what feelings and concerns were involved in the physical illness. As soon as the healer could penetrate the field enough to know that forgiveness and letting go were involved, images and feelings would come up in the person being healed that would reveal to them what was involved. All of this could go on without the healer's awareness of any specifics. Jesus said that often, once the person begins to recognize, accept and let go of the issue, at some level he opens up the field enough to voluntarily share with the healer what he or she was struggling with. Again, we were cautioned never to push or to venture in where we were did not feel welcomed, for that was considered a serious offense, and abuse of the trust placed in us. In this particular case, the man continued to desire his privacy, and that was to be respected.

The conversation then took a turn that I could not have anticipated. Jesus began talking about changes coming for us in the healing work we would be doing. I have mentioned how we had been very systematically trained in the science of healing, over a period of several years at this point. We had been trained how to read the energy field, how to recognize and identify disturbances in normal energy patterns, and how to work with these patterns, understand them and heal them. We also learned how to support each other in healing, even when this healing was done at a distance. Time and space did not matter in this healing work. We had been carefully prepared, and had learned by this time many of the subtleties of the work. Jesus had given our training, and we had much opportunity to practice both on each other and on the many people who had asked Jesus for healing. Our training had taken place both during the day and by night, and we had learned much.

Jesus now told us that there would be a time, in the not too distant future, when we would find our training and skills in this area would be enhanced greatly by the inpouring of the Spirit of God into us. We would be astonished by what we would be able to do. For these several years, we had been developing our bodies, our minds and our spirits as instruments of healing. Now that our instruments had become much more highly developed, they would be able to receive a much greater influx of energy. We would be able to utilize this energy in the mission of healing and demonstrating to people how God can operate through his missionaries on earth. He said he did not know when this would come about, but we could look forward to this as a marker. The works we would then be able to do would be much greater. We would also be able to operate much more independently.

I had long since given up any thoughts of ever being able to have the highly developed healing abilities of my Master. I know from speaking with the others that they, too, felt they would not be able to do great works on their own. I know I was at my best when I was able to contact the Kingdom of God within me, and I was best able to do this when I found that space inside of me where I could summon and perceive Jesus. We had gone out and healed on our own, it is true, but I could only do this when I was particularly clear myself. Then, I could feel his voice or his energy coming through me. When I compared myself to him, I blocked the flow of energy through me, and was not able to receive the gifts of Spirit he could transmit through me.

The news he gave was exciting, and a collective burst of exhilaration went through us. In the excitement of receiving the news, no one thought to ask more about the situation, such as how this would be coming about, or why. I know that, for myself, I simply preferred to think it was one of the benefits that would be coming as a fruit of our hard labor. Since I had learned to think that with Jesus, all was possible, I did not stop to question the mechanism by which this would be made possible, or why this would be made possible to us now. In the privacy of my dreams, I began to put the pieces together. Jesus would prepare us more as the days and weeks went by, but for now, the news seemed entirely positive. I watched Jesus as he quietly took in our reactions, and wondered why he seemed so serious about something that seemed so joyful. Inside of me, I sensed that for now, I should keep this questioning to myself, and that I could approach him later. At present, he seemed very deep into his own thoughts. The rest of the group was reacting exuberantly. I now had very mixed feelings, and did not know whether this was my perpetually serious nature, or whether I needed to take seriously that which was disquieting to me.

All was changing, there was no doubt of that. The signs were showing up everywhere. I did not like what I was feeling. I experienced a great deal of anxiety at the heart chakra region. I knew that I felt fear, and I did not dare look at the reasons behind the fear in my energy pattern. There were the outer and the inner preparations, but I have learned over time that it takes many repetitions of information about the future in the energy field before I can really allow the information to settle in enough to trust it. If I receive something directly, I can process it directly. It seemed however, in this case, that information was coming from many angles. Most of it was not spelling out directly what was coming. Instead, the pieces needed to be put together. I believe that my mind knew the whole at some deep level, but in my humanness, I could not bear very much truth. I could not bear to think that Jesus would be gone at any time in the very near future. When I put together what was happening around me, and my recent dream experience, I concluded that if he were to be going away soon, that "soon" could mean in several years or in a decade, even. For, after all, when I had expected to spend an entire lifetime with him, 2 to 3 more years or 10 years was a very short span of time to have with him. We had been to Jerusalem before, so it might be a later trip to Jerusalem in which he would be sentenced to die. In this manner, I continued to talk myself out of my feelings.

That night, I had a difficult time getting to sleep, as I puzzled out for hours these various pieces coming through my consciousness. The fear and the anxiety that I felt were great. Though I knew I was very tired, my mind could not rest. It was as if I felt I had to resolve these important issues in my mind before I could allow myself to rest. I settled them by deciding that there was still much time, and I finally drifted off to sleep.

I awakened, sobbing, out of a dream. The dream was as follows:

"I am walking around the Sea of Galilee at night, alone. I am terribly sad. Jesus is gone, and I cannot find him anywhere.

I hear him calling me, but as soon as I get to where I think the voice is coming from, I hear the voice coming from a different direction. I know he is dead, and that he is speaking to me from beyond.

My grief and my despair are so great that I want to collapse and die. It is only the sound of his voice calling me that keeps me moving. It is as if he is the only force that keeps my steps going. I have never before felt so desolate, and so full of despair. I am angry, too; angry that I have ever lived and loved, for the ecstasy of my love has now been replaced by a loss which I feel I cannot bear.

I hear him singing a song to me, in an exquisite voice. The song raises me to another level of consciousness, in which I see that what is must be, and it is by his movement into the next world that this world will be transformed. I hear in the sound of the notes that there is much to celebrate.

When the song ends, I fall down on my knees on the ground, and I begin sobbing. I know I have many choices to make, both for myself and for others, and that the road ahead will be very difficult. I want to close my heart, to make the pain go away, but I know this is not possible."

It was still dark when I awakened. My heart was so pained with hurt and anxiety that I knew I would not be able to sleep again that night. I got up from my sleeping spot, wanting to scream at the top of my voice, and walked to a spot away from the others, where I could not be heard. There, I sobbed and sobbed, as the reality of what was occurring finally sank in fully.

I bargained and pleaded with God, begging him to take me instead, for whatever little my life was worth. I knew inside, however, that the events that were to take place had already been set in motion. After a time, I prayed for strength and courage to get through what would transpire. I asked for the wisdom I would need to help the others.

I knew that if I had a role to play in helping others, the very role would help me to forget myself enough to find the will to survive and carry out what I must do. I prayed for such a role, and that I might be given the guidance I would need in order to carry it out. I heard an answer to these prayers, in a deep voice that said to me: "so shall it be given." I felt relief in knowing there would be this something to give my life meaning and help get me through.

Then I recognized, that in this voice, there was also an affirmation that Jesus would be departing, and very soon. Once more I broke down sobbing. I must have stayed here, sobbing, for hours. I lost track of time. It seemed an eternity that I lay there like this. I must have eventually fallen asleep, for when I roused, the sun had already risen and the day's activities had begun. It quickly hit me what dreaded realities I had encountered the night before, and my heart sank. I tried within myself to gather my strength and my courage. I went to find water to cleanse the trails of my tears and the puffiness off my face, before going to join the others.

CHAPTER 46

JAMES LOOKED QUIZZICALLY AT ME as I re-entered the group of people, who were now gathering for morning prayers. I could not respond, but went to sit by him. I felt as I sat down the incredible warmth and comfort of Jesus' energy surrounding me. I knew immediately that he knew what I had been going through, and he was sending me love and courage. As much as I welcomed this energy, in my reception of it a new wave of sadness went through me, with the recognition that it was exactly this I would be losing.

"On the physical plane, yes," I heard in my head, "but not on the spiritual. I will always be there for you to reach me."

I heard and accepted this, but in a part of my heart, I was dying and closing down. I know this now, but I did not know this then.

Jesus spent time that morning teaching, as he had done often in the earlier days. It seemed now that there were repetitions of earlier, familiar events, and their very familiarity was very comforting. We listened attentively as he spoke on patience, which he described as one of the most difficult virtues to attain. Unlike moral conscience, which could be highly developed even in a young person, patience was something that had to be cultivated over time. It superseded many of the other virtues in that it was in many ways the solution to them. For example, he spoke of greed and of envy, which he described as a failure of faith, and an inability to be patient and to trust that all good things would come in their own time. Instead, people became grasping, and could not or would not wait. They coveted that which they did not have, and lost contact with their own souls. This made a great deal of sense, and I wondered why I had never seen this before.

Additionally, Jesus said that in patience lies the resolution to much of the ill will generated between men. He explained that much of the error in the world is created when man tries to force the creation of that which he does not have or is not ready for, and violates the rights of others in an attempt to gain what he lusts after. He said that women, because of their natural biological rhythms in childbearing, were much more attuned to the need for patience. For, after all, he stated, what good would it do if a woman were to try to shorten the time which nature decreed is necessary for the child that is developing inside her? In this, she learns to wait, and to respect the timing necessary for the full development of the child she carries. Men, he said, have no such physiological imperative in which they learn patience, and so it is more difficult for them to learn these lessons. He said this was an important component of why men develop their aggressive traits so much more strongly than women, for they have no natural internal or biological rhythms to tame them.

Jesus went on, saying that for all persons, whether male or female, patience is a fruit of the long struggle to learn to love through the heart. It is born of the struggle to attain one's special destiny on the earth plane, by loving others and by loving God. It is through the heart that this combination of earthly and spiritual concerns is mediated. Through this process, over the years, and with all of the slowness with which flowing water wears down a stone, patience is developed. It is a by-product of the commingling of love and wisdom.

"In many ways," he said, "it is easier to love than it is to be patient. God's will is done in the timing of the divine, which none may know or predict in advance. As humans, on this earth and in these fleshly bodies, it is all we can do to try to live as truthfully as we can, and to try to live out that which we see has been assigned to us. We must not make the mistake of assuming we can create our own time frame for the sacred events of our lives. Only in patience do we ascertain that we are doing what we are meant to do, and that we are on God's timing, not our own."

I knew instinctively as he spoke that there were many great mysteries on his mind, and that each of us received his words at the level we were able to comprehend. I sensed that there was much weighing on him, as I knew there was on me. I could only begin to guess at some of the truths that were hidden inside the words that he spoke. At an immediate level, I resonated very strongly to his words, and I knew my impatience was a mark to me of the relative immaturity of my soul. I knew much through intuiting, and was short on the kind of patience that gives a long-term perspective on the time that it takes for love and divinity to manifest and mature through the souls of men. As an old man now, I am not sure that even now I have learned the lessons of patience, for I have been many years waiting for the return of my blessed friend, and still eagerly and impatiently wait for him.

As the lesson wound down, we finished with a prayer that each of us might be taught patience in our own lives and in our missions, and that we each be given the strength, courage and wisdom we would need in order to develop that patience. I knew with certainty, as this prayer was closed, that patience would be the lesson of this lifetime, and of many lifetimes to come, and also that it would be a much more difficult lesson than I could ever imagine. My heart suddenly felt heavy with the weight of what I knew I had ahead of me to learn, and I entreated Jesus' help in this matter. Immediately, I felt his presence within me, encouraging me that he would always be there with me to help me on my way, if I would but call on him.

As we closed our prayers, it took me a long time to come back to the group, and to the day. I got up slowly, and with trepidation. James stayed with me. When the others had moved away, he asked me what was upsetting me so, and where I had been earlier this morning. Since the group of us was to be traveling today, I told him I would like to talk with him, but since it would take some time, I preferred that we wait until we were walking. I debated just how much I would tell him, but then it seemed it would be best if I just told him everything I was thinking and experiencing, for this would have a tremendous impact on us all. James stayed close as we gathered our things. I was grateful for his solicitude, as well as for his presence. His presence helped keep me composed as I went about my tasks, and his cheerful demeanor helped brighten my spirits. James was very witty, and his natural ebullience had helped me over so many rough times that I could not possibly number them. I had learned to see a sense of humor as a tremendous strength and coping skill, and appreciated very much his ability to take a situation and see the humorous side. James was a very deep and thoughtful man, and I knew his humor was a tool he developed to keep in balance. Over the years, I drew from this side of him on many occasions, and tried to incorporate what I could of his fun-loving self.

As we began walking, it took me a while before I was ready to begin sharing with James. I was grateful he did not push me in any way, for he knew that sometimes it took me time before I could compose my emotions and my words. Writing was always easier for me than speaking, for I could take my time to collect my thoughts and emotions before I committed them to paper. Speaking was much more difficult. I have always believed I am much more persuasive and articulate when I write than when I speak. It often seems there are no words for what I wish to articulate, and because of the pressure of delivery to another person that is inherent in speech, I regularly feel I am groping for words I cannot find. When I write, I have the time to allow the concepts to come up from the depths, and from there, the words form in my consciousness.

I told James all I could piece together, from the dream, to the experience we had on the mountaintop, to my observations both before and after that experience. I told him how terribly afraid I was, and how all of the pieces pointed to a reality which I felt I just could not accept. He listened until I had finished speaking my mind. He took in each of my words and weighed them. When I was done, he shuddered terribly. I knew immediately that he had also been fighting against drawing the same conclusions as I had.

He said to me, "Brother, I have not seen and heard all you have seen and heard, but I have been witness to many of these same things, and others, and Jesus himself told us directly. I do not know how to understand these things, and I certainly do not know how to accept them. I share in your pain and your confusions, and in your deepest wishes that we might have as long as possible with our Master before he is taken away from us, if this is what must happen. There is so much which we do not, and cannot understand. We are limited by the force of our desires from seeing the fullness of the truth that is presented to us. If this thing which we dread is true, and if it must happen, then we must do all we can to strengthen and to prepare ourselves, for he has charged us with carrying on his work for the rest of the time we are alive on this planet." He then went on further, in this same vein.

I admired so much the wisdom of James' words, and the directness of his vision. He was, above all, a very practical man. He could see straight through to the heart of a matter, and figure out a way through, when I might be groping in the dark. What he said made perfect sense, and helped to renew my sense of purpose. I had not been able to see my way past my grief and my fear. It was as if James could see through to my core, and find a way to help lift me out, even in this case when he was feeling disconsolate as well. His strength in this matter was an inspiration to me. I knew he was right.

I had to pull myself out of the morass of my emotions, and move myself into a place where I could function effectively in the role I had chosen, and which had been chosen for me. I did not know how I would do this. I decided that for the meantime, I would allow myself to lean on James' straightforward manner and direction, until I found my own firm footing through my overwhelming emotions. I did not know at this stage that his strength in this critical circumstance had at least as many, and perhaps more, constraints and limitations than my own. We had always taken turns providing support and strength for each other, and never would this be truer than in the events that would follow. For now, I thanked God for having provided me with a brother who was not only a brother in blood, but in soul. I prayed we would both be given what we would need in order to help us through the times to come.

CHAPTER 47

As we journeyed southward, people joined us along the way. They were of many types, and all had in common an uncommon faith in the divinity that they saw manifest in this man. Their reasons for joining were many and varied. Jesus had healed some in person or in a dream; others had dreams compelling them to seek out Jesus. Some were merely curious. Most had a story of a deep inner awakening to tell, an awakening that was activated by Jesus in some manner or another. I loved to listen to the stories people shared, for each person was moved in such a different way, and each way had its own beauty and truth.

We spent several days in Ephraim, a town and a region very dear to me. James and I had distant relatives here, and found time to spend with them while we were there. They had many questions to ask of us. Their neighbors also gathered around to hear what we had to say. A young child of one of the neighbors was sick with some malady that the local physicians had not been able to cure. The girl had been sick for almost ten months, and had not seemed to improve at all during that time. James and I used our healing abilities to work with the child. Almost immediately, she was able to rise up from her cot, something she had apparently not done for some time. All marveled at her miraculous recovery. We gave testimony to the powers of God that Jesus was teaching all of us to invoke.

We shared how Jesus had learned to be an instrument through which God's works manifested, and that he taught us how we could also manifest God's power through healing. They were very curious about this, for previously only the religious elite laid claim to knowledge about God. Now, Jesus taught a very different perspective, which said all who wished to know about God could experience divine reality for themselves.

They knew that James and I had been simple fishermen, and had not spent endless hours of our lives in the temples, reading the holy scriptures. Rather, we had learned about God through a man who had learned to manifest the divine through the instrument of his body. We talked of how the message Jesus brought with him was very different than that which was prevailing, with all of the endless rules one was supposed to follow in order to somehow meet and approximate the divine order. In the prevailing model, one met the divine through molding one's outer form; in this model, union with God was attained by reaching within. The change was radical indeed. For some people, it made immediate sense, but for others, it was a very difficult idea to grasp. I had, at this point, no idea how much further this change would be developed and radicalized after Jesus' death.

If I were to assess the impact we made on these good people from the comments they made to us, I would say that we brought to them new hope by demonstrating a living, breathing manner of reaching God, and of bringing God's presence to earth. Of course, this is exactly what Jesus brought to us. I was gladdened that my brother and I could convey the same message in a way that touched other people's hearts and souls. Here was a vital, living presence of God who could be, and was, effective in the present.

This was not the first time we had been out teaching and healing on our own, for we had done this for a while now. However, with all I had been learning recently, this now took on new meaning. I knew this was how things would be in the future. I would not have Jesus to use as my anchor and mainstay in the same physical way. I would not be able to go back to him in the evening, or at the end of a few days' journey, and tell him of what I had done. He would not be there to share with me his responses, which had always been enlightening. I would not be able to use his physical and spiritual presence as a tool for attunement. It was impossible to imagine how things would be in the future without him. My heart pained me greatly to think of these things. I tried to think in terms of time, and how much longer he would be around. In my mind, I always tried to maximize the time left, for I believed there was so much that all of us had to learn. I reasoned that it would not be God's will for Jesus to leave us before he had taught us what we would need to know to carry on effectively after he was gone.

The mood of the family and neighbors around me was exuberant and very animated, and contrasted with the sad thoughts I was having. James, who usually could at least match the high spirits of any good-natured crowd, was also more quiet than usual. I knew he was pondering these things as well. We did not wish to dampen their rejoicing spirits, for after all, they were celebrating a healing and a renewal of their faith. James and I, on the other hand, were greatly saddened with what we were learning. It had grown very difficult to mask our anticipatory grief and sorrow. It took only a glance at each other to know we were both ready to leave. We said our goodbyes, and made our departure.

It was late afternoon as we made our way back to the group. We spoke a few words as we set out, but quickly fell into a silence in which it seemed we both were feeling and thinking the same things. There was nothing to say to each other. It was great comfort to have James with me, as our brotherhood was a powerful sustaining bond. It was probably the only relationship bond I had which was strong enough to help sustain me in preparation for the greatest of sorrows. For once, I did not feel I could turn to Jesus to help me with what I was experiencing. I needed to attain some perspective and some detachment, and I felt myself pulling back inside myself.

As we neared our group, James turned and asked me if I thought we would be all right when it came to that time when we would have to cope with what was coming. I said we had to believe that this would be true, and, after all, did he not say he would be back after three days? I realized I was doing my best to console James with something we had both heard, but I also realized I was very confused. On the one hand, he had told us he would be back after three days, but I also remembered my dream, and the other events, feelings and circumstances that had been accumulating. These portrayed life without him in the flesh. These were mysteries to me. No matter how hard I thought on them, I could not reconcile them or resolve them in my own mind. I wished I were smarter, so I could figure all of these pieces out, and form them into one comprehensible whole. Yet, at present, I could not do this at all. The complexity was overwhelming.

I decided my best strategy was to continue to accumulate information. If possible, I would go to Jesus, and see if he could help me understand that which seemed so incomprehensible. I did not know if I would have the strength to hear what he might have to say, though I did decide it would ultimately be much better for me to know what we would be facing. At this point, it felt intolerable that the future was so veiled. I had never before experienced this inexorable need to know the future, combined with such anxiety and apprehension about that which I might learn.

Still, I told myself, this dread that you are feeling may be powerful, but is it not true the whole reason Jesus is here is to instill faith, hope and joy? If he must depart, then it must be for the higher good, and there must be a profound reason why this must be. God would not allow him to come, just to leave those who loved him only with a profound sense of sorrow and loss. There would have to be a deep reason for his going at such an early stage, much as there was reason and purpose for his incarnation. There could not be anything in this that was not planned and not necessary to his mission. Yet, no matter which direction my thoughts would take, I could not understand why he would be taken from us so early. It made no sense at all, and it seemed tremendously unfair to all to have him taken away.

I wondered if he wanted to go, if this life were burdensome to him in the extreme. Did he grow weary of the foolishness of men and of the many burdens they wished him to remove? I stopped myself in this thought, for after all, did he not have infinite patience and compassion, and did I not see this every day I was with him? But, I reasoned, surely the human part, that lives with the limitations of the physical body, must be exhausted. It must take an act of will every day to choose to remain in the physical state, rather than to go on to those other realms where he would be so much freer to work. I understood that he chose to descend on earth to do this work, and that this was his ultimate sacrifice. I could also not help wondering how much being incarnate must limit him. Would it limit him to stay on earth longer, when he could be possibly much more effective on other planes, and in other worlds? If he could do so much while restricted within the confines of the human body, how much more could he do if he were unhampered by this condition, free to act in whatever manner he chose?

My mind felt stretched, a familiar feeling that had on many other occasions come up in connection with Jesus' abilities and powers. I believed that my thinking was clearer than it had been, perhaps because in these past few moments, I had managed to detach myself from my own pain and sorrow. I thought I was intuiting some glimpses into the Higher Plan. If what I was thinking were true, then it would surely be much easier for me to let go of that which I could not hold onto in any event. It was difficult to let go of my personal pain and individual perspective on these matters, as my love and adoration of him was complete, and given out of the fullness of my heart, with no holding back. I felt extremely vulnerable, and almost desperate to find some meaning and explanation that would help me to see clearly that which seemed destined to happen. I believed that the more I knew and understood about all of the aspects of this situation, the more mastery I would have over my reactions. I knew I would have to be strong, and I knew I would be given the strength I would need to get me through each situation as it occurred. Yet, the more I tried to grasp the full import of the circumstances with my mind, the more I lost contact with what my heart was feeling. It felt too much to bear. I shifted my attention away from my pain, fearing that I would be swallowed up within it.

I rejoined the group reluctantly, in body only. My heart and spirit were very far away. I did what was necessary, while lost in the intensity of my thoughts and feelings. So many people had need of Jesus' wisdom or and healing; he was always surrounded. I looked at him with great sadness, knowing he would be gone, and fearing I would be lost without him. I was fortunate to have so many loving friends and relatives, yet the human love they gave was so different from the unconditional human and divine love Jesus gave without reservation.

As the embodiment of Love, Jesus brought with him a completeness to the human experience that had never before been fully experienced on earth. Those of us who were touched by this Love would never again be the same way we were before this happened. I wondered about the imprint this Love would have on the collective human psyche, and how this would manifest in all of us after he had moved on. I wondered how he would impact on us from the other side, and what kind of contact we would have. I remembered that he said he would always be there for me, and I hung onto the word "always". I had to believe he meant this literally. I remembered what he had shared with me about future times, and how he had let me know that we would have a very special connection in those times. My mind wandered to many different places, in an attempt to console myself and help myself to realize he would continue to be there, though in a completely different form.

I sought him out as it grew late, but there were people still around him. I needed to be close to him tonight. It did not matter if we were talking, but I needed the closeness of the physical connection. I knew that the spirit connection would provide whatever continuity there would be, and I asked inside myself if it would be there often. I felt his spirit in immediate response, and heard his voice inside of my head, telling me he would be there as often as I needed him to be, whenever I called on him. I fell asleep, still troubled, but reassured that I would not be losing him forever.

CHAPTER 48

TIME PASSED RAPIDLY. I counted each moment I had with Jesus as a precious gift. I wanted to ask him more, and yet I did not want to know. I wanted to think there was much time together stretching out in front of us, and though there were many clues that there was not, I overlooked them in my desire to not feel the pain.

In what was to be our last journey together in the flesh, just the two of us, he asked me to accompany him one afternoon as he walked. The group had stopped at a resting place in the countryside, and we wandered off, much as we had done in the earlier days. It was clear that Jesus had much on his mind. I was eager to hear what he would have to say; yet, at the same time I dreaded his words. I planned to ask him directly about those things I had been thinking, yet I did not know if I would find the courage to do so. My sleep had been deep and seemingly dreamless recently, yet I would wake up with the impression that I had been learning a great deal during the course of the night. It had been frustrating to not be able to remember, and I was looking forward to a more conscious encounter.

Oh, how I adored him! I would gaze at him, and try to memorize every detail of his being as we walked. It was as if I felt I would never have to let go of him if I could just remember every detail of him; how he looked, how he sounded, how he felt, how he smelled, how his energy body presented itself, and how he inspired me always to the highest possible levels of my being. I knew he was aware of what I was doing, and accepted it as something I needed to do. I was so much in awe of him that I was not aware of any difficulties he might be having with what was happening. In my obliviousness, I was aware only of my own pain and struggle. There were moments in these later days when I would come out of this, but overall, I could not imagine what he might be experiencing. If only I had known, or allowed myself to know, what lay ahead for him!

I came out of my daze long enough to realize he had been quiet for a long time. He seemed sad, perhaps sadder than I had ever seen him. I felt deeply for him then, for I knew he carried far greater sorrows than any of us mere humans would ever know. I tried to imagine what he might be feeling, and soon he began talking to me.

He said he knew I had been thinking through things a great deal lately, and that it was true what I had been thinking, all of it. He complimented me, saying that no matter how upset or concerned I grew about a thing, my head remained clear, and I was able to reason through what I saw. This validation made me feel wonderful, and awful, both at the same time, for he complimented my mind at the same time that he confirmed to me that which I dreaded most.

He said that the human part of him was weighted down with what he knew was coming, and that I accurately perceived sorrow in him. He told me, in what was to be a rather lengthy discourse, all he would later tell the twelve of us, as to what was coming and why. He would have to die in order that the greater dispensation would come to pass; so the Holy Spirit could descend upon earth in a way never before imagined by the minds of men. That which would happen in the short run would be very painful for all, including for him. However, all would happen in the service of the Divine Plan and the Divine Will. I must never forget that what would happen was mapped out eons ago, and must be fulfilled to the letter.

He had chosen us for many reasons. We would withstand the trials of these days, and we would go on in his name, teaching that which he had taught us, and would continue to teach us, from another dimension. He would die a cruel death at the hands of ignorant men, but these same men would be doing necessary work, in freeing him up to move into the greater part of his mission. I had great trouble understanding what he was saying, but I kept my silence, and allowed him to continue. I must never lose faith, he said, that all that was happening, had to happen. I must never allow that which I would witness to keep me from loving and forgiving. He told me it would be easy for me personally to grow bitter and shut down my heart from loving freely in the personal sphere, because that was something I had carried with me from previous times, and had a propensity to do whenever I felt hurt over something. This would not manifest as clearly in the area of my work, he said, because I had a tendency to keep these areas separate, insofar as I could. However, he said, it would be of vital importance to me to continue to love from my heart, and, when necessary, to allow my sadness to wash over me, but not to dam up in me.

I heard the words he said, but I do not know whether I truly understood them, then or now. So much has happened, and I have never felt as whole since, as I did in those days. Yet, this is another story, and I must return to the one I am telling...

As if he had known my thoughts about him, he told me that it was true his time during his mission on earth was short, because there was so much more he could accomplish from other spheres. He had come to understand that he had done as much on this earth plane as he could, and he was now summoned to move on and to fulfill, not end, his destiny. The greater work was only just beginning. That which he had done here so far was merely the laying of the groundwork of that which was to come. There would be a time, he said, when his Kingdom would be fully established on earth. None could imagine the shape it would take. Each of the twelve, and all of the other disciples, would play a vital role in disseminating the teachings, and in providing a crucial link between the human in the flesh and the Spirit within. We would be responsible for demonstrating that link repeatedly in this life and in many lifetimes to come, in the many roles we would take on. In this life, we would teach, and heal; some of us would write, myself being one of those. By our presence and by our gifts, people would know us. We would also be hated and reviled, as he was, and some of us might suffer greatly for our truths.

He told me he knew I had been greatly concerned about losing him as my trusted friend and counselor. It was all I could do at this point to hold back the tears that were welling up in my eyes. He said he knew it would not be the same ever again, but he would always be with me. Our bond would be everlasting and not subject to the rules of physical death. Whenever I needed him, I had only to call on him, and I would feel his Spirit and his Presence with me. There would be incarnations where I might forget about this entirely, but I would remember in some deep part of me always. He wanted me to know how very much he had loved me also, and how important it had been for him to have me there by his side in these recent years.

I could not believe what I was hearing at these moments, for I had always felt that I had taken so very much from him, and had not been able to give very much back.

"No," he said, continuing from my thought, "you have given your love to me, even when it hurt you personally. You have been my truest friend on this sojourn. I have many admirers and many followers, and many are those who love me. But, on this plane, there are not many who are my friend as well. And you, you are that. It has given me great comfort and great joy to have you with me, in this dimension and in those others where we travel. Your physical presence beside me at night when we lay beside each other has been as much of a joy for me as it has been for you; do not ever forget this. I have needed you, too. You have brought me much gladness. You have helped to humanize me. When I see your face, I feel as close to being home on this earth plane as I can be. I feel received and seen by you, for the whole of who I am. Only Mary, my mother, also sees me in all of these ways. You and she are bound together by many ties. I have needed to tell you these things, so you will know and remember them, for it is not only you who have benefited from this affiliation."

I was weeping at this point, in sorrow and in gratitude. He put his arms around me and comforted me. He wrapped me in pure Love and Light. For a while, I wept even harder. Gradually, after some time had passed, I began to feel strengthened by the love he sent me, and I began to feel whole once more. I was momentarily embarrassed by my weakness, but immediately he told me I must never be embarrassed by my sorrow, for it is a part of the love that I feel, and there is only strength and good in loving. To not have sorrow means that one has not loved, and there is absolutely no reason to rejoice or to have pride in that.

There was more to share, and though I was exhausted in my emotions, I tried to absorb as much as I could. There were instructions as to what I must do in this life, and challenges I would face. He gave me words of courage that let me know I would meet these challenges, and gave me insight as to what lay on the other side of these obstacles. Although I did not know of what he spoke, I committed to memory as best as I could that which he was saying, that I might have his words to draw upon at those times when I would need them most. Again, he encouraged me that I could contact him whenever necessary, and that I need never feel I was alone in what I would be facing.

We took some time to look at some future lives, where I would once again be playing a role in carrying out the work. Several of these we had discussed on a number of occasions now, but it was as if I needed some final thoughts and words of inspiration, even though these lifetimes would not occur for many centuries to come. His words informed and encouraged me. I hoped that in some manner I would be able to retain them so they would help to inspire me in those times when things grew difficult. He let me know there would be times so discouraging that I would wish to end it all, but that if I persevered, the rewards of my persistence would be great. I would have guardians to help me through, if I would only allow them to do so. He himself would always be available if I would but keep my heart open enough to let him in.

I was much more comfortable considering those times when I would continue to be in a male body, for my physical identification with my male nature was so strong. I could, in my mind's eye, see myself as a scholar, or a leader of men, or as a male religious leader. But I still faltered when I projected myself forward as a female, and saw myself doing those things only men were permitted to do in our time. We had discussed this on a number of occasions now, but this time he said something he had not said before.

"John," he said smiling, "you do not even know how much woman you have within you. It is part of you which makes you so balanced, that you know and draw upon both the woman and the man sides within you. When you are in a woman's body, you will still have the same combination of man and woman within, and it will not feel that so much has changed as you might think. It does not matter in what sex the outer body chooses to manifest, for the work you might do will be the same. It is our times now that say that power can only be carried by the man; this has been different in the past, and will be different again in the future. Look around you at those men in power; do not many of them abuse it in the most horrible of ways? This is because they have over-identified with the male side within them, and they do not know the value of the loving heart and the gentle spirit. These are traits that women know instinctively and reflexively. These traits issue forth from them naturally, as do the progeny from their wombs. These are not traits that would lead them to positions of influence or power in a society such as ours, for these are values of the home and the hearth. As you have seen, the natural piety of women is often far superior to that of men in the temples who preoccupy themselves inordinately with detailed rules and regulations by which people are supposed to live their lives. These men become so engrossed in their details and formalities, that the heart and spirit are lost. It is women who stay close to this naturally, and who will be able to retrieve the true nature of the Kingdom in a time when men will have all but destroyed themselves."

"Do not think that you will be striving to achieve in an inferior vehicle; nothing could be further from the truth. In those times, it will be because you are in a female body that you will be closer to the fundamental truths that will be needed to guide the hearts of men. There will be many opportunities for you to incarnate as a female, in order for you to become accustomed to the vehicle. You will have much man in you then, and you will have much work to do in order to accept yourself as being incarnated in the female. This will coincide with the struggles that men and women both will have in society as a whole with the question of the feminine. It will not be a struggle that you will be facing on your own. These distinctions of male and female are ones that come about as a result of the descent onto earth of spirit into matter; these are not distinctions that have any great importance in the higher realms. What is important is that the balancing of the female and male principles is achieved; and this will not come about easily or without great struggle. I came in male form because this is how I needed to manifest in order to achieve the greatest good for the greatest number of people. Within a female body, I would not have been free in these times to do that which I had to do, nor would people have accepted me in the same manner. In another time, this might have been different, but not now. Mary, in her devotion and her piety, preceded me. Through her receptiveness to the Divine, she was the first person on earth capable of the total surrender and preparation necessary in order that I might be brought into the flesh. Her role must not be underestimated, for it was only through woman that I could manifest. And when once more I manifest, it will once again only be through the feminine that this will be made possible."

I knew now that he was speaking in great mysteries. I comprehended most of what he said, and I knew more than I have put into these pages. Yet, I knew the mysteries were far greater than I could comprehend in this lifetime. I felt my mind spinning in that familiar manner that it did when I knew that the subject under discussion was stretching me beyond the reaches of my mental capacities. I have tried to capture in these words most of what I heard on this day, for not only was it the last truly personal conversation we would have in the flesh, but it also seemed that we covered a great deal of material in the most condensed manner possible.

CHAPTER 49

WE SLOWLY MADE OUR WAY BACK. I had the greatest reluctance to end this time together, but I knew he had much to attend to. My mind was weary, and was probably not able to absorb much more. It seemed I had so much left to ask him. Yet, in a strange way, I suspected I knew now as much as I could understand.

There was one more subject, though, that I felt I needed to ask Jesus about. That subject was the most important one of all, that which would be happening to him, and how this would manifest over time. I also wanted to know specifically in what ways I might be able to be of help. My friend and Master did not think it wise to give me much more of the details than I had already; he said he wanted me to focus on the overall Plan and how to continue to implement it. One of the twelve, he said, would be responsible for the betrayal, but I must understand that this, too, was part of the plan, and as difficult as it might be, I must forgive him. He would not tell me who, and I realized immediately that if he had, I would have done everything I could to change what was coming, even if I knew in advance that my efforts would be futile.

As to what he personally would undergo, he said it would be a time of great suffering for all. I must remember it would be necessary to endure this in order that the greater glory of God be made manifest. As to what I could do, he mentioned that there would be no point if any of us jeopardized our own well-being as well. We would be needed for many years to come, to spread his words, and to teach of the new life he would be bringing back with him.

He asked of me one more thing, probably the first time I can remember that he asked something so personal of me. "Mary will not be dissuaded from viewing the crucifixion, no matter what, and I ask that you be there, for her and for me. My spirit will rest more easily knowing you will be there. Your prayers and your love will be of great help."

I was stunned by the request, but was glad to be able to be of help in this way. Would I have the strength to be of any service at all? Why, why must this terrible thing happen to the most loving of all men? This must be the most horrible thing ever to happen upon the earth, and to he who brought such great blessings to mankind. My eyes, still swollen from the tears I had shed earlier, once more released streams of sorrow. I told Jesus that of course I would do this thing, and it was the very least I could do for him. I only wished it could be me instead of him who would have to undergo this horrible torture. We both fell into silence. Of course, only he could do that which had to be done.

The pain and the hardship loomed large ahead of us. It felt more than my heart could bear. I could not even imagine what thoughts he must be having about these days to come. Yet, still, there was redemption on the other side of all of this horror, and he reminded me of this, that I might keep this in perspective: "There will be days of suffering, and eons of gladness."

I found myself hungry once more for information, for details about that which would come to pass after he returned, and for how long he would appear. I felt so desperate, and needed something to look forward to, to hope for, and to help me to endure the time that stretched out before me. He gave little more in the way of details, saying only that he would be back for a time, as I had seen in my dream. He explained that he would return to show that he could not be killed, and that the Love he came on earth to manifest would continue to reveal itself through him. Then, he would be gone into a realm where he could bring God into the hearts of every man and woman who called upon him. There he would fulfill his purpose, in a manner that he could not do as a physical man walking upon the earth, for he could then manifest through every individual as Spirit. This, then, would be the true meaning behind his death, for he would be released to do the higher work for which this was preparation. He had to come in order that the Spirit of God could be made manifest on earth, and grounded thereon. History would be changed, by the appearance on earth of the eternal manifesting through time. He had to depart in order that the Spirit of God could reveal itself through the hearts of men, not only in this time but in the many times to come.

This was the essence of what he had to say to me as we returned to the others. I tried to anchor every word of what he was saying into my mind. I would want to remember these words for the rest of my life, and I knew I would use them in my teaching. I wanted my mind to function extremely well on this day because of the importance of the words, yet in my emotional body I was saddened more than I had ever been before, at the prospect of the loss of my friend and Master. These feelings seemed selfish to me in light of what I had just been hearing about the meaning and the importance of what would be transpiring. In this manner, I tried to keep perspective on all of this, and yet I fear I failed terribly. The personal loss seemed so huge, and in those moments when I allowed myself to feel the extent of it, I did not know how I would ever be able to bear it.

I knew that what was important was that no matter what I was feeling, I had to carry on with the work, and I would have to find a way to do this. I made a silent prayer request that I would have the strength and resolve to get through this.

I wanted to focus on what was necessary now, and tried to put my focus outward. After all, what would be my pain next to his? It would be he who would be undergoing this horrible ordeal, and nothing could be done, or should be done, to alter the events to come.

My mind was racing once more, and I was desperately wondering what else I could do to help him through this. Reading my thoughts, Jesus responded to me that there was nothing else I could do now, other than to continue to love. However, he was concerned about what would happen to the community of apostles and disciples after he had gone. He thought Peter would be the best person to help the community stabilize and develop, even as it spread out over time. I agreed completely with this choice, for Peter's natural charisma and leadership ability, plus his naturally outgoing personality, were just the right character traits that were needed for this kind of organizational task.

I knew I would not well suited to this, nor would I be nearly as good at this as Peter. I would be better suited to a role as teacher, healer and proselytizer. I was clear about the relationship that I had with Jesus in this life, and I would not have traded anything for this. Still, I was a man of some ambition, and I quelled any envious pangs that came up with what I knew of the opportunities I would have in other lives to play out roles that were important. Even in the midst of all of this, I still found myself having to deal with some of the more grasping aspects of my nature! I felt Jesus' energy smiling through me now, patiently understanding my struggle, accepting these crazy battles I put myself through in my lesser moments.

At that point, an idea struck me so strongly that I was temporarily stunned. I realized that it was this divine acceptance Jesus had of the human condition, and of human frailty, that enabled those with whom he came into contact to release themselves temporarily from the struggle. They could then fly into that realm of freedom, where all is seen and understood, and accepted and loved. I did not have to hate my flesh and my weakness: it was through this Love that I was transformed. If even for a moment I could be greater than who I was, for that moment the divine could shine through me, and I could feel radiant with his Love...

This revelation was very powerful to me. I basked in it, and let it penetrate into the fibers of my being. How blessed it was to be able to let go of fear and struggle, and move into acceptance, understanding and love. This was truly his gift to us, and I wanted to remember this forever. I hoped that in some small ways I would be able to transmit this same feeling to others when they were also struggling with their humanness.

As we approached the area where the group was staying, a young woman hurried up to Jesus, with an urgent request for Him. I wanted to hold onto the afternoon for as long as I could, and I barely heard what she had to say. Yet, with this interruption I realized I would be saying my goodbyes in many ways now, with many kinds of different occurrences. Every event now would be colored with a very different emotional layer on top of that which was actually occurring. I observed myself distancing from the moment, and attempting to put it in perspective of the larger scheme of things.

If I had been able to change things at this point, I would have wanted to find a way to hold onto the strength and the courage to face events that he had imparted to me today. I think that was what I was trying to do when I wanted to hold on to the afternoon. Although there had been much grief, in these afternoon moments I had been given the strength and sustenance to carry on in what was to be. I had faced the truth squarely, and had seen that I would be able to carry on in faith, knowing that which I knew. I sensed that this was a very special state. I had no idea that I would not be able to fully retain it.

As we passed back into the energy of the group, and Jesus attended to the problem that was pressed on him, I found comfort in the old feelings, which included anticipation for the future. I was at odds with the prevailing group thought because of what I now knew. I tried to find a place where I could feel comfortable in the morass of conflicting ideas and feelings. It was more comfortable here in the short run. I observed my mind as I settled down for the evening, and marveled at my continued wishfulness that things would never change, in the face of the most powerful evidence to the contrary. I realized, in observation, how fragile a thing is the human mind, and how clouded over it can become by human needs and desires. I, who had always considered that my mind was exceptionally strong and clear, now found myself in a position where I watched the illusions sweeping over my mind and attempting to settle therein. And perhaps worse than this, I observed my desire to have them settle in, and comfort me in my pain, believing that they might somehow prevent me from having to face the inevitable.

As I fell asleep that night, next to Jesus once more, I pondered these many things. With his energy surrounding me and within me, I was strong and courageous. Yet, I remembered that I had seen the weakness of my own mind, and wondered what I would be like when he was gone.

CHAPTER 50

THE DAYS AND WEEKS THAT FOLLOWED FLEW BY IN A HAZE. There was much movement and activity. Internally I was stunned, yet there was much to do, and I tried to keep my focus outward as much as possible. I was saying my goodbyes at every step of the way, and had to work in order to keep from being melancholy. James and I buttressed each other during this time. His good humor was one of the prime ingredients that helped me to get through this time.

Jesus had many people to attend to. I noticed that he began at this time pulling away by himself on more occasions than previously. When I noticed him doing so, I always sent a prayer with him. I could not imagine what he must be undergoing, but I knew that within him there was much pain and sorrow. The energy field around him was generally more expanded since that afternoon on the mountain when God spoke; yet I noticed in the recent few days, it had grown larger and brighter than ever. How I longed to know what occurred in those times when he communed with the Universal Spirit; how I longed to know what filled him and expanded him so!

Mary, his mother, was with us now, as she knew this would be his final sojourn. He had told her what would be happening, because he knew her grief would be infinitely greater if she did not know ahead of time, and if she were not able to participate in these times. Mary told me later that when he told her, she already knew. Many signs had come to her that pointed out the coming events. When she saw him at her doorstep on that day when he came to speak to her, she knew it was now time for the prophecies to be fulfilled. No words needed to be spoken between them; there had been an immediate shared emotion of dread, grief and anticipation, and great sorrow as well as elation. The human parts felt the dread, the grief and the sorrow; the spiritual parts knew the anticipation and elation.

I looked after her specially; I cherished and adored her as I did her son. I was happy to be around her, and to help and support her. Now that she was without a husband, she had no man to look after her. I made a point of making sure that she knew she had a special ally in me. For me, it was as if by being close to her, I was also close to her son. I found her warm radiance irresistibly draw me into the fullness of her energy field. They felt so very similar energetically. There was always such great comfort in being within the space of the energy field of either one of them.

In that space, there was a warm blanketing of love and compassion, which expressed itself through the human vehicle, but was clearly divine in origin. There was no mistaking this, for no merely human love can approximate the joy and the bliss that emanates from the divinity within.

Perhaps I should say a few more words about Mary before I go on with my chronicle. Her stature in my eyes has only increased as the years have gone on. At this point, I regarded her with an awe and reverence that I reserved only for Jesus. How perfected a vehicle she must be, that she would be chosen to provide the womb and the home which bore such a child. It was she from whom he would learn his earliest lessons about life and love and humanity in all of its vicissitudes. Her faith was perfected. She emanated such a sweetness and compassion that to be near her was like basking in the warming rays of the sun on a chilly day. In her presence, I felt myself transformed into a man of less roughness, and more wholeness. I felt more relaxed, and comfortable in being myself when I was around her. When I was around her, the world seemed in perfect order, and it seemed that all was occurring as it should and as it must. The only other person who gave me this feeling was Jesus. The only time I could achieve this state on my own was when I was in a state of deep meditation and prayer. Yet, around either of them, I could move into this state with ease, and transition into it almost without noticing that a transition had been made. I knew that testified to the perfected levels of communion that both of them had with God, and this necessarily conveyed itself to those who were exposed to their energy fields.

Mary was indeed beautiful, both on a physical level, and on all the levels of her field. As she grew older, and as she came into the fullness of her being, she grew even more beautiful. She inspired me with her movements and her grace, and with the love that flowed unceasingly from her heart. Never have I known such a woman as she, and perhaps never again will there be a woman with her fullness of spirit. She was blessed, and blessed the world in turn with her gift, which she freely gave. She was always tender with me, and there was a great affection between us. Like James, she knew how to nudge me out of my intense seriousness, and to move me into a lighter-hearted view of the world. She would tease me gently; this never failed to move me out of my mind and into the reality of the usually gentler environment that surrounded us.

At this time of which I am writing, our relationship was still young and developing. I sought out her company when I could, and made sure that whatever her need, it was attended to. I do not know how this protectiveness for her developed, but it was extremely strong in me, and felt instinctive. I trusted it, and followed it. Never did I feel from her that my solicitude for her well-being was unwelcome or intrusive; in fact, almost from the very beginning of our relationship, I felt that she welcomed me and my attentions, and she was grateful for them. Others attempted to win her favor by ingratiating behaviors; but she always sensed where there were ulterior motivations, and was very good at shutting these others out by the firmness of her inattention to them.

I could spend many pages writing about Mary, and her virtues and integrity of character, but this would be another whole story. I was glad she was on the journey. I was also concerned about her, and made a private resolve that I would look out for her throughout. As I made this mental resolve, I heard Jesus' voice inside my head, speaking a resounding "good", and I took note of this. Something inside me said this decision was very important, and I resolved I would do my very best to carry out whatever I had to do. I felt honored and blessed to have the privilege of knowing and being close to her and her son, and wanted to do whatever I could to make their passage through these perilous times easier. In this way, I would not only be serving them, but I would be forgetting myself as well. I knew I would on many occasions want a reason to move out of my own pain.

An incident that to me, well summarizes Mary's spirit occurred during this time. We were resting under a tree, after a long day of walking. She asked me about my mother, Salome, who had married her brother, Zebedee. She wanted to know how it was for my mother to have her two sons gone from her home, and from the family business. I told her of how it was when we first accepted Jesus' call, and how my mother had been prepared in advance by a dream. I told her that Salome had at times joined us, as had Zebedee, and that they were both very excited at the great good thing that was happening. I knew she was sad not to have our company on a daily basis, but she was very happy in spirit for us, and for the important work we were undertaking. I told her that there were times when she became overzealous for us, but that overall her heart was glad for us. It gave her pride to think that she and Zebedee had raised us well, that we should be chosen as emissaries for the message of love Jesus was bringing into the world.

I asked Mary what it was like for her, to be in the position that she found herself, both as the mother of this heavenly messenger, and as the human being on earth who knew him most intimately. She grew radiant as she thought about my question, and answered that in him she had found the answer to all of life's questions. In Jesus, she found a Love she had not ever imagined, even in her most prayerful moments. She felt a communion with Jesus from the time he was in the womb, and had felt connected with him spiritually and mentally ever since then. She could contact him whenever she chose, a communion that inspired and guided her through everything she did. Through Jesus, her heart grew larger than she had ever thought possible, and her awareness became almost iridescent with the complexities of understanding the perfection that is in all things and all people.

She turned suddenly sad, and began talking of the sacrifice to come. She knew it must be, and that it would take all of her strength and her prayers to withstand it. She knew she must see it through, and show all who were there that she never stopped believing in him. The sadness of the moments must not be allowed to interfere with the greater purpose and Truth. Through her sorrow, she would shine with the Light he brought into the world, and would continue to bring, in even greater measure, from the other side. His bodily defeat would mean nothing in the face of the spiritual victory that would begin manifesting at the moment of his death.

She was strong and serene as she spoke, and I knew she did not waver in her convictions. Her strength and her courage warmed me, for if a mother could speak thus of the bodily death of the child of her flesh, then who was I to be so concerned about my personal loss of my dearest friend? The light of her spirit was unwavering and true, and provided a beacon for me that would prove to be an unyielding source of support and strength for me in the months and years to come. On this occasion, I took her hand and shared with her how she inspired me, and how much I admired her faith and courage. We smiled at each other through moistened eyes, and through a shared love.

As the days went on, and when I began to lose my courage, I thought of Mary, and the far greater sacrifice she would be offering and suffering. I remembered her equanimity in the face of this great catastrophe, and was lifted up by the remembrance of her spirit. Her warmth and devotion only grew as time went on. She had far more courage than I to fully confront and suffer her pain. My heart, though open, was not nearly so free. I wanted to block my pain with clouds of obscurity and forgetting. When I thought of Mary, I could allow myself to be present to my experience. She inspired me to the fullest possible experience of my human self.

It was a paradox that in my fully human self, I found God within me. Though this was the same truth Jesus had taught me in many ways, my assimilation of this feminine experience felt very different to me, in a way I cannot fully explain. All I can say is that when I found this through her, it was like I went down through the depths and the darkness, and emerged once more into the Light. With Jesus, the experience was a more direct experience of the Light, though I was always aware, even if on the fringes of my awareness, that this Light transmuted the darkness. Mary's way was more of a mystery to me, and intrigued me greatly. At the same time, I had a tremendous fear that, left on that path on my own, I would be swallowed up forever in the darkness before I could emerge into the Light.

Mary was intrepid and fearless in all she did. She was now facing the future that was almost upon us with this same spirit. She looked a bit older, and somewhat weary. I could feel that within her she was marshalling and galvanizing her vast interior resources for that which was to come.

CHAPTER 51

I WILL NEVER FORGET THAT DAY BEFORE WE TRAVELED into Jerusalem. I awoke suddenly, before dawn, with a mixed sense of fear and dread. A chill washed over me. I knew that events had been irrevocably set in motion. I wanted to go back into a sleep state, into unconsciousness, but my state of alertness was far too great. I walked outside, for we were staying in the homes of followers in Bethany, and looked at the starlit sky.

I prayed to God for the strength and the courage that I would need. As I prayed, I felt myself expanding, as if my body had no boundaries at all, larger and larger, until I reached the sky and stretched endlessly outwards. No longer was I one isolated man, alone and afraid. I was one with the Universe. As my heart beat, it beat with the pulse of the One Being, over and over again. The feelings I experienced ranged from a state of great bliss, which moved into detachment and acceptance, back to bliss again, and then to detachment. The only state I have ever experienced which was in any way comparable was that day on the hillside with Jesus when he allowed me to experience his state of being one with God.

On this occasion, however, the experience felt more exterior than interior somehow. I felt a sense of peace unlike anything I have felt before or since. It felt like floating in a sea of unlimited consciousness, with the knowing that all that exists is in God, that every pulse of man is a pulse of God, and that there is in reality no separation between them. In this state, I felt utterly free and unconfined, not desirous of anything. I stayed in this state for some time, oblivious to time, or to my surroundings. I would start to wonder if I should come back, but then I would let go of my concern, and continue to wander in the vastness of that undivided universe. I felt more freedom and more release in those moments than I have ever felt since. Eventually, I began to hear the noises of dawn, the animals and the people stirring, and I saw the first light of dawn appearing on the horizon. I came slowly out of my reverie, and as I did so, I knew that my memory of this experience would help me through times when I felt constrained and limited in the flesh.

There would be a lot of activity today, and many preparations. Mary and Martha were busy preparing a feast in their home. People began coming in and out at an early hour with the items that would be needed. The twelve, plus a few others, met early in prayer and meditation. A special emphasis was placed this day on the immense good that had been bestowed on us all. There was a strong need to consolidate in our minds all of the wondrous blessings that had been given to us and through us, and to take stock of how much we had grown in Spirit. We thanked God for the opportunity to know and work with each other in the Lord's work, and prayed for many such opportunities in the time to come. We asked for strength and endurance in the trials ahead. Peter bestowed a special blessing on Jesus, to help lighten his burden in the time ahead. We did not know the exact timing of the events to come, but we all knew that the time was soon.

Lazarus was the most vocal of all of us. Since he had been raised from his tomb, he was fervent in his beliefs and offered all his support to Jesus. He vociferously challenged those who did not understand or believe what had happened. He felt the miracle that had been worked on him was testimony that could not be refuted. His spirit had been in a state of suspension, he said. He had been bathed in light, and communed with spirits and angels. He had been informed that he would not be moving on, but was to re-enter and re-animate the body at Jesus' command, as proof that Jesus worked with the powers of God. His testimony about this was very enlightening, as I had not understood what had happened to him during those four days that he had been dead. I recalled my initial disbelief that Lazarus had actually died. All of us thought that he must have been merely sleeping.

Yet, during the actual raising of Lazarus from death, Jesus manifested an energy of an entirely different order than I had yet seen in any of the many healings I had witnessed. The vibrational level and intensity were matched only by what James, Peter and I had witnessed on the mountaintop not so long ago. I could feel in those moments that the powers of the Universe were at his disposal, and was awed. Lazarus commented on the same thing. He said that his feeling as he was commanded back into his body was that the entire history of mankind was being raised above itself, because of the glory of God, and for the glory of God. He was a man transformed, and served as proof of the living presence of God in the midst of men.

I was fascinated to hear Lazarus' comments. There was now no one more ready to support Jesus and his work than Lazarus. It was fitting that in these days we were meeting in his home. The entrenched political powers had been very upset by the raising of Lazarus, for they felt that Jesus' following would now swell interminably. They were afraid for their position, and for their power. We had heard many rumors, and even had informants who kept us abreast of the latest with Caiaphas and his men. We knew Jesus was perceived as a dangerous nuisance. It was tragic that he was so misunderstood, for he wanted nothing to do with political power. He only desired that the hearts of those who ruled be guided by the wisdom of God, and not by their greed or quest for power.

This morning, we took a long time in discussion after our prayers. This was memorable to me, because we had time to be together, to plan and to learn some last lessons from our Master in the flesh. We were unhurried today, despite the activity around us. Jesus took his time in instructing us. I was never more aware than today of his ability to speak on one level, and at the same time to be present within each of us, giving more personal instruction. I knew that as this was occurring in me, it was also happening in others. This ability always amazed me.

While he taught, I looked within, and I envisioned and experienced a permanent space being carved inside my heart, that would always hold room for Jesus. This space had been there, but now was being set or fixed somehow. I knew at the time how important this was for me, because I knew well my tendency to obstruct my feelings when I felt pain over some loss. This image felt like a gift, for I knew it could never be completely blocked. I knew that I would need only my will to access this place, and it would be opened to me. I remembered that experience long ago when Jesus had unblocked the many obstacles I had placed over my heart over many lifetimes, and how on that day I accepted him as my Master. And now, almost three years later, he was giving me a gift that would help me to remember the lessons I had learned. It was the perfect gift. I was deeply touched. I wondered what the others were experiencing, and if they were as touched by their experience.

We did not focus today on the events of the near future, though they hung over us like a dark cloud. Instead, the focus was on the future beyond these times, in which we would be carrying the Word of God to many people in different lands. Each of us had particular talents, and we were to use them as best we could to individualize the manner in which the message was being delivered. We knew the Holy Spirit would descend upon us, that we would be inspired to speak, to teach, and to heal, and that we would not need to fear the Holy Spirit would fail us.

Our afternoon was leisurely. This leisure was much needed and appreciated. By the time of the late afternoon meal, we were relaxed and in good spirits. The meal was a sumptuous feast, and we enjoyed each other in a way that we had never, before or since. There were some serious moments early in the evening, with Mary anointing Jesus' feet, and Judas protesting the costliness of the ointment, but this seriousness soon faded. Maybe it was because of the incredible tension we were facing, and maybe it was because we knew there would never be a time like this again, but the house was full of laughter and good cheer. The buoyancy of love between us and for Jesus knew no bounds. It was, as I look back over my life, perhaps the most joyous of all the times I have experienced. It was as if we had all chosen to live as fully as we could in the moment we were now sharing, to forget our past and our future and just concentrate on what we had before us, in these rooms. There was gaiety and joy, and a kinship that was moving and easy. It felt as if we were reaping some of the fruits of our labor in being able to enjoy each other so, and to luxuriate in the loving glow of this man who had brought us all together.

Jesus was very cheerful, and laughed a great deal. This was the first time I had seen him enjoy himself so fully. I loved it that he had this opportunity. His life and his task were onerous, and though he was always a man of good cheer, it was not often that he had time to relax socially in this manner. We were all glad to see him enjoy himself.

The evening came to an end all too soon. Martha reminded us of the lateness of the hour, and how the Master would need his rest for the journey tomorrow, as would the rest of us. We reluctantly pulled ourselves up from the spots we had been enjoying, and broke up the socializing. I went to my pallet, energized by the evening. It took me a long time to fall asleep, caught between the good cheer of the evening and the dread of the days to come.

CHAPTER 52

I AM NOT GOING TO REPEAT HERE WHAT OTHERS and I have said about the entry into Jerusalem, and the events that followed. I intend to track some of what this was like from an insider's perspective, and how we passed through these days, knowing what was to come.

In the morning, we held an especially moving prayer circle. It seemed as if the entire heavenly host was with us during this time, and I felt immeasurably strengthened and fortified. We entered Jerusalem in full consciousness of that which was to be, though most of us were not aware of the significance of the myriad of details that made up the pattern. Each of us understood according to what we could absorb and bear. I know that, for myself, this capacity could vary greatly with the day or the hour.

The moments now had an additional resonance: from my perspective, it seemed that the events were unfolding not only in this time, but also in absolute time, in which others had viewed them from other times and other places. I also knew that these events would be recorded for the many generations to come. This gave them an added depth, and an added density somehow, in a manner that I cannot explain in a more adequate fashion.

It was heartwarming and gratifying to witness the large crowds who had turned out to greet Jesus, and to praise him. Many had heard of his raising of Lazarus from the dead. This caused a great number more to join the ranks of those who would glorify him. This also caused a great reaction in the hearts of those who feared for their worldly power with Jesus near. I saw all of this, with my heart and my mind focused on the days ahead, and the difficulties we would all be facing. When Jesus spoke to us and to the crowds, it was with great intensity, and with the focus of a man who has much left to say and little time left in which to say it. I attempted to soak in every word, as I am sure all of us did who knew what was occurring. It was easier to focus on the words that were being said than on the reason that he was saying them now.

As we passed by the gates of Jerusalem, my heart nearly stopped beating. I experienced feelings of finality here. A part of me wanted to die at this moment, and to not have to go through what was coming. Then I remembered how Jesus had asked me to be present throughout this, for his mother and for him. Once more, my reason was restored. I wondered if his asking me to be there for him had more to do with Mary, and his knowing that I would need every possible motivation to keep on going, than it did with any real need he felt he would have for me. My idealization of him was strong, and it was hard to imagine him being so vulnerable, though I knew that the pain he would be undergoing would be excruciating. I hoped I would be strong enough to stand tall beside Mary, so she would have a man to lean on in this horrible hour to come. She was the dearest of all women, and would be in grievous pain, no matter how well prepared she was.

We had many friends in Jerusalem, and many offers of housing. The times were perilous, and it was good to have safe refuge. Many people had need of Jesus now, and many more than ever were eager to hear his words, or just to stand in his healing presence. We headed over to the Mount of Olives, which was to be our station over the next few days. The weather was balmy. It was good to have a place away from the noise and din of the city in which to relax and prepare. Most nights we stayed here to sleep, although Jesus did spend one night away, a particularly long night for me. On that night, however, we did meet in the sleep state, which helped me tremendously.

On the other nights, we slept outside on the top of the hill. We slept in a garden, around a table. He and I slept facing each other, his energy enfolding me. Though there was someone on his other side, he always slept closest to me. There was never a more comfortable sleep than this for me, for in this sleep was perfect peace, with the energy of divine serenity permeating through my consciousness. No matter how troubled I was feeling during the daytime, his energy never failed to calm me into a tranquility which reassured me that all that happened was in divine order, and would unfold perfectly, in its own time. Later, I would think back to these days and marvel at the serenity I found in this sleep. For the rest of my days, I suffered from disrupted sleep, sleep in which I could never again find perfect peace.

One morning, when everyone was off doing something, I went back to the sleeping area in the garden to retrieve my journal. It had showered after we had arisen. I looked at the puddle of rainwater on the spot where Jesus had slept. He slept in this same spot by me each night. His spot was almost at the end of the table, in the most comfortable spot, and my spot was at the end of the table, facing him. As I looked at the puddle of rainwater, I noticed there was a faint oil slick in several spots in the water. I realized that this was from oils that had stained his robe while he was traveling.

In a reverie, I watched a small black snake slither across the area. He had a funny way of moving; by balling up, then stretching out and slithering, then continuing this routine until he was out of sight. I stood there for what could have been a minute of time, or what could have been an hour. Tears flowed down my cheeks as I realized that these spots of oil on the water would soon be all that was physically left to attest that the Master had lived. At this moment, it was as if he had already gone, and these traces were all that remained. I was disoriented, and did not know if I was in a dream state, or if this was waking reality. I recognized, in a sudden insight, that the snakes' movements represented the teachings on reincarnation. The balling up of the snake represented the moments of death, and the between-life state. The shooting out and slithering of the snake represented the physical lives in between. This image gave me comfort, for it reminded of how infinitesimally small this time was in the scope of things. No matter how painful and tortuous a time this might be, it was in the service of the greater plan, which would unfold over the course of many lifetimes.

After I came out of my reverie, I stayed at this spot for what seemed to be a long while. The others were in morning prayer. I longed to join them, but could not. I was caught in this other world, perched between this time and the other times, and needed to feel separate from the events occurring now. I had needed perspective, and a sense of the grander design, and here, as I stared at these oil spots, I found what I was looking for. As insignificant as it might seem, the image of this oil slick was a particularly powerful one for me, one that came back to me many times over the course of my lifetime when I remembered these final days. The water would soon dry, and the oil would soak into the ground, but the image was to remain with me as a reminder of the temporality of all things, especially the life of the Master.

James and I were particularly close at this time, and spent much time together. The disciples were involved in many different activities during these final days of Jesus' life, and we were not always together in a group. There were many requests for prayer and healing from the many followers who had greeted Jesus on his way into Jerusalem. All of us took part in these healings. Of course, all who came wanted to be personally healed by Jesus, but the volume of people was too high, and we were filled with Spirit and able to do the work as well. Paradoxically, it was a time of promise for us, for we were working at peak levels, and were full with the sense that we could do this work with which we were charged. It is true that at this point we were dependent on the spiritual energy Jesus channeled through us. However, he had promised us that in the near future, the Holy Spirit would descend upon us, and we would then be able to do this work on our own, in this land and in others. So now, we had a taste of that which was promised to us for the future time, and it felt glorious and free. There were times when James and I were almost ecstatic at what was happening through us, to help others. At times, we were almost like young boys in our enthusiasm, but then we would look at each other, or something would happen that would bring us back to the reality of the time in which we found ourselves, and our enthusiasm would be tempered by the sobering truths of the time.

Peter organized men to help keep the crowds away from the location where we had settled. His organizational and leadership skills were exemplary. He had tremendous instincts for such work, and always seemed to anticipate the need for it before problems arose. My sense of this was that a part of him was permanently attuned to what might be occurring in the background or backdrop of whatever situation in which we found ourselves. This seemed to be a sixth sense for him. I worked hard to try to cultivate a similar kind of awareness, but I was always much more proficient at tuning in to the events in my inner reality or in the world of spirit, than I was at keeping alert to events on the periphery of my physical world. Peter's gatekeeping gave us the time and freedom to rest, and to converse and plan in these crucial days. Much of our time was spent in crowds, working, and this could be extremely exhausting. We truly needed the time that he helped us to keep to ourselves, in order to rejuvenate and rest.

Jesus was active as I had never seen him before. He was in good spirits, and seemed to have tremendous amounts of energy. Yet, by nightfall each night he seemed worn, and drawn. He was invited to dine at the homes of many supporters in Jerusalem, and accepted those invitations that he could, taking the core group of us with him. This included the twelve of us, plus his mother, Martha, and the other Marys. Though he was invited to sleep at the homes of his supporters, he returned with us. He told us he had no home on earth except with us, and that he felt it important we be together as much as possible in these days. The women were encouraged to stay in the comfort of these homes, and mostly they did so.

By night, we prayed under the stars, and fell asleep gathered near each other. Each night before I fell asleep, I would gaze at the vastness of the sky above me. In it, I would recognize the immensity of God's plan, and feel the wonder that it could be designed in such a way that an individual man such as I could be touched in such a profound manner. The human, fearful part of me wished I could leave the earth along with my Master, not only so that I would never have to face the pain of losing him, but also so I could leave behind the many limitations of the body, and move into those vast spaces where freedom and movement were to be had. I knew this was not to be for many years, and I knew I would have to reconcile these ethereal yearnings with the corporeal reality I would be facing.

I wanted to solidify in my mind the memory of lying under the night sky, along with all of the feelings that it evoked, so that as time went on I might be able to recall the mystery and the grandeur of those evenings spent under the sky beside my Master. I was transfixed when with him, and when I was within that energetic atmosphere that he carried with him, I was in a state that I compare to heaven on earth. I truly believe Jesus lived in a natural state of bliss a great deal of the time. This state translated to every cell of my body when I was near him. In this state, it was possible to be completely merged with him, and to be subsumed by this feeling of complete harmony, yet at the same time to feel completely separate and supremely aware of my individuality. I adored him completely, and without reservation, and yearned to lose myself completely in him. Yet, paradoxically, as I did so, I became more fully myself. In thus becoming more aware of my true self, I became more fully aware of the false boundaries I placed on my selfhood. I loved him more than I ever thought possible. This gave me the greatest joy, and it also terrified me horribly.

Mostly on these nights, I did not remember any dreams. It was as if there was so much going on in the outer world that my nighttime response was to go deeply into a state of no remembering. Only there could I forget completely that I would soon be losing this man whom I loved so dearly, and on whom I had so grown to depend. Part of me wished that he and I could spend the nighttime together too, in those dream journeys I so loved, but I knew he had much to prepare for, and so did I. I, too, needed the time away, even if it was only at night, to be separate and to bolster my sense of selfhood at a time when I felt I was in danger of crumbling away, lost with the loss of my beloved friend and teacher.

On this one night, however, I had the most extraordinary dream. I have remembered it clearly always. It has carried me through some of the most difficult of times. I dreamt this dream on the night preceding what was to be the last full day we had with Jesus. It was the next evening that we had our last meal together. I have lost the memory of how the dream began. I know only that it began with some preliminary scenes that seemed rather ordinary; maybe this apparent ordinariness is why I have not retained this part in my memory.

My first memory is of being with Jesus and a number of the disciples, in a small dusty town where we are gathered, listening to him.

"People from the town begin to gather around us, to hear what he has to say. Jesus is teaching that the Kingdom of God is within, and how each person can access that part of themselves through prayer and meditation. I remember those times when I have felt his presence deep inside of me, and how his words or his guidance was unfailingly correct.

Then, he is gone, and I know that the twelve are scattered over many different places. There are people around me, people who seek to hear and understand the teachings of Jesus, and who have heard much about him and the works he did. He is physically gone from the earth, and I feel a great responsibility to carry on with his work.

For a moment, I feel great fear and hesitation, wondering how I can possibly ever convey his greatness through my own much lesser voice. I say a quick prayer, and suddenly I am filled inside with his presence, much as in the days when he walked on the earth. The surety of his presence and his energy replaces my fear and my hesitation. I feel replete with this inner light. I speak, and I say that which needs to be said. I pray, and I heal, and the Christ within me does that which needs to be done. I serve as a channel for this energy, which heals me as it heals others. The energy comes in abundance, and I know there will be as much as is needed. I trust in this completely, much as I trusted the Master when he was on earth.

During this time that I am working, I rejoice in the knowing that the Master will always be there to guide me and to work through me, and through others who will call upon him. It is a great comfort to me to feel his spirit moving through me, and to know he will never be gone from me. I have missed his physical presence grievously. I rejoice also that I will continue to strengthen through him, and that I will be able to impart this to others. I am on the other side of the darkness of my grief now, where I can truly feel and know that all that happened was not in vain, but for the most glorious and transcendent of reasons."

I awakened, filled with the sense that all that was happening was occurring in the completeness of the Divine Plan, and knowing that all fear and worry was a squandering of my energy. I took the dream to be a deep reassurance that I would be able to carry on not only as I was supposed to, but with a joy and a sense that Jesus Christ would always be there with me, in all of my endeavors. I was tremendously relieved to know this, and also to know that one day I would no longer feel that my grief was so overwhelming as to overshadow my consciousness.

It went through my mind that perhaps this dream was only telling me what I would want to hear. I momentarily wondered what I would do if the reality of my situation turned out to be drastically different than the dream version. This thought only stayed with me for a moment, however, for I recalled those times when I had dreams with similar qualities in tone and in feeling. I remembered that these dreams had come to support me and give me courage. They had not failed me, but rather had always presented me with the truths I needed to hear. The beauty and the encouraging power of these dreams made a deep impression on me. In this instance, I knew from a place deep within that this dream, as well, came to bring to me important truths.

As completely as I trusted Jesus, and his reassurances to me about the paths in my future, I look back now on this dream and the power it had on me. I realized that because it had come from within me, and not from another, the impact was stronger. It was one thing to hear him say to me that he would always be with me, if only I would call on him. It was quite another to have a glimpse into my future, and to see and feel this very thing for myself. I find it easier to hold onto that which I feel from inside, than that which I hear as an idea, even though in this case I had absolutely no reason to doubt what Jesus had told me. There were times when I held onto this dream with all of my mental capacity, for there were times when I was so grief-stricken and desolate that I could not see my way through the darkness. On this very morning, I had little idea how extremely important this dream would be to me in future times. Yet, instinctively I knew I must write it down as soon as I had the opportunity, and that it would be with me for some time to come. The morning was very active, and I found no time in which to write. In the middle of the afternoon, I stole a few moments and recorded my dream.

CHAPTER 53

ON THE EVENING OF THAT FINAL SUPPER TOGETHER, my heart was breaking. In these last days, I realized more than ever that my joy was constant in Jesus' presence. As I have said many times, it was always a delight to experience his energy, to learn from him, and to soak up his wisdom. I felt utter devotion and love for him when I was with him. Now, as I sat beside him in these final hours together, I wanted to be as close to him as I could, to absorb what last light and hope and strength I could from him. In the human experience, it was all that I would have of his direct, humanized divine energy to last me through so many lifetimes. I could not get enough. I rested my head on his chest, to take in all I could of his heart energy. I wanted to remember forever how he felt, and what his energy was like. This was the only way I knew to directly experience the physicality of his being.

When he washed our feet, I felt both honored and overcome by grief. I wanted to believe that none of this was true, and that his leaving had all been one of my imaginings. How could such a thing happen, to him of all people? How could this happen to me, and to all of us who needed him so? My mind was a cloud of swirling thoughts. I tried to escape from the pain of my heart into the thoughts of my mind, but there I found only confusion, and no clarity. Only within my heart did I find clarity, and that clarity felt more than I could bear. I did my best to keep myself collected on the outside, though there were times when I could not keep the tears from gathering in my eyes.

When I found out that it was Judas who would betray him, my reaction was blind rage and disbelief. How could my brother be so deluded, so mistaken? His betrayal was not only a betrayal of Jesus, but of all Jesus had taught him. I felt he was also betraying all of us, and all we stood for. My thoughts towards him were not at all charitable. I had never before felt that I wanted to kill a man, but now I understood that feeling as it surged within me in a sudden mad wave. Immediately, I calmed as I listened to Jesus' voice in my head, telling me that this is how it must happen. He said Judas would need the forgiveness of us all, for what he did, he did out of ignorance and lack of understanding. This I could not mentally fathom, but the energy that accompanied these words had an extremely calming effect on me. I knew I would be wrestling with this for some time to come, but for now, there were more important things on which to focus my attention and my energy.

As I sat beside Jesus, I felt bathed in the radiance of his light, and cleansed by the purity of his soul. I wanted to remember how this felt forever. I hoped that the courage it gave me now would still be available for me in those later times when I would have need. His energy was different than usual, somehow even more powerful and vibrant. At times during the meal, there was a good deal of noise and talking, and all I wanted to do was to be quiet and take in all I could of his presence. I felt, or at least hoped, that my attention and my caring provided some degree of support for him too, in these crucial times.

. When we partook of that first communion, I actually felt I was taking in his energy, and that it became part of me. It was as if the blood that ran through my veins was somehow quickened, and the density of my flesh was lifted into a higher vibratory rate. It was an experience that moved me out of the normal range of experience, and into something that partook of the mystery of his incarnation into flesh. Through this ritual, we were incorporating his divinity into the substance of our own flesh, much as he translated his divinity into flesh through incarnating into the body of Jesus. It was as if the entire room lifted up, in a collective experiencing of this mystery. For this moment, through his ability to transmute his divinity into the wine and the bread that he fed us, we experienced the divine within us. From this time on, flesh and blood would forever be mixed with the divine, accessible to all who sought this union.

283

The room was hushed for some brief moments, as we experienced the awe and the epiphany that had been brought about by this experience. We were all similarly affected by this ritual, which would come to symbolize his handing over of the new covenant between God and man.

As he spoke to us at length, I was painfully poised between wanting to absorb and remember his every word, and the inner turmoil of my emotions, which kept vying for my attention. He was never more charismatic or filled with Spirit than on this night. In all he said, there was much hope in the midst of the great sorrow. It was hard to know how to react, for I knew the work ahead of us would be vital, but my breaking heart seemed to command the bulk of my attention. As tremendously important as the work was, I was overcome with the impending personal loss of my closest friend and my Master. At some point on this evening, I made a decision that the work had to come first, and I would deal secondarily with my personal grief. As he prayed for us, I felt renewed strength and resolve to carry through with whatever I must do. After all, was he not the perfect model for us, he who was going through such personal trials and sorrow in order to show God's way to the masses?

As the evening came to a close, we left and made our way back to the garden where we had been staying. Jesus asked James, Peter and I to stay awake as he went and prayed. None of us could stay awake for more than a few moments. I have oftentimes wondered how I could have possibly fallen asleep, and how I was not able to do as he requested on such an important evening. I know now that the weight of the thing to come was so heavy, that those moments of unconsciousness in slumber were my defense against the painful awareness of what I felt I could not possibly bear. For many years, I could not forgive myself for this thing, for reacting as if the most important thing was my pain. What about what he was going through, the immensity of what he was facing, and his need in these moments for the prayerful support of his friends?

CHAPTER 54

WHEN THEY CAME FOR HIM, and when Judas betrayed him by his kiss, I was completely sickened. We were powerless to help. We had known this would happen, and had to happen. I knew that Jesus had asked me to be present with him, and for Mary, through the ordeal on the cross. What was now paramount in my mind was that I needed to do whatever was necessary to make sure this would happen.

I sprang into action as I never had before. I slipped away into the stealth of the night, and followed behind from a distance as they took away my beloved Master. I felt surges of hatred for them. Even in these moments of his trials, I felt Jesus' presence within me, guiding me into compassion and a more balanced state of mind. He reminded me that these men were only instruments in the greater plan, and they had no idea of the role they were playing. I took in the correction, and focused once more on Jesus and how he was faring. He was in some distress, but I could tell by reading his energy field that he remained in a state of focused prayer.

He wanted me, I heard inside my mind, to remain as an observer, but not to do anything that would draw unnecessary attention to myself, or put myself at risk. I would have done anything he wanted me to do at that point, anything. Now that all of this was in motion, it was real and horrible, and I could not wish it away. I felt more energy surging through me than ever. All of my senses were focused on attuning to the events that were occurring. Never had I felt so powerless to help someone I loved. All that I could do was follow, and watch.

I was able to get in to the home where he was taken to see Caiaphas, but then he was taken away again. I stayed among the crowd, and watched the horrible thing that they did when Pilate offered the crowd the choice of who should be crucified. I wept in my agony for him. Truly, it was the ruler of the world that opposed him, for Jesus was contrary to all the world knew and strove for in its everyday dealings.

Throughout all of this, I tried to maintain energetic contact with, and prayerful support for him. As he was judged against, reviled, and beaten, he kept his heart continually open, loving God, and trusting God and the purpose of this thing that was happening. I think that his vulnerability, and the lack of hatred or scorn that he demonstrated, made the people around him hate him even more, for they saw him as weak. Where was this all-powerful man now? And yet, as I observed him energetically, I was amazed at the tremendous strength he had in his heart, keeping it open in love despite the terrible things they were doing to him. This would continue to impress itself on me over the course of the day, a lesson I would never forget. I saw that the outward display of strength of a man is nothing, compared with the inner strength of love which comes from God through man. There was simply no power that could compare with it. Yet, who could see this on this terrible day in which he was mocked, scourged and murdered?

When I heard where they were taking him, I ran to find Mary. I could not get near him now, and I wanted to honor my commitment to him as far as she was concerned. I followed my intuitive sense, and found her quickly. She needed no explanation; she knew what was happening and why. Her face was lined with tears. She would not hear of not going, as Jesus had predicted. Several of us sadly trudged the way to Golgotha in silence. The bravery and courage in her soul inspired me; there was nothing in all of this that she would not face, and face squarely. How perfect a mother she was for this man!

We stood in front of him for many hours, for what seemed like an eternity. We prayed for him constantly, that God would give him strength to bear his agony, and that it be over soon for him. None of us wanted to give the Roman soldiers the satisfaction of our tears, though there would be many tears shed later. Many now were falling inside of us. My heart felt torn in half. I have never known such agony as I knew in those moments. What a wondrous man he was, and how little he deserved this heartless brutality! A lifetime lived to bring love into the world, only to be met with such hatred and horror! I wanted to take his pain away, yet there was nothing I could do but pray and send my loving energy to him. I knew I had to be strong now, and rise above my pain.

When he looked up, saw us, and told Mary that I would now be her son, and that she would be my mother, I felt honored and blessed. I knew he would want me to look after her for the rest of her years, and to ensure that her needs were well met. It was a great honor, which I was honored to fulfill.

The moment quickly passed, as his spirit prepared to move on. The sky grew dark and ominous, and remained that way for hours. At that time, it felt as if the world were ending. When he spoke his final words, "it is finished", the earth quaked and shuddered at the loss of its divine son.

For a moment, I did not care if I were to be swallowed up into the earth, for my reason for living was gone. Slowly, I remembered Mary, and the work ahead, and I came back to my senses. I think, however, that in some way, the sky of my inner world remained darkened, and was not restored to the light of day. If I were to be completely honest with myself, I would have to say that this is true, even unto this day, so many years later. There was a vast emptiness and sorrow where so much joy and love had been. I had never known such desolation and such grief.

The lance piercing his heart was the final brutality, and the final indignity. Words could not describe the horror of the situation, and the despair I felt at this loss. We prayed that his spirit would pass over safely. Through prayer, we rallied our forces to do that which had to be done.

All of the disciples gathered and prayed over the course of the day, were astounded at this thing that had been done. None of us thought it wise for one of us to go to Pilate to ask him to release the body to us, for our chances of receiving it were small. Instead, Joseph of Arimithea, a rich man in good stead with the powers of the world, requested the release, and was granted his request. The women went to help with caring for the body. We met in collective grief and disbelief, and prayed for strength and understanding.

I could not find his voice when I called on him. This had never happened, and it was extremely disconcerting to me. I felt completely lost without him, he who had been the center of my world for so long now. I tried to remember what he had always told me, that one could always hear God if one listened, but now I did not hear. I tried to keep up appearances in front of the others, but inside I was having horrible doubts. What if this all had been a tragic mistake? What if this were not the time in which this was supposed to have happened? Then I would grow calm, and remind myself that he knew his time had come, and if I did not trust in my own perceptions in this matter, I could certainly trust in his. My mind would not be stilled for long, especially when I was by myself. If I had to be present for others, I could be much stronger than when I was on my own.

I remember a time after the crucifixion, when I was with Mary. We were trying our best to cope with our sorrow. Her grief was intense, and she alternated between sobbing and wailing. I felt deeply for her grief, and felt my own as well. The strong sense of responsibility that I now felt in looking after her, rose from deep within me. I suppressed the expression of the full extent of my own feelings, so that I could be strong for her, and be someone on whom she could depend. She would from then on, until her death, live with me. I wanted her to know she could completely trust me and rely on me.

As I sat with her, I sensed the depths of my grief. It was an indescribable grief; it seemed there could never have been another heartbreak such as this one. I felt the grief much more deeply than I could ever have imagined. I felt I had to restrain my expression of it. I thought in these moments that Jesus had been so wise in telling me I was now to look after Mary, as her son. Our shared grief was great, but our love for him was greater, and bound us together. Looking after her gave me purpose. I repeatedly thought, "I must be strong for her." However, she was strong in those days, and pure and loving in her expression. I have often wondered in the days since, if it were not her free-flowing expression of sorrow that enabled her to love so freely and so purely. I wished I could have been as open as she, but that was not my way.

She talked about how she knew he would be back. Through him, God would forever be glorified. She was immensely proud of he who had been born from her womb. She knew that all of this was for the glory of God, and for the triumph of the divine in the many generations to come. She also had a mother's tremendous sorrow at the pain her son had borne, and at her personal loss of her son. She acknowledged openly those kinds of thoughts that I had kept to myself. I shared with her that I had many similar feelings. We talked about the sacrifice that was being required of us. Although it felt enormous to us, it was a small thing compared to what he had to endure.

So much went on in these days, much of which is a blur to me now. I slept little, and constantly felt stretched beyond my limitations. I would try to focus my attention forward on his imminent return, and would be pulled back into the morass of my feelings of desolation and abandonment. I remembered my dream, in which I had those very feelings, and in which he did return, but only for a little while. It was enormously exciting to me to think of seeing him again, yet this excitement was tempered by the recognition that this would only be for a little while. I doubt that I was very useful to anyone during this period, though I certainly tried to be as attentive to Mary as I could. I also spent time with the others.

This was the first time the disciples had truly been without a leader. Jesus had gone off on occasion, but his presence had always remained with us. Now, it was different. We had some struggles with initial organization. Peter was not himself, and we now had a looser organization than when he was more fully in charge in the past. Nevertheless, we met, and prayed often for Jesus' imminent return. These were the most difficult of times…

CHAPTER 55

THE DAYTIME WAS EXCRUCIATINGLY PAINFUL, but the nighttime was even more so. Where once I had fallen asleep in the loving energetic embrace of my Master and my beloved friend, now there was only emptiness, grief and desolation. By day, there was shared comfort, for so many of us were grieving, but by night, I was completely alone with my loneliness for him. The horrible sight of him on the cross, suffering as he did, was an image that had firmly implanted itself in my consciousness. It kept coming back to me, over and over again. The pain and the agony that he suffered throughout the entire ordeal must have been horrendous. In order to accomplish what he had to do on the spiritual plane, he had to stay conscious and in his body, and thus be fully aware of the physical pain.

Time after time, I went through my impressions of what had happened. I had watched him and his energy field carefully throughout the long ordeal. At the time, I was in so much pain that I could not sort out my impressions. Now, by night, when it was so quiet and I could not sleep, these impressions went through my mind. I was obsessed, inside of myself, with figuring out the energetic patterns, so that I could understand what he had been doing while he was on the cross. Deep inside of me, I knew it had been extremely important work. I had to understand. I would not let go of the thing until I understood, for that was how I was.

I finally realized that in those final hours, he was working extremely hard energetically at transforming, on a metaphysical level, the darkness and the hatred and the evil that had placed him there, despite all of the tortuous pain it gave him. The period when it grew dark outside was when he had to move into the pain and darkness, and be completely

290

within it. He moved into the darkness and pain with all of the courage that he had. I think this might have been a far greater task for him than to face the cross itself. For now, he had become the darkness. The world outside became dark as he descended into the region which had not yet been redeemed by the Light. His cry of "my God, why hast thou forsaken me" was his cry as he fully entered that world of pain and error and darkness, where he could see no light. It was his cry and his prayer that the Light be shown to him. In the moment of the nethermost darkness, when he could no longer see God, he called out to God. He had to be fully present there, in that unholy region, for it was out of this chaos that the miracle would take place.

Once fully there, with his light and love and power, he transformed the darkness. He transmuted it into something now forever changed. From now on, the darkness of the world would be redeemed, through him, through his Light. This work that he did there, while on the cross, would change history forever. God was now present in all matter in an unprecedented manner, and could free men's souls from the darkness that had hitherto trapped them.

As one by one the pieces of this tapestry came to me, I was amazed and overcome by what I learned. I thought at first that surely this was too grand to be true, and too powerful to be possible. Yet, this is how I understood the energy, with the help of the guidance that was given to me in response to my prayers. Now I understood why he said "it is finished", for he did not mean just the finish of his life on earth, but also the finish of the task which he was accomplishing.

Once more, I was stretched beyond my capacity to understand with this information. It made sense, and it excited my intellect, but I cannot say that I could fully grasp the enormity of the thing. Perhaps only the mind of God could do that. What I do understand is that mankind was redeemed while Jesus was on the cross, and the above is the best that I know how to understand and to explain what happened and how. The concepts involved are huge, and I have spent much of my lifetime attempting to better understand them. I have wondered if perhaps I have been guilty of being overly imaginative in this matter, yet as I have thought about this over the years, I think not. The capacities of Jesus were in every way beyond the range of human experience as we understand it. The redemptive work began on this plane, and continued as he moved on to the next.

When I would return from my mental journeys, I found myself in extreme pain, and miserable. This gulf between my spiritual understanding and my personal pain at my loss was a great chasm, and I had much trouble reconciling the two. The pain and anxiety in the region of my heart chakra were great. The anxious feeling in my chest pounded so strongly that it kept me from sleeping. I would be exhausted to the point where I could not keep my eyes open at all, yet when I lay down and closed them, my pain and anxiety were so powerful that my mind stayed dreadfully alert. How was it that I could be so comprehending of the absolute necessity of that which was happening for the greater good of all mankind, and still be so terribly upset, and feel so abandoned and desolate? I do not think I have ever had an experience of greater contrasts than this. I was in total awe of the grandeur of the thing, and I was in the deepest of personal pain and agony, both at the same time, and over the same series of events. My rational mind could barely comprehend this. I sorely wanted, and attempted, to focus on the positive and the spiritual aspects of this thing, and yet my pain kept moving me back into my body and my broken heart.

It was comforting to know that others were struggling with the same paradox. Mary, whom I revered, confided in me that she too found the same struggle confusing at best, and excruciating at the worst of times. She, however, was more comfortable with the contradictory feelings. I learned from her about accepting the coexistence of both polarities. My own tendency was to want to focus on the spiritual understanding, and push away the human feelings as somehow lesser than the former. Her gentleness of spirit, and her perfected heart taught me that rapture and anguish are both necessary and equally perfect as aspects of the human condition in coping with this situation. She could contain both within herself perfectly. Around her, I did not feel I was selfish to experience pain at my personal loss. I saw another aspect of the divine in her full expression of sorrow at her personal loss, something I had not seen within my own sorrow. Through her, I learned more of the enormity of the wisdom of the human heart.

Mary stirred up much tenderness and protectiveness within me. I felt joy to be now so closely associated with her as to be considered her son and protector. From now on, she would live in my home. I felt privileged to be able to be thus positioned, and knew there would be much I could learn from her. I vowed to take the very best care of her that I could, and to give her the best of comforts and company for the rest of her days.

CHAPTER 56

WE ALL ANXIOUSLY WAITED FOR JESUS' RETURN. We knew he would return in some form, but did not know what form that would be. I was living for the moment when I would have contact with him again. I wondered what it would be like to see him or hear him, and how it would be to be around his energy again. The days seemed to stretch on endlessly, and the nights even longer. I did not know what to expect, though I did know it would never be the same. I was most eager, however, to reestablish some kind of contact with him, for it puzzled me terribly that I had lost the connection we had always had, and which he said we would always have.

When first we heard from Mary Magdalena that he was no longer in his tomb, Peter and I rushed to see for ourselves. We searched throughout the tomb, and found no trace of him. It was exciting to see the cloth that had been around him, and was now folded up, for we knew he was once more among us, and would make himself known to us when he so willed. Since there was nothing now that could be done, we left. He then appeared to Mary Magdalena, who was awestruck to see him.

On that evening when he showed himself to us, we were full of gladness to see him. It was a miracle that he was once more among us! He gave us the gift of the breath of the Holy Spirit, and the power to forgive sins. He had a new, expanded power now, which manifested to us in different ways during the time he was with us.

On this, our first sight of him since he had risen, he showed to us the wounds in his body. He had a much different presence now: I could almost feel his body as having materialized out of light. He explained to us that the body he had taken on is like a sheath he was wearing, much as one would wear clothing. His body was physical, yet not fully physical, as we know physicality. I wanted to touch him, but could not.

My feelings about seeing him were extremely mixed, and were extreme in intensity. I felt great joy to see him, to feel his presence, and just to be around him again. Yet, with this closeness and joy, I felt intense grief, for I knew the closeness I was now feeling was only temporary. Also, I could feel close to him now, but in another way, I had never felt so far away. Though he was in a body, it was a different kind of a body. I had never been more aware of the distance between us. That I was seeing him again also meant I was losing him again. I knew from what he had said, and from my dream, that he would only be here for a while, and then he would again be gone. I did not have any idea how long a time he would be here. Of course, I hoped that it would be long, but inside of me I knew his stay would not be prolonged. I felt tremendous anxiety in my chest at the thought of being physically abandoned again.

He did not stay with us this time as he had before. Instead, he came and went, according to his need. We did not know when we would see him again. I found myself always in a position of eagerly and anxiously awaiting his return. I worked very hard to tame my mind, so that I could make efforts at contacting him, to see if the connection could be re-established. To my great joy, this did happen. In my calmer moments, I could relax into a direct connection that both reassured me and gave me strength.

Through this connection, I received direction and instruction both during this period, and throughout the rest of my life. While Jesus was still on earth in this altered form, the connection was stronger, and was imbued with his personality as well as his spirit. The quality of the connection changed later, into a more purely spiritual connection, though I did occasionally use this channel for personal information as well.

Part of the information he shared during this time on earth was that this connection would be available to all who called on his name. He would be returning to the higher dimensions in order that this could be made a reality. It did not matter who called on him, as long as they believed in him, and wanted sincerely to make the link. This would then become the basis of the new dispensation. Through calling on his name, each person could individually discern their truth, and reach God within them. No longer could the religious authorities lay claim to a special relationship with God, for each person could have this relationship on their own. This move to a personal relationship with God would be a radical shift in consciousness, something that would take many centuries to make. The old ways were firmly entrenched, and the new ones would not be easily discerned or comprehended.

Jesus came back to teach us many things. It was miraculous to us all that he was once more among us, and we could not get enough of his presence and his teachings. We had been starved for him during the three days he was gone. Though we had tried to keep his spirit alive, there was no denying the grief and the desolation we felt. Now, we were hungry to absorb whatever we could, in the remaining time we had with him.

The second time he appeared to us, he went over many things, past, present and future. He said it was not enough that we understood what had happened in our lifetimes. It was important that we had a context in which to place the events with which we were familiar, and which we ourselves would be creating as the years and the centuries went on. Each of us was aware that our discipleship was not a thing limited to this physical body and to this lifetime. All of us knew generally, and some of us specifically, lifetimes in which we would be carrying forward the work for which we had been so well trained. The commitment we had made to the work was a very deep one, made at a soul level. Though it would not always be in our best soul growth interests to have this work as our focus, there would be lifetimes in which this would benefit us individually, as well as help us to serve others collectively. The information we had about specific lifetimes would stay with us, and was not something we would generally share the particulars of with others, for there was no need.

Jesus reviewed with us those parts of the ancient scriptures in which there were prophecies concerning him. This review of ancient scriptures was an exercise of extraordinary interest to us all, for we learned where he had been referenced, and in what ways. As we were not religious scholars when he had chosen us, most of us were quite unaware of the extent and the particulars of the prophecies that had been made concerning him. As for myself, I knew these prophecies existed, and very generally what they said, but I knew very little else.

One of the things on which we spent the most time in discussion was his explanation of the energetics of the crucifixion, the resurrection, and how he, as Christos, would be operating from the higher planes after he once more left this earth. This energy that he had embodied while on earth would, through the process of transmutation that had begun while he was still on the cross, manifest everywhere as the access point through which every individual could connect directly with God. He would be as a living column of light in the soul of every man, woman and child. To find God, all they would have to do would be to call on him. This was possible because he, in his life, and especially in his death, had transmogrified matter, imbuing it with the divine light force. From the place in the higher planes where he would soon be, he would serve as a link between man and God, thus providing man with a direct access via this channel that had not heretofore been available.

I have condensed here what he took much time and care to explain to us. What struck me the most in all of this, was the impression made on me that in his coming, this earth and its history had been fundamentally energetically altered, in an unprecedented manner. There had been many Masters before him, and there would be many after him, but none had been involved in this kind of a cosmic transformation. The implications were staggering. I could only begin to fathom them at the time. Even now, so many years later, my mind is stretched to its limit when I ponder on how this will affect humanity in the times to come.

He said he was the way to the God, and that he was the truth and the life. On the energetic plane, this is exactly true. He created for us a direct channel through which we can freely access God, if only we call on his name. That channel has been very carefully prepared. As time goes on, and as what he taught becomes more firmly established on earth, that channel will expand and become more established. Through that channel, the Holy Spirit can be received on earth. As more people work to access that channel, the more easily will that channel be accessed. Through the increasing reception of the Holy Spirit, the light and the love shared between people will be greater.

As we were accustomed to working with energetics, the descriptions he offered were consistent with all we had learned so far. I had seen so many miracles in my short life that something like this, though of an almost inconceivable magnitude, seemed believable and consistent with other things I had seen. Everything he had ever told us had turned out to be true. We had seen the Holy Spirit working through him on innumerable occasions. There was no reason to suppose that what he said now was not true as well.

Now our task was, through prayer and meditation, to access the Christ within us. Through this channel, we would receive the Holy Spirit, and let it work through us. We had experienced this many times through him while he was living on earth; now it would be incumbent on us to continue to do the same as before, only now relying on him in a different manner. We would need to draw upon everything we had learned about healing and energetics from him. That learning would be condensed into a specific ray of focus; on receiving the energy through the channel he had created for direct transmission of the Holy Spirit. We would be given a very great gift in the future of the Holy Comforter, and with this energy, we would be sent out to heal and work many miracles of our own, to glorify God.

I think that it was easier for Jesus to work with the higher energies while in this more rarefied physical state, than it had been while he was in the denser human body. As we sat with him, at one point he told us to focus very carefully within our own minds, and we would be able to mentally scan the specific focus that our missions would take within this lifetime. Somehow, through amplification of our own soul's purpose, he was able to set it up so that each of us saw in our minds the path our lives would take. We also saw any particular focus that was laid out for us. This review reminded me of the scanning journey that he had taken me on so long ago when we had taken a walk up into the hills. Now, however, this journey was being orchestrated for a number of us at once, in highly specific ways. When I thought about it later, I reflected how it was truly amazing that he could have led each of us simultaneously into a scanning of our individual soul's purpose and path.

What I saw for myself both surprised and amazed me. One of the things I saw was me sitting at a wooden table, with candles lighting the room. I was writing. I knew as I saw myself here that writing was something I loved very much to do, and it would be something I would do often. There was a sense of fulfillment and purpose to this work. I also saw myself in many scenes, out among people, teaching them, healing them and generally sharing with them what I had learned from the days I had spent at the feet of the Master. There were many great joys associated with this work.

I also knew from this scanning that there would also be many great sorrows to come. I received that the world had not learned its lesson after the killing of Jesus; there would be many deaths to come in the course of this work. I saw Mary, the mother of Jesus, around me for many years, and I saw Mary Magdalena close to me as well. There seemed to be, in fact, a community of women around me. There appeared to be great joy and support in these associations. I saw many other things as well, but the above seemed to be the pivotal points. All of these points were concerned with carrying forth the work that had begun with Jesus. I saw many scenes on this day that, years later, when the actual events did occur, I remembered.

The private moments I had with Jesus were extremely limited, for the little time he had while he was back was needed for group work. He was glad that Mary and I had found comfort in each other, and he said we both would find comfort through frequent communication with him. Mary, he said, would lead a more quiet life than I, and would oft be in communication with him. Many would depend on her for inspiration and guidance, as well as for the serenity and steadiness of her faith. I would be much out in the world, yet because of my quieter nature, I would not as readily become embroiled in the kinds of controversy with which the others would find themselves involved. This was for a purpose as well, for it would be part of my task to look after some of the women. I would learn much from them, as they would benefit well from their association with me. If I were to become discouraged and weary, they would provide me with great support and encouragement, and help strengthen me on my path. In many ways, the circle of prayer from this small group would provide the nucleus of the new faith, and the journeying apostles would serve as the radii emanating from the core.

Jesus encouraged me to write freely of what I had witnessed, and to let myself be inspired by Spirit as I wrote. He knew that I had been keeping journals as I went along, and told me he saw I had both a public and a private version that I would want to document. It would be my choice whether to make public my personal account, he said, but it would teach me much if I were to follow through with the actual writing. One day, he said, I might decide I would want others to see it, but that would be up to me to decide at the time. We spoke briefly of times to come, but did not dwell on this. Much had already been said, and I felt as prepared as I could be for those distant times. He reminded me that he would always be there for me to contact, and one day he would return for all the world to experience. In that time, I would be present to witness his return.

I began weeping, recognizing that his departure was again imminent. He filled me with his love, and in this fullness, I felt both immense joy and immense sadness. There were no words for this love, for there could be no greater human love than this; nor were there words for this sorrow. All that I was and had become, I owed to him. I wanted so badly to depart with him, and to follow him where he was going, but I could not.

CHAPTER 57

SOME DAYS LATER, WE HAD OUR FINAL BREAKFAST TOGETHER. This was to be our final meal. He had appeared on shore while we were out on the Sea of Galilee, and we went to the shore to meet him. I had the most eerie feeling about the encounter. Something was quite different; all of my senses told me this, though I did not know quite what was happening.

I felt a horrible anxiety and dread, and yet I told myself that what was occurring was my reaction to being around he who was so different than the physical man with whom I had grown so comfortable. If I were to say now what was causing the anxiety at that time, I would say that it was because in my deepest self I knew I was losing him again, this time from the physical plane forever. At the time, I denied to myself my own prescience, and forgot that which I knew. As I have explained before, I was quite adept at this when it came to the subject of Jesus' departure from this world.

I was struck with his warmth on this morning. He was always a tremendously compassionate and feeling man, but today he was even more so. How my ideas about God had changed through knowing him! Before meeting Jesus, I had always seen God as remote and detached. I thought God's perfection lay in his distance from human affairs. Through Jesus, I had learned so very much. Through him, I had learned that God expressed himself through caring and compassion; that in his very essence he was love and compassion. Out of this love and compassion streamed the wisdom that fully embraced the human condition, and strove always to bring it to its highest possible level. Divinity and humanness were not separate at all; to the contrary, humanness fully expressed was divinity incarnate. This had been a revelation to me, and never again would I regard my flesh in the same manner. Today, as he was freed from the constraints of the fully corporeal human body, it seemed he was freer than ever to express love, much as several days before he had seemed freer to work with other higher energies.

In my anxiety, I was feeling vulnerable and dependent, which was quite uncomfortable. I felt him come into my heart, and reside there, reassuring me of his love and of his accessibility to me. I knew somehow that the others were also having the same experience of him, for the energy in the group shifted into a greater serenity and composure than in the moments before. I loved that he could express his love so generously, so we would all be affected in such a demonstrable manner.

No sooner had I experienced this inner shift, and group shift in energy, than I experienced another shift, this one into a very different state. I can best describe this state as expectancy, a pause that felt pregnant with anticipation of what was to come. I did not know whether something would be happening in the next moment or in the next hour, but the sense I had was that this time was a cosmic pause, a transitional moment in which the past was completed and the future was about to begin. I felt suspended between two worlds, not knowing what to expect. I knew only to wait, and to trust the moment to fulfill itself as it would. I found myself wanting to hold on to the present, and to somehow try to prevent it from moving forward, even though of course I knew this was impossible.

I surrendered to God's will. As I did so, I felt a similar pattern in the group's energy configuration. I wondered how this came about, and it dawned on me that we were following in the energy pattern that Jesus was setting down for us at this moment. I looked over at him, and recognized in his greatly expanded energy field that familiar pattern of surrender I had seen and emulated so many times before. Now, because his physical body was less dense than previously, and thus offered less resistance to the spiritual energies working through him, I observed an intense radiance about him. This radiance compared with, though it was not equal to, the radiance that James, Peter and I had observed around him on the mountaintop, when God spoke. He appeared almost translucent for some moments. Then my consciousness altered back again to a more normal mode of perception, and he once more seemed somewhat more solid.

He led us in a long prayer, asking God to always lead us in the direction where we could best serve. He asked that we would be moved to love our fellow human beings always, and to forgive them as we ourselves would seek forgiveness. He thanked God for the time we had together on earth, and asked that the Holy Spirit be present to each one of us when we would call upon it to guide us and support us. He asked for our continued education and enlightenment as we walked in the Lord's Way. He asked that we would serve as instruments of God's will wherever we walked on the face of this earth. He prayed also that our eyes would be opened to the understanding of what had happened thus far in his mission, and that we would continue to learn as he moved on into the subsequent stages of his work.

The most important work lay ahead of us, he said, and we would need all our courage and strength to move through these times. We would be going out into the world and teaching about him, and baptizing in his name. He came to teach the world about love; central to his teachings about love was what he had said about forgiveness. It would not be difficult for us to love those who were dear to us, he said, but our life's work would be intricately involved with an endless practice of forgiveness, especially towards those who persecuted us. He prayed for our continued strength to get through this. He prayed that we would continue to seek inspiration, and for us to remember that through him we would reach the Kingdom of Heaven both while we were still on earth, as well as when we would move beyond.

As he went through this prayer, I was left with the very clear impression that this was to precede his leave-taking. I tried to deny this with my mind, but my heart and my senses knew clearly that what I felt was true. Part of me was much better prepared for his departure this time than previously, especially the spiritual part of me. However, in my emotional body, I was in a state of dread and sorrow, and attempted to raise myself by focusing on the spiritual purpose of these moments. I was never more aware of the split within myself between the emotional body and the spiritual body than in these moments. I so desperately wanted to give myself over to my spiritual awareness, and to the high vibrational level he was manifesting. I wish I could say I was successful in this. Instead, I felt such despair, and dread of impending abandonment, that I was aware only of wanting to die. I did not want to live another moment on this earth without him. I imagined myself willing myself to die, somehow being successful at this, and being fortunate enough to depart and move on into the next stage with him, where I could be with him forever. I knew this was wrong and selfish and not at all in line with that which was set out for me, but at the time I did not care about any of this.

All I knew is that at this moment I had no will to live. I equated, on a purely personal level, his leaving with the ending of joy and with the extinguishing of the sun that brought light and warmth into my life each day. If I could have lain down on the ground and simply died at this moment, I would have done so. It would have been so much easier to have been able to be the first one to leave, rather than to have been the one who was left behind.

I do not know how I thought I could hide these reactions from my dear brethren, but I tried as best I could. The difference between the outer and the inner man could not have been as much as I wanted it to be. I felt Jesus approach me, surrounding me both inside and out with love and courage. What surprised me most at this point was that, instead of welcoming his approach, as I had always done before, I wanted to repulse him and to keep him as far away from me as possible. I did not want to allow him to lend to me understanding or love, for that would maintain my attachment to him. All I wanted was to allow the darkness to close in around me, so I could move into oblivion and not feel any longer this pain that was killing me inside. Any enlightenment or elucidation that I had received from him over the years, I now suddenly wished away. I wanted to be completely by myself, and to be as horrifically miserable as I felt myself to be. It was certainly the most despondent of states that I found myself in, in the midst of the misery of grief and loss. I felt I had completely lost my orientation, in the center of this desolation. Now I was groping my way in radically new territory, territory I both hated and despised. What had happened to all of my spirituality and my training now? Was I not the weakest of men that I could not raise myself to the level of the higher vision? I believed there were no answers to these questions, and that I had sunken to new depths in my inability to bring myself to a point of understanding and wisdom.

I do not know how long I remained in this state. I eventually tired of it, and found what was going on around me more interesting and compelling than my inner state of despair and turmoil. Jesus was talking with Peter, and asking if Peter loved him. I was touched as they went through this, with Jesus asking Peter three times if he loved him, and Peter responding three times that he did. Each time, after Peter said that he did love him, Jesus responded to him to look after his sheep. I knew Peter had been unable to forgive himself for denying three times that he knew Jesus, when Jesus had been arrested. Here it seemed was his opportunity to correct his mistake, and to re-establish himself with Jesus. No words needed to be spoken about what had gone before, and it was understood now that, in this way, Peter was forgiven and once more given his charge in establishing the church that was to come. I was happy and relieved for Peter, for he was so well suited to this, and he had been so unhappy with himself for what he had done. Each of us had many failings. My own had never been so apparent to me as during this recent time. I felt lifted by Jesus' forgiveness of Peter, for I knew in those moments that he had forgiven us all.

Jesus had more to say to Peter about what was coming, and asked Peter to follow him. Since that very first day when I had met Jesus, when we dialogued with the inner voice but not with the outer, I had often experienced this kind of communication with him. On this particular occasion, he impressed on me that he wanted me to come also, so I followed. Peter was quite surprised to see me. When he asked Jesus about my following them, he had no idea that I had been asked through the inner voice to come as well. Neither he nor the others understood the answer that Jesus gave, but I understood it quite well because of conversations we had shared. What Jesus said to

Peter was allegorical and not literal, though no one could have known this. Jesus said that if he willed that I were to remain until he returned, then that was up to him. In saying this, he spoke on several levels, first letting Peter know that he wanted me to come with them. His words were taken by the others to mean that I would not die, for we knew it would be many years before Jesus would return, though no one knew how many. I knew that Jesus' statement referred to that future lifetime which he and I had discussed numerous times. I would be present on earth, though in a different body, in the time when the Christ Spirit would return to earth. This was not something I thought I should discuss with the others, since he had not chosen to discuss it with them. And so I kept my silence on this matter, as it seemed right to do so.

We spent what seemed to be a very brief time, but which I know was in truth much longer, discussing arrangements for the times to come. Whereas before we had organized around Jesus in the physical body, now our center of organization would be around him in Spirit. In this world, Peter would be the center of our new system. This was not new information, but what followed was a review, using the technique of scanning in our minds, key points about disciples and locations, mapping out where people were to go, and where they would establish centers of teaching and worship. Each of the twelve, now eleven, had been given this information individually, but now we were given the overview, as well as more general information about the task of the other disciples who had been gathering around Jesus. It was exciting to be seeing and otherwise experiencing this information, and I was gladdened by the extent of the outreach that would be made within our lifetimes. It was not nearly what I had imagined in those earlier times, when I had thought Jesus would be literally a King over the peoples of the earth, within our lifetime. Now my view was expanded, and I realized that the Kingship was to be a spiritual one, ruling people's hearts and souls. This would take many lifetimes to accomplish. The many miracles we had seen thus far, during Christ's presence on earth, represented an acceleration of energies and a winning over of people's hearts to a new way. This was necessary in order to begin the arduous work that lay ahead. This acceleration would continue during our lifetime, but would decrease for a time, and then again a time.

Peter was pleased with what he saw, and with the position he would be taking. This was clear from his demeanor, and from the expanded energy I felt around him. I also sensed that he was immensely grateful not only to have been forgiven, but also to have been restored to this high position. I learned from him, as I had also learned from Mary Magdalena, about the power of forgiveness. When a person is forgiven, and honored for the soul they truly are, rather than seen for the blemish that had appeared temporarily, they are given a second chance. This second chance is not something they had expected, or dared to hope for, and so it is especially sweet and dear when it arrives. That person then has strong potential to give the most earnest and dedicated of service.

I, too, failed my Master on that final night, when he so needed me. I, too, had the opportunity in those final hours to make good on my failings. Individually, in our own ways, we had failed our highest selves, and the forgiveness that had ensued had freed us up to become whole again.

My consciousness was split. I made intense efforts to focus on what was occurring around me, but in my heart I felt I was dying. I was conscious that I was gasping for breaths, and I knew instinctively that my difficulty in breathing was due to the energy shift as Jesus was preparing to move on. I felt him with me in every breath I took, and I felt his presence acknowledging the extreme difficulty I was having in being alive at this moment in time. His support meant everything to me at this time when I felt I had nothing to live for personally. I allowed him to surround me with his loving energy, which enabled me to expand into the necessity of my spiritual destiny within this lifetime. This helped me to keep perspective, and to acknowledge that my personal struggles were small in comparison to the larger context of meaning in which I found myself.

I went back and forth between these two perspectives, and conceptually, with his assist, was able to prioritize the levels on which

I needed to work. Just as he had, I needed to let my personal pain and suffering be secondary to the mission which I had been invited to accomplish on this earth plane. As I thought about it again, my personal suffering once more seemed small and inconsequential in comparison to what he had suffered, and I felt ashamed. No sooner had I felt this feeling, than I felt him infusing me with the knowledge that I had no reason to feel ashamed. It was my love, which caused me to suffer now, that brought me the closest to the divine. How beautifully and how poignantly he made it all fit together for me! Now, none of the pieces were split apart, but were healed in a beautiful circle in which I understood that love and suffering in the human condition were inseparable. I felt spiritually, mentally and emotionally complete, in a rapture that I shared with him for a few moments.

Now came the time I had dreaded and feared. We had rejoined the others, and walked to a place sacred to us, where the energy felt clear and powerful. We gathered in a circle, in prayer. As we prayed, the energy level rose, through our prayer, to a point where we were all connected in light and in ecstasy, and then, in God's will for us all. I heard inside of my soul the words: "Goodbye, John, I have loved you dearly."

I could barely contain my mounting emotions. I responded that he meant everything to me, and that all that I did, I did for him. I told him I had never loved as I loved him, and that all my prayers and love went with him. I felt at those moments that he knew this beyond a doubt.

As he ascended, he grew less dense, and more transparent. I knew that what we were witnessing was miraculous. I sensed no pain in him at these moments, but only joy and transcendence. He rose by stages. It seemed that as he rose, he was accompanied by legions of helpers and angels. The beauty and the wonder of what was happening before our eyes were astounding. What did it mean, and how were we to understand it? At this point, it almost seemed not to matter, for the event seemed something meant only to be taken in. I knew he was rejoining his essence with God. As this occurred, I knew he must be experiencing the bliss of reunion that most of us spend much of our lives longing for. We were completely transfixed by his ascension.

The energy field within and about me shifted as his energy shifted. I began to experience the most wondrous release. It was as if every cell in my body was lightening. As this happened, I became more free to experience the divine side of my nature. This shift, far from being temporary, was a major energy shift that continued far beyond this time. At this moment, it was as if, through the process that he was initiating, I was undergoing an initiation of my own. I felt transported into another realm, one he had shown me often in our dreaming journeys. In this realm, the body did not encumber, but merely served as a convenient vehicle for individual self-expression, expression that was ultimately of the divine. In those moments, it felt as if I was going on this marvelous journey with him, with my energy expanding into a realm where only he could take me.

I have no doubt but that the others were having a similar experience at this time. As a Supreme Master, Jesus was uniquely gifted at transmitting the most sublime of experience to many persons at the same time. The possibilities in these moments were undeniable. He was showing us our future, the future in which we would become so spiritualized and so cleansed, that we would no longer need to encumber ourselves with the tremendous burdens of incarnations in the human body. This future, however distant, of the human soul, was clearly impressed upon me. I felt transported on wings of light along with him. I longed to merge with him in an ecstatic experience of the divine. But, as I strove for this, I felt myself falling, falling back into the human experience, back into the pain and suffering of the human body, back into the huge gulf that separated us and which caused me so much pain, and back into the agony of the reality of what was occurring before my very eyes.

It was as if for a few moments I had been allowed to take flight on the wings on an angel. Then, abruptly, my wings had been clipped, and I fell from a great height to the ground. I came crashing back to my reality, to the recognition that he was truly leaving, soon to be gone forever, and that my best friend was nowhere to be found in the physical universe. The darkness began crashing over me again. I felt myself weakened, without any awareness of the light forces I had felt so strongly only moments before. As I felt myself being overcome with this darkness, which I now know to be grief, I forced myself to join the consciousness of the group, which was valiantly struggling to stay focused on spiritual purpose. I do not know if I succeeded in this, for I remained caught in a bitter struggle that left me little mental energy to assess my pitiful state. There was tremendous contrast between the glory and the wonder of his deliverance into the hands of God, and my own fall into the void wherein I found so much darkness and sorrow. At the time, I chose to understand this as a personal shortcoming, but since then I have learned much more about the darkness, and about grief.

We remained transfixed, unable to move, and not daring to disturb the wondrous and yet also terrible moments that had transpired. The beauty of his soul had touched and transported us to places we had never dreamed were possible, either within our souls, or outside, in the dimension of human interaction. I felt as if my soul were poised on a precipice, ready to jump off and follow him into the great light of God. However, in feeling and recognizing my terrible pain, I wondered if this precipice was not the point of departure for a dark and excruciating journey. I could not decide, and recognized a level within my own soul, where both of these were equally true. At the same moment that I recognized this, I tried to comprehend these paradoxical thoughts, but knew this would be a futile effort.

I focused back on the outer world, on what I had just seen and experienced, in the context of all I had ever experienced about this man/God Jesus Christ. I felt within me the extraordinary wonder of his presence, and the miracle of his existence. I felt with surety that the earth had been blessed with every breath he took. With a sudden gasp, I recognized that my sorrow at my personal loss was intensely deep, far deeper than I would be able to comprehend in this lifetime. In this knowledge, I felt I could easily collapse and die. I chose to move on in my awareness, on to a recognition that every soul on earth would benefit by what he had brought to us, and what he would continue to bring to us. I could not begin to grasp the enormity, the complexity and the beauty of what he had brought us. I felt humbled by the recognition that no particle of dust on earth would ever again be the same.

And so, I end this chapter of my story. In many ways, this is a beginning, a beginning of new hope for humanity, and a beginning of the bringing in of new ways to our corrupted flesh and spirit. I wish that everyone who so desired could understand the marvelous ways of our Lord, and could recognize that he manifested the true meaning of love and friendship on our tiny world. I hope that my good fortune, the wondrous instruction I received, and my many errors would prove helpful to those who would come after me. I pray also that Jesus be remembered both as a past figure, and known as a present spiritual teacher, by all those who would seek to know the ways of God.

ABOUT THE AUTHOR

CAROL D. WARNER, M.A., M.S.W. is a Licensed Clinical Social Worker in private practice in Falls Church, Virginia. She received her B.A. in English Literature from New College in Sarasota, Florida in 1974. She traveled around the world for a year, learning about world cultures and religions, before getting her Master's Degree in Religious Studies from the University of Virginia in 1978. In 1983, she received her Master's Degree in Clinical Social Work from Smith College in Northampton, Massachusetts. Because of her dual background in both clinical and spiritual traditions, she combines spirituality and clinical work in her psychotherapy practice.

Carol Warner has worked with and studied dreams for more than 25 years, and has been in varying positions, including Chair of the Board, and Chair of the Ethics Committee, on the Board of Directors of the Association for the Study of Dreams for many of the past 17 years. She considers dreams to be a gateway to the soul, and to the understanding of the soul's purpose. She is also student of the Course in Miracles, of the Alice Bailey readings, and is a Holographic Memory Resolution (HMR) practitioner.

ISBN 155212718-4

9 781552 127186